UNDERSTANDING HUMAN KNOWLEDGE

Understanding Human Knowledge

Philosophical Essays

BARRY STROUD

OXFORD

UNIVERSITY PRESS

OXFORD

UNIVERSITY PRESS

Great Clarendon Street, Oxford OX2 6DP

Oxford University Press is a department of the University of Oxford.
It furthers the University's objective of excellence in research, scholarship,
and education by publishing worldwide in

Oxford New York

Athens Auckland Bangkok Bogotá Buenos Aires Calcutta
Cape Town Chennai Dar es Salaam Delhi Florence Hong Kong Istanbul
Karachi Kuala Lumpur Madrid Melbourne Mexico City Mumbai
Nairobi Paris São Paulo Singapore Taipei Tokyo Toronto Warsaw

and associated companies in Berlin Ibadan

Oxford is a registered trade mark of Oxford University Press
in the UK and certain other countries

Published in the United States
by Oxford University Press Inc., New York

© Barry Stroud 2000

The moral rights of the author have been asserted
Database right Oxford University Press (maker)

First published 2000

British Library Cataloguing in Publication Data

Data available

Library of Congress Cataloging in Publication Data
Stroud, Barry.
Understanding human knowledge: philosophical essays / Barry Stroud.
Includes bibliographical references and index.
1. Knowledge, Theory of. I. Title.
BD161.S713 2000 121–dc21 99-059002
ISBN 0-19-825033-9

1 3 5 7 9 10 8 6 4 2

Typeset by Best-set Typesetter Ltd., Hong Kong
Printed in Great Britain
on acid-free paper by
T.J. International Ltd
Padstow, Cornwall

To my mother and to the memory of my father.

They did everything to make many things possible.
So I had only to make something actual.

CONTENTS

INTRODUCTION

I collect here fourteen essays published over twice as many years
in a number of different journals and books. In bringing them
together in one place I hope to make them more conveniently and
so more widely available. Each essay was written to stand on its
own, independently of the others, and I have not altered the texts
from their original appearance. But I hope that each might gain
from being read in connection with others that deal in similar ways
with closely related questions. Those written later develop or
explore some of the earlier ideas in directions that were not fore-
seen at the time. I thank the original publishers of the essays for
permission to reprint them here.

The essays centre on the task of understanding human knowledge, as it is pursued in philosophy. What has come to be called
'epistemology' is the attempt to explain how we know the things
we know. It would seem that any successful explanation of our
knowledge should carry the implication that we do in fact know at
least many of the things we think we know. That conclusion would
be the denial of philosophical scepticism, which says that we know
nothing, or (within a certain range) that we know nothing of a
certain sort. So it would seem that a serious philosophical interest
in human knowledge, either in general or for this or that restricted
range of subject-matter, cannot be separated from a concern with
the truth or falsity of scepticism for the domain in question.

I say that is how it would seem, but in fact many philosophers
declare that they have no interest in scepticism. That is understandable, since many philosophers have no interest in epistemology either, and there is no reason why they should. But many who
claim to have no interest in philosophical scepticism also put
forward philosophical theories of human knowledge, or of this or
that region of it. Those theories are positive answers to some question, and it is presumably the same question to which scepticism
gives a conflicting negative answer. Many of the essays in this
volume focus on the importance, and the difficulty, of identifying
that question or issue, and of arriving at an answer we can find

satisfactory. What exactly is the philosophical question? What is problematic, or to be explained, about human knowledge? What does a philosophical theory of (this or that domain of) knowledge seek?

Without some idea of an answer to these questions there will be no firm way to assess philosophical theories of knowledge, or to understand what they are meant to do, or even what they say. It is presumably not enough for them simply to say something or other that is true about human beings and how they know things. I think the issue can be identified more sharply by using the challenge of philosophical scepticism as the criterion and asking what it would take to show that scepticism in this or that area is not true. That would identify a task for the theory of knowledge, and a question for it to answer. That strategy would require an understanding of the challenge raised by philosophical scepticism, and of its source. But when that question, and the conditions of a successful positive answer to it, are more clearly understood, it comes to seem undeniable that scepticism is the right, in fact the only possible, answer: we could know nothing at all in the domain in question if knowing required what the sceptical challenge demands.

This leads to attempts to expose that epistemological question as meaningless, or as imposing impossibly high standards, or as in some other way illegitimate. If that could be shown, scepticism would be no threat, even if it seems like the only answer to that question. Many different diagnoses have been offered. In the view of J. L. Austin, which was shared by many linguistic philosophers in the 1950s and later, there is simply no intelligible epistemological enterprise. It is the result of nothing more than misuse or misunderstanding of a few familiar words, and of concentrating obsessively on a few half-studied 'facts' of perception. No serious philosophical issue is really at stake, and no substantive philosophical pay-off could be expected from it. The most that can be done is to 'dismantle the whole doctrine before it gets off the ground'.[1] That is a matter of 'unpicking, one by one, a mass of seductive (mainly verbal) fallacies, of exposing a wide variety of concealed motives—an operation which leaves us, in a sense, just where we began'.[2] Where we began is presumably wherever we were before we took a philosophical interest in the possibility of human knowledge.

---

[1] J. L. Austin, *Sense and Sensibilia* (Oxford, 1962), 142.   [2] Ibid. 4–5.

I think there is much more than that to be gained from a study of the sources of the philosophical problem of knowledge and its attendant scepticism. But at least this dismissive view is consistent in finding unintelligible or ill-formed not only scepticism and the question to which it is an answer, but also theories of knowledge that appear to give more positive answers to that same question. That is better than trying to show that the question is meaningless or of no interest and then giving what looks like a positive non-sceptical answer to it. That is what it seems many philosophers have continued to do. But when some of the 'concealed motives' of philosophical scepticism are brought to light and properly under-stood, I think it can be seen that many responses to it, and many diagnoses of its failings, are superficial or off target, and do not really get to the heart of it. Seeing how and why that is so can amount to what I regard as a real advance in philosophical under-standing. In *The Significance of Philosophical Scepticism*[3] I consid-ered a number of promising-looking responses to see how far they could go.

I have included here only essays which for the most part do not take up ideas and themes most emphasized in that book. There are two or three exceptions, but almost all the rest were written after the book was finished. I have arranged them almost chronologi-cally, except for placing first 'Scepticism and the Possibility of Knowledge', which appeared in the *Journal of Philosophy* in 1984. It can serve as an introduction to the problem of identifying the challenge of scepticism as I presented it in very general terms to a symposium at a meeting of the American Philosophical Association.

'Transcendental Arguments', which was published in the *Journal of Philosophy* in 1968, describes and begins to explore a very ambi-tious and potentially devastating response to scepticism. It would prove a priori, in the spirit of Kant, that we know many of the things we think we know, and that our having such knowledge is a condi-tion of our being able to think anything at all. If that were so, no one could even think that scepticism is correct and be right. That would be a very reassuring conclusion for those who seek an under-standing of how human knowledge is possible, and it would also help explain what can be felt to be the depth of scepticism: the

[3] (Oxford, 1984).

question is about the very conditions of the possibility of human thought.

The essay casts doubt on the prospects of revealing the impossibility of scepticism by transcendental arguments which would establish conclusions about the way things are in the world, especially when they are severed from the idealism that their success appears to depend on in Kant. The essay now seems to me very compressed, and to try to do too many things at once to succeed in all of them, but I think the basic dilemma still stands out clearly enough to carry conviction. It is an assessment of a certain streamlined, or what Strawson called 'scaled-down', Kantian turn or strategy in philosophy, not of the philosophy of Kant itself, which would be a much more complex story. What can reasonably be expected from an epistemological strategy along some such lines is a recurring topic of many of the later essays.

'Doubts about the Legacy of 'Scepticism' has not been printed before. It was my response to Thompson Clarke's 'The Legacy of Skepticism'[4] in an American Philosophical Association symposium in 1972. In that paper Clarke illustrates the way in which use of the same form of words, even apparently with the same meanings, can be seen to have a different point, or different implications, in the ordinary affairs of everyday life from what it has in the philosophical investigation of knowledge. This is one thing that makes it so difficult to identify uniquely the elusive, peculiarly philosophical, question of knowledge. The distinction lies behind the difficulties I mention in 'Scepticism and the Possibility of Knowledge', and is one of the main themes of *The Significance of Philosophical Scepticism*. Part of this essay appears in slightly different form in the last chapter of that book. Despite the overlap, I publish it here because it expounds some of the central views of Clarke's important, rich, and difficult paper, and focuses attention on one of the crucial issues on which its success appears to depend.

'Taking Scepticism Seriously' appeared as a long review of Peter Unger's *Ignorance: A Case for Scepticism*[5] in the *Journal of Philosophy* in 1977, but without that title. I there lament the fact that most philosophers at the time did not take scepticism seriously enough, but Unger certainly takes it seriously in that book, even to the point of believing it, or at least saying he believes it. He shows

---

[4] *Journal of Philosophy* (1972).   [5] (Oxford, 1975).

in interesting ways how his believing that he knows nothing is compatible with his speaking and acting as all the rest of us do in everyday life. He goes further and claims not only that he does not thereby violate or distort the meanings of the epistemic words we all use, such as "know" and "certain", but that our understanding of the meanings of those words actually commits us to scepticism. I argue that something more is needed to get us all the way to that philosophical conclusion, and make some suggestions about what it is. This too is close to the account in *The Significance of Philosophical Scepticism*.

'Reasonable Claims: Cavell and the Tradition' has not been previously published in exactly this form. A shorter version, amounting to some two-thirds of what is here, appeared in the *Journal of Philosophy* in 1980 as part of an American Philosophical Association symposium on Stanley Cavell's *The Claim of Reason*.[6] Some of the ideas of this essay also appeared in different form in the last chapter of *The Signficance of Philosophical Scepticism*. I include the longer version here because it gives a fuller appreciation of some of the most distinctive and most important aspects of Cavell's response to scepticism, beyond what I mention in my book. I believe Cavell's reply at the APA meeting was largely based on this longer version.

'Transcendental Arguments and "Epistemological Naturalism"' was published in *Philosophical Studies* in 1977. It is in part my reply to Jay Rosenberg's 'Transcendental Arguments Revisited'[7] in an American Philosophical Association symposium under that name. The 'epistemological naturalism' in question is Rosenberg's somewhat Peirce-like view of enquiry, and is not meant to include everything that could be given that label today. In this brief essay I focus a little more on the requirements of the Kantian project itself, and come back to the question of the special status of those conclusions or 'principles' that would be established by a successful transcendental argument—what in 'Transcendental Arguments' I call the 'privileged class of propositions'. Exploration of the possibility of establishing some such conclusions, perhaps of different status and varying strengths, but all within a broadly Kantian or 'transcendental' strategy, runs through several of the later essays.

In 'The Allure of Idealism', which appeared in the *Proceedings*

---

[6] (New York, 1979).　　[7] *Journal of Philosophy* (1975).

of the Aristotelian Society: Supplementary Volume in 1984, the Kantian project gets more detailed attention, and I try to bring out more fully how idealism is implicated in it and required for its success. I also expand a little on the profound disappointment, not to say unintelligibility, of transcendental idealism as a solution to whatever problem of knowledge of the objective world we might have felt at the beginning. The essay was presented in a Joint Session symposium with Jonathan Lear in which he went on from Kant to defend a very Kantian reading of the later works of Wittgenstein, even arguing for the presence of something very like Kant's 'transcendental deduction' in *Philosophical Investigations.*[8] This was in effect to make a case for Wittgenstein as an idealist. I give some reasons for thinking the case cannot be supported. But Lear raises an important question about what exactly we can expect to get from Wittgenstein's writings, and especially from his drawing attention for philosophical purposes to what he calls facts of our 'natural history'. Some of my essays on Wittgenstein in *Meaning, Understanding, and Practice: Philosophical Essays*[9] touch on this question.

'Understanding Human Knowledge in General' was published in M. Clay and K. Lehrer (eds.), *Knowledge and Skepticism* (Boulder, Colo. 1989). It returns to the question of the conditions of a fully satisfactory answer to the distinctively philosophical problem of knowledge, filling in with some detail the outline offered in 'Scepticism and the Possibility of Knowledge'. I give reasons for thinking that, because of the way we apparently want to understand human knowledge in philosophy, there is and could be no satisfactory answer to the question. This turns in part on the extreme generality of what we seek. Because we want to understand how *all* knowledge of a certain kind is possible, we cannot rely on any knowledge of that kind we might think we already possess in order to explain how we know anything at all of that kind. It seems as if a satisfactory explanation must then explain how we can get from knowledge of some other kind to knowledge of the kind in question. But no such step seems available.

Some theories of knowledge would deny that such a step is needed; someone who has knowledge of the kind in question does

---

[8] See his 'The Disappearing "We"', *Proceedings of the Aristotelian Society: Supplementary Volume* (1984).
[9] (Oxford, 2000).

not have to know that the step is justified in order to have that knowledge. I explain the point of that 'externalist' strategy and argue that, given the problem of knowledge with which we began, 'externalism' alone would still leave us in an unsatisfactory position. We would not really understand how we know the things we do, even if we do know them. The position we would be left in, and its unsatisfactoriness, are difficult to describe accurately, for reasons I try to explain, and perhaps even illustrate.

'Epistemological Reflection on Knowledge of the External World' was published in *Philosophy and Phenomenological Research* in 1996. It is my response to Michael Williams's *Unnatural Doubts: Epistemological Realism and the Basis of Skepticism*[10] as presented in a symposium devoted to that book at Northwestern University. Contrary to Williams, it stresses the 'naturalness' or apparent irresistibility of the general reflections that lead to philosophical questions about knowledge, and so to the subsequent scepticism. Williams holds that those reflections depend from the very beginning on abstract philosophical assumptions and theories which distort or obscure the phenomena in ways that guarantee the unsatisfactory result. He and I agree that what is needed is a satisfying diagnosis of the source of the appeal and apparent inevitability of scepticism in philosophy. We differ about how to do it, or what rewards can be expected from it. I express doubts about the details of some of his diagnoses, in particular about the role of what he calls 'epistemological realism'. But if there are philosophical assumptions or theories at work in leading us to scepticism, I think understanding what seems to support them, and why it is so easy for us to fall into them, is likely to prove philosophically rewarding. I would put more weight on the demand for complete generality that is felt to be essential to the philosophical project, and on the (perhaps all too human) urge to get outside the human condition which it seems to be an expression of.

'Skepticism, "Externalism", and the Goal of Epistemology' was in part a reply to Ernest Sosa's 'Philosophical Scepticism and Epistemic Circularity' in a Joint Session symposium, and was published with his paper in the *Proceedings of the Aristotelian Society: Supplementary Volume* in 1994. It stresses the unavoidability of a concern with scepticism in any attempt to defend a philosophical

---

[10] (Oxford, 1991).

theory of knowledge, and argues again for the idea that scepticism is probably the only right answer to the epistemological question. Sosa disagrees, and defends a version of 'externalism' by opposing the idea that it must leave us ultimately dissatisfied—something I had argued for in 'Understanding Human Knowledge in General'. But the reasons I gave for that verdict there are not really taken up and assessed by Sosa, so in effect I give them again. The point is elusive, and requires a certain difficult imaginative projection. I do not know how well I succeed in bringing out what I have in mind.

'Kantian Argument, Conceptual Capacities, and Invulnerability' appeared first in P. Parrini (ed.), *Kant and Contemporary Epistemology* (Dordrecht, 1994). It begins with something of a review of the problem of transcendental arguments as I saw it at that time, and of the development of P. F. Strawson's views on the subject. In 'Transcendental Arguments' I had taken his discussions of objective particulars and of persons in his *Individuals*[11] as giving perhaps the clearest and most persuasive arguments of the kind I thought could not succeed. In his *Skepticism and Naturalism: Some Varieties*[12] in 1985 he conceded that perhaps they could not go as far as he at one time had appeared to think. He thought we should settle for 'a certain sort of interdependence of conceptual capacities and beliefs', without supposing we can reach conclusions as to how things actually are.

The rest of my essay gives reasons against retreating so far so quickly, and giving up all hope of arriving by general argument at conclusions that enjoy some special status or other, and so have some special standing in our conception of the world and in our knowledge of it. The question is what is possible down that road: perhaps there is a way to disarm certain forms of philosophical scepticism without having to go as far as establishing truths about the independent world. I give the name "invulnerability" to that special status and begin to explore different forms it might take and different ways in which it might be shown to belong to some of our beliefs.

The depth and potential power of a broadly Kantian strategy lie in the fact that it begins with the very conditions of thought and experience. If scepticism is correct we have no knowledge, but even

---

[11] (London, 1959).   [12] (London, 1985).

to consider the question or to entertain the sceptical challenge we must at least have certain coherent thoughts. We must think of ourselves and others as having a set of beliefs about the world even to be in a position to contemplate drawing the sceptical conclusion that none of those beliefs is reasonable or amounts to something we know. In 'Radical Interpretation and Philosophical Scepticism' I examine Donald Davidson's account of belief and belief-attribution to see what anti-sceptical lessons can be drawn from it. The essay was first published in the Library of Living Philosophers volume, *The Philosophy of Donald Davidson*, edited by L. E. Hahn (LaSalle, Ill., 1999), but written several years before that.

On Davidson's view our beliefs about what the world is like in general and our beliefs about what thoughts and beliefs there are in the world must go hand in hand. This puts limits on how far we could find the contents of the beliefs we attribute to people to deviate in general from the way things are. My essay is an exploration of those limits, and where they would have to lie in order to provide an effective defence against the threat of philosophical scepticism. I argue that the actual truth of most of our beliefs cannot be derived solely from fulfilment of the conditions of our attributing them to ourselves and others, at least not without a doubtful transcendental argument that would appear to depend on some form of idealism. I try to indicate how an anti-sceptical argument could still succeed by demonstrating, not the truth, but only what I have called a certain kind of 'invulnerability' of the beliefs in question.

Discussion of the idea of 'invulnerability' is carried a few small steps further in 'The Goal of Transcendental Arguments'. That was my contribution to a conference which 'revisited' transcendental arguments once again, this time in Sheffield, England, and was published in Robert Stern (ed.), *Transcendental Arguments: Problems and Prospects* (Oxford, 2000). It first gives a quick review of some of the special features of transcendental arguments, overlapping to some extent with earlier essays. It then adds a distinction between two different sources of the kind of 'invulnerability' I have in mind, or two different ways of showing that certain beliefs have it. Being indispensable to any conception of an independent world at all would render a belief invulnerable to exposure as mere illusion, but beliefs can be invulnerable in a similar way even without enjoying that kind of indispensability. Exactly what kind and degree of resistance to scepticism can thereby be secured is certainly a question for further investigation. In illustrating the idea in this essay with the example of the colours of things, I invoke the much fuller treatment of the whole strategy given in my *The Quest for Reality: Subjectivism and the Metaphysics of Colour*,[13] where epistemological scepticism is not really the issue at all. I draw heavily in that book on ideas first presented in the essays 'Kantian Argument, Conceptual Capacities, and Invulnerability' and 'Radical Interpretation and Philosophical Scepticism'.

'The Synthetic A Priori in Strawson's Kantianism' has not been printed before. It was presented at a conference on Strawson and Kant in Reading, England in 1999. Kant's question of how synthetic a priori judgements are possible was in part a question of how philosophical results with the distinctive status of those he reached in the *Critique of Pure Reason* could be reliably arrived at, and metaphysics set on the secure path of a science. The question depends on a clear distinction between "analytic" and "synthetic" judgements, and on the assumption that if something is known to be necessarily true then it is known a priori. Kant's answer was that transcendental idealism is the only possible explanation of our knowledge of such truths. This paper asks whether there is a parallel question about the more 'austere' Kantian project pursued by Strawson with no appeal to transcendental idealism or, apparently, to a priori knowledge.

I try to show that conclusions with a very special, distinctive status can be reached if necessary connections can be discovered between the possession of certain concepts or conceptual capacities and others, and if certain specified conceptual capacities can be shown to be required for the possibility of any thought or experience at all. The distinctive status of those conclusions can be described without making use of any "analytic–synthetic" distinction, and without supposing that we know them a priori. There remains the question of how we can know of the kinds of necessary connections that the project requires. I suggest that when certain traditional reasons for thinking that necessity is uniquely problematic are overcome or set aside, what remains might be no

---

[13] (New York, 1999).

more than a special case of the general question of how we can know anything. Issues touched on here overlap with those in earlier papers in this volume on transcendental arguments and the Kantian project, and with discussion of the idea of 'invulnerability to unmasking' in the two immediately preceding papers.

Scepticism and the Possibility of Knowledge

Scepticism in recent and current philosophy represents a certain threat or challenge in the theory of knowledge. What is that threat? How serious is it? How, if at all, can it be met? What are the consequences if it cannot be met?

I obviously do not have time to go into all these questions, or into any of them thoroughly. I can only sketch a point of view in the hope of provoking some discussion.

The first question is clearly the place to start. I believe the true nature of the sceptical threat is still not properly understood, nor are the consequences of it not being met. That is one reason we have tended to give inadequate answers to the other questions. It is still widely felt that scepticism is not really worth taking seriously, so it hardly matters whether the challenge can be met or not. That kind of reaction seems to me to rest on a philosophical misconception.

Many would dismiss scepticism and defend not taking it seriously on the grounds that it is not a doctrine or theory any sensible person would contemplate adopting as the truth about our position in the world. It seems to them frivolous or perverse to concentrate on a view that is not even a conceivable candidate in the competition for the true or best theory as to how things are. I would grant—indeed insist—that philosophical scepticism is not something we should seriously consider adopting or accepting (whatever that means). But does that mean that it is silly to worry about scepticism? I think it does not. A line of thinking can be of deep significance and great importance in philosophy even if we never contemplate accepting a 'theory' that claims to express it.

One reason that is so is that philosophy thrives on paradox, absurdity, dilemma, and difficulty. There are often what look like good arguments for surprising or outrageous conclusions. Taking

This essay was first published in the *Journal of Philosophy* (1984).

the paradoxical reasonings seriously and re-examining the assumptions they rest on can be important and fruitful when there is no question at all of our ever contemplating adopting a 'theory' or doctrine embodying the absurd conclusion.

The point is clearest in the case of antinomies—explicit contradictions. We know we cannot believe the conclusion; it couldn't possibly be true. To take The Liar, or Russell's paradox seriously is not to hold open even the remote option of believing that someone who says he is lying speaks both truly and falsely, or that there is a set that both is and is not a member of itself. Such 'theories' would be worse than outrageous as things to believe, but that in no way diminishes the need to take seriously the reasoning that leads to them.

The same is true even when the conclusion of the paradoxical or surprising reasoning falls short of explicit contradiction. The Eleatic doctrine that nothing moves, for example, need not be in any remote sense a live intellectual option for us in order for us to be rightly challenged, overwhelmed, perhaps even stumped, by Zeno's argument that Achilles can never overtake the Tortoise. The mere idea of something's being true at a time can seem to generate the absurd result that there is never any real alternative to what happens, that things are fated to happen as they do. We can be impelled to investigate that line of reasoning without thinking that otherwise we would have to adopt the 'theory' that we have no control over what we do or what happens to us. Again, it seems undeniable that adding one more molecule to a table would not turn it into a non-table, any more than pulling one hair from a bushy head would make it bald. The discomfort I feel in the thought that an exactly similar step can be taken again, and again, does not show that I in any way consider accepting a 'theory' according to which there could be a table the size and shape of the earth, or that a bushy head and a bald head are the same sort of thing.

Those modern philosophers most closely connected to the sceptical tradition and most impressed by sceptical reasoning—Descartes, Hume, and Russell, for example—do not hold that believing the conclusions of that reasoning is a real option for us. The ancient sceptics themselves seem not to have accepted, or to have contemplated accepting or declaring the truth of any 'theory' either. They were highly anti-theoretical philosophers, and their strictures would have extended to any theoretical pronouncements put into their own mouths by their opponents as well. But none of that shows that sceptical ideas were not worth taking seriously or were not of great philosophical importance.

The importance of scepticism came always from the uses to which its ideas were put—different uses at different times. It is now widely understood to represent a certain threat or challenge in the theory of knowledge. That is not to say that everything in epistemology as we think of it today, or even in that challenge, can be traced back to the sceptical tradition alone. Exactly which sceptical ideas were important in defining the modern philosophical concern with human knowledge, how and to what extent they were used, and to what effect—all these are intriguing historical questions. Clearly, it is complicated. The role of sense-perception in our knowledge of the world became an important issue even for those apparently untouched by scepticism—by those in the atomist tradition, for example, from Galileo to Boyle and Locke, as well as by Descartes himself in his studies of optics and the physiology of perception. I want to concentrate for the moment on the problem or challenge itself. I think that, whatever its historical source, it has come to define, or perhaps even create, the philosophical concern with our knowledge of the world.

What do we want from a philosophical theory of knowledge? What is it supposed to do? It seems that we simply want to understand how we get the knowledge we have—to explain how it is possible. But I don't think that is enough to uniquely identify the philosophical problem.

Take what is usually called in philosophy 'our knowledge of the world around us'. Now it seems obvious, without any philosophical preconceptions, that there are countless ways of coming to know something about the world around us. I can find out that there is a bus-drivers' strike in Rome, for example, by waiting in vain for a bus or by reading a newspaper or by getting a letter from a friend. How many different ways of finding out is that? Is reading a newspaper only one way, or possibly many? Is reading it in the *New York Times* a different way of finding it out from reading it in the *New York Post*? It seems hopeless to try counting. Obviously we do not just want a list of sources. What we seek in philosophy is not just anything that is true about how we get knowledge of the world around us.

The philosophical interest in knowledge is general, and in at least two different ways. We are interested in all of our knowledge of the world taken all together, or in some domain characterized in general terms. To ask only how we come to know some things in the domain, given that we already know certain other things in it, is not to ask about all knowledge of that kind in general. And we don't just want a heterogeneous list of ways of coming to know. We want to find a single way, or a small number of very general 'ways of knowing'. To explain how they work will be to explain, in general, how knowledge of the kind in question is possible.

Is that enough, then, to identify what we are interested in in the philosophy of knowledge? I don't think so. Suppose we eventually establish contact with some beings elsewhere in space. We receive some regular signals, we send back similar messages, and eventually find ourselves communicating with something somewhere. We take the opportunity to find out about them. We ask them where they are, what it is like there, what they are like, how they send out their signals, how they receive ours, and so on. Suppose they do the same with us. One day there appears on our receiving screen the question: 'How do you come to know of the things around you?' We send back the answer: 'We see them with our eyes, we touch them with parts of our bodies, we hear the noises they make . . .'. That might be just what those beings want to know. Perhaps for them it's all a matter of sonar, or something we do not even understand. But even if that answer is just what the aliens want, is it what we want in philosophy?

I think we recognize that the philosophical question is not simply a request for information of this kind. What we want, rather, is some kind of *explanation* of our knowledge—some account of how it is possible. But what kind of explanation of its possibility? Our friends in space could send back a message pressing us for details. 'Exactly how does seeing work?' they might ask. 'What has to happen after light strikes your eye in order for you to know something about what is reflecting the light? How can you recognize the objects around you and pick them out from the background? Please send detailed explanation.' We could send answers to some of their questions. We might even send them as much as we can of our science as it is and let them figure it out for themselves. Maybe they would send back better explanations than we've now got. That would be super naturalized epistemology, if not supernaturalized epistemology.

But would it be what we seek in philosophy? Sending them that information would be like sending them what we know about motion and acceleration, from which they could easily deduce that Achilles will have no trouble overtaking the Tortoise. Would that meet Zeno's challenge? What puzzles us in that case, if anything does, is how it is possible for Achilles to overtake the Tortoise *if* what Zeno relies on at each step of the argument is true. We want to know how overtaking is possible given those undeniable facts invoked by Zeno. That is how that challenge is to be met—not simply by reminding us of the obvious facts of motion and acceleration, or, worse still, by running off and overtaking a tortoise oneself.

The same is true in the case of our knowledge of the world. It is not enough simply to know something; and not just any explanation of how such knowledge is possible will do. It is true that we come to know of the things around us by seeing and touching them, but that is just the sort of information we could send to the aliens in space. Only they or others similarly removed from us would seek that kind of answer. The philosophical question has not yet been reached.

We want a general answer to the question. It should be expressed in terms of a general 'way of knowing'. And we find that general source in what we call 'the senses' or 'sense-perception'. The problem then is to explain how we can get any knowledge at all of the world around us on the basis of sense-perception. But again, not just any explanations will do, any more than just any relevant information about motion and acceleration will answer Zeno's question. When our friends in space request such explanations we do not understand them to be asking a philosophical question about our knowledge. What *we* want is an explanation of how we could get any knowledge of things around us on the basis of sense-perception, given certain apparently undeniable facts about sense-perception.

The difficulty comes in philosophy when we try to see exactly how sense-perception works to give us knowledge of the world. We are led to think of seeing, or perceiving generally, in a certain way. What is in question is our knowledge of anything at all about the world, of any of the truths that are about things around us. The difficulty in understanding how sense-perception gives us knowledge of any such truths is that it seems at least possible to perceive what we do without thereby knowing something about the things around us. There have been many versions of that fundamental idea. But whether it is expressed in terms of 'ideas' or 'experiences' or 'sense data' or 'appearances' or 'takings' or 'sensory stimulations', or whatever it might be, the basic idea could be put by saying our knowledge of the world is 'underdetermined' by whatever it is that we get through that source of knowledge known as 'the senses' or 'experience'. Given the events or experiences or whatever they might be that serve as the sensory 'basis' of our knowledge, it does not follow that something we believe about the world around us is true. The problem is then to explain how we nevertheless know that what we do believe about the world around us is in fact true. Given the apparent 'obstacle', how is our knowledge possible?

It is an 'obstacle' because it seems to make our knowledge impossible, just as the facts cited by Zeno seem to make overtaking impossible. If several different possibilities are all compatible with our perceiving what we do, the question is how we know that one of those possibilities involving the truth of our beliefs about the world does obtain and the others do not. That would seem to require an inference of some sort, some reasonable hypothesis or some form of reasoning that could take us from what we get in sense-perception to some proposition about the world around us. That hypothesis or principle of inference itself either will imply something about the world around us or it will not. If it does, it belongs among those propositions our knowledge of which has yet to be explained, so it cannot help explain that knowledge. If it does not, how can our acceptance of it lead to knowledge of the way things are around us? If it itself implies nothing about such things, and we could perceive what we do without knowing anything about such things, how is our knowledge to be explained? If we are in fact in that position, how is our knowledge of the world around us possible?

The problem is too familiar to need further elaboration here. I have wanted to stress only how very special a question it is about the possibility of knowledge, and what one must do to bring it before our minds in its proper philosophical form. That alone is thought to be enough to show that the question is frivolous or idle. The alleged 'obstacle' to our knowledge is thought to be easily avoidable. Even if that quite special question cannot be answered satisfactorily, there is felt to be no good reason to ask it in the first place. The 'assumptions' on which it is based are held to be wrong, misguided, and in any case not inevitable.

One familiar criticism is that the whole project is based on the mistaken assumption that there are or must be sensory 'foundations' of our knowledge of the world which are in some way 'epistemically prior' to the knowledge they serve to support. Abandon that assumption, it is suggested, and the whole problem, or the need to answer it as formulated, disappears. 'Enlightened' epistemologists have accordingly moved beyond that quaint doctrine known as 'foundationalism'. They seek a 'non-foundational' theory of knowledge.

There is not time to go carefully into that complicated issue here. I think the suggestion does not penetrate very deeply into the sources of scepticism; it seems to me to get things almost exactly upside down. And regarding it as simply a matter of deciding to adopt or not to adopt a certain 'assumption' is just another way of not taking scepticism seriously. But if we ignore or reject out of hand the familiar traditional question I have tried to identify, what is left?

Suppose we abandon, or never reach, the idea or hope that our knowledge of the world around us is to be explained as being derived from some knowledge or experience that is not itself knowledge of the world around us—something that is 'prior to' or 'underdetermines' the knowledge we are interested in. What would we then need a philosophical 'theory of knowledge' for? It might seem that we would simply have liberated ourselves from an unrealistic restriction, and we could then go ahead and simply explain how our knowledge is possible. But if we are free to explain it in terms of sense-perception that *does* amount to knowledge of the things around us, can we ever properly understand *all* our knowledge of the world—how any of it is possible at all?

The 'liberated' question can easily be answered by saying that we know of the things around us by perceiving them. We see them, we touch them, we hear them, and so on. We even read about them in the newspaper. But that was just the sort of information we could send to the aliens in space. Is that the sort of thing we want to find out about our knowledge of the world when we wonder, as we do in philosophy, how any of it is possible? Obviously not. We already know all that. If it were the job of a 'non-foundational theory of knowledge' to give us answers like that, it would be even more

tedious than sceptical 'foundational' theories are now widely held
to be.

I do not say that such 'enlightened' 'theories' or explanations
could never tell us anything we do not already know. Obviously,
when they got down to the physiological details, they could. But I
think there is something we aspire to in the philosophical theory
of knowledge that such explanations would not give us. We want
an account of our knowledge of the world that would make all of
it intelligible to us all at once. We want to see how knowledge of
the world could come to be out of something that is not knowledge
of the world. Without that, we will not have the kind of doubly
general explanation we seek. I think scepticism in epistemology
now represents, and perhaps always did represent, the possibility
that such an explanation is impossible; that we cannot consider all
our knowledge of the world all at once and still see it as knowledge. Given that project, the threat is that scepticism will be the
only answer. That alone would not straightforwardly imply that we
can know nothing of the world around us—that we can never know
whether there is a bus drivers' strike in Rome, for example. But it
would suggest that a certain kind of understanding of our position
in the world might be beyond us. Taking that possibility seriously,
trying to see whether it is so, and if so why, would then be what
taking scepticism seriously would amount to. To dismiss it simply
on the grounds that we do know many things and that it would be
ridiculous to believe we do not would be like assuring us that
Achilles will overtake the Tortoise, and that it would be ridiculous
to believe that he will not. And we will be in a position to dismiss
it on the ground that it is absurd even to seek the kind of understanding philosophers have sought of our knowledge only when we
understand better what that goal is, why we seek it, why it is unat-
tainable, and what a philosophical 'theory of knowledge' that did
not aspire to it would look like.

2

Transcendental Arguments

In recent years there has been widespread use of arguments described as Kantian or 'transcendental' which have been thought to be special, and perhaps unique, in various ways. What exactly is a transcendental argument? Before looking closely at some specific candidates it will be useful to see some of the general conditions that such arguments must fulfil.

Kant recognized two distinct questions which can be asked about concepts.[1] The first—the 'question of fact'—amounts to 'How do we come to have this concept, and what is involved in our having it?' This is the task of the 'physiology of the human understanding' as practised by Locke. But even if we knew what experiences or mental operations had been required in order for us to have the concepts we do, Kant's second question—the 'question of right'—would still not have been answered, since we would not yet have established our *right* to, or our *justification* for, the possession and employment of those concepts. Although concepts can be derived from experience by various means, they might still lack 'objective validity', and to show that this is not so is the task of the transcendental deduction.

For example, Kant considered it

. . . a scandal to philosophy and to human reason in general that the existence of things outside us . . . must be accepted merely on *faith*, and that if anyone thinks good to doubt their existence, we are unable to counter his doubts by any satisfactory proof (B xl).

The transcendental deduction (along with the Refutation of Idealism) is supposed to provide just such a proof and, thereby, to give a complete answer to the sceptic about the existence of things

This essay was first published in the *Journal of Philosophy* (1968). I am indebted to many friends and colleagues for their criticism of an earlier version, and would like to thank in particular Martin Hollis and Thomas Nagel.

[1] I. Kant, *Critique of Pure Reason*, tr. N. Kemp Smith (London, 1953), A84ff.

outside us. We can therefore get some understanding of Kant's question of justification by looking at the challenge presented by the epistemological sceptic.[2]

Since the traditional epistemologist asks how it is possible to know anything at all about the world around us, he is not interested only in the specific question of whether there really is a tomato on the table. Consequently, he will not be answered if we simply appeal to one alleged matter of fact in order to support our claim to know another. You cannot show the sceptic that you're not hallucinating, and hence that you know there is a tomato on the table, simply by asking your wife if she sees it too—hallucinations of your wife's reassuring words are epistemologically no better off than hallucinations of tomatoes. At every point in the attempted justification of a knowledge claim the sceptic will always have another question yet to be answered, another relevant possibility yet to be dismissed, and so he can't be answered directly.

Doubts about whether some particular hypothesis is true can often be settled by following the ordinary, well-known ways of establishing matters of so-called empirical fact. But the sceptic maintains that the whole structure of practices and beliefs on the basis of which empirical hypotheses are ordinarily 'supported' has not itself been shown to be reliable. As long as we have a public objective world of material objects in space and time to rely on, particular questions about how we know that such-and-such is the case can eventually be settled. But that there is such a world of material objects at all is a matter of contingent fact, and the sceptic challenges us to show how we know it. According to him, any justification for our belief will have to come from within experience, and so no adequate justification can ever be given. Transcendental arguments are supposed to demonstrate the impossibility or illegitimacy of this sceptical challenge by proving that certain concepts are necessary for thought or experience; but before trying to see exactly how they are thought to do this it will be instructive to consider a possible objection to what has been said so far.

If transcendental arguments are meant to answer the sceptic's

---

[2] When I speak of 'the sceptic' I do not mean to be referring to any person, living or dead, or even to the hypothetical upholder of a fully articulated philosophical position. I use the expression only as a convenient way of talking about those familiar philosophical doubts which it has been the aim of the theory of knowledge, at least since the time of Descartes, to settle.

question and if, as many believe, that question makes no sense, then there will be little point in considering the exact nature of these alleged arguments. This line is reminiscent of that taken by Carnap.[3] He, like Kant, distinguishes between two types of questions—ordinary empirical questions on the one hand, which are raised and answered from 'within' a framework of concepts, beliefs, and recognized procedures of confirmation, and, on the other hand, questions raised by the sceptic or metaphysician about this framework, raised, so to speak, 'from outside'. To ask whether there are any objects more than ten billion miles from the earth is to ask an 'internal' question to which there is an objectively right answer. It is a genuine 'theoretical' issue which can be settled by discovering the truth of certain empirical statements. But to ask simply whether there are any objects at all is to ask an 'external' question about the existence of the system of spatiotemporal material objects as a whole, and this is not a 'theoretical' question with an objectively right answer at all. It is a 'practical' question, a request for a *decision* as to whether or not we should think and talk in terms of material objects. Since there is no set of true propositions that would answer an 'external' question, the issue cannot be settled by gathering evidence.

The belief that 'external' questions must be answered in the same way as ordinary empirical questions is what leads the epistemologist to the sceptical impasse. Carnap avoids scepticism by denying this and claiming that statements like 'There are material objects' assert nothing about the world at all and, hence, that we couldn't conceivably lack knowledge of their truth value. They have no truth value—they merely serve to express a policy we have adopted or a convention with which we comply.

If this conventionalist line is to be successful there must be no *need* for us to conceive of the world in terms of material objects in space and time; it must be perfectly possible for us to find the world and our experience intelligible in other terms. But transcendental arguments are supposed to prove that certain particular concepts are necessary for experience or thought; they establish the necessity or indispensability of certain concepts. Therefore conventionalism of this sort will be refuted if a sound transcendental argument can be produced. If there are particular concepts that are

[3] R. Carnap, 'Empiricism, Semantics and Ontology', Appendix A in *Meaning and Necessity* (Chicago, 1956).

necessary for thought or experience then it is false that, for every one of our present concepts, we could dispense with it and still find the world or our experience intelligible. A sound transcendental argument therefore would show that it is wrong to think (with the conventionalist) that the only possible justification of our ways of thinking is 'pragmatic' or practical, and equally wrong to think (with the sceptic) that they can be justified only by collecting direct empirical evidence of their reliability. Although these look like difficult demands to meet, they represent the minimum conditions that Kant set for the success of a transcendental argument.

Recent attempts to demonstrate the 'absurd' or 'paradoxical' nature of sceptical questions have taken various forms. It has been argued that seeing a tomato in the clear light of day, when other people say they see it too, when I can reach out and feel it, is simply what we *call* 'finding out that there is a tomato there'. This is the best possible case of knowing of the existence of a tomato, and since situations like this certainly do occur, it follows that we *do* know that there are tomatoes, and hence that there are material objects. But from the fact that this is the best possible case of knowing of the existence of a tomato the most that follows is that 'If this isn't a case of knowledge of the external world then nothing is', or, in the more familiar example, 'If this isn't a case of acting of one's own free will then nothing is.' But the truth of such conditionals does not threaten the sceptic; it is precisely because they are true that he is able to challenge all of knowledge by considering only one or two examples. In addition to establishing conditionals of this sort, then, one would also have to show that it is false that there is no knowledge of the external world. But any attempt to show that by an appeal to other empirical facts would lead back onto the sceptic's treadmill.

Defenders of the paradigm-case argument have failed to see that the sceptic need not deny that we can make all the empirical distinctions we do make (e.g. between what we call 'hallucinatory' and what we call 'nonhallucinatory' perceptions), or that we all apply certain concepts (e.g. 'of his own free will') in certain circumstances and withhold them in others. In Kant's terms, these are answers to 'questions of fact' and so are not sufficient to answer the 'question of justification'. It is not a sufficient refutation of the sceptic who doubts that *p* to present him only with a conditional to the effect that if *not-p* we couldn't possibly do *A*. What is in question is whether we ever 'validly' or 'justifiably' do *A*. This is shown, in the extreme case, by the obvious weakness of the argument that runs: If no one ever acted freely, then the ascription of praise and blame would be impossible. But we do ascribe praise and blame. Therefore it is false that no one ever acts freely.

In order to demonstrate the absurdity of scepticism, the paradigm-case argument had to rely on a theory of meaning to the effect that, at least for some words, if those words are to have the meaning they do have in our language, there must actually be things or situations to which they have been, and perhaps still are, truly applied. If this were true of the word "*X*", for example, then from the fact that the question 'Are there really any *X*'s?' makes sense it would follow that the answer to that question is 'Yes'. This has been thought sufficient to demonstrate the 'absurdity' of the sceptic's question.[4] But this theory of meaning is highly doubtful, for reasons that will be given later. In the meantime I shall examine some subtler and more persuasive recent anti-sceptical arguments.

The first half of Strawson's *Individuals*,[5] which is certainly Kantian in tone, gives the impression of relying on transcendental arguments to establish the absurdity or illegitimacy of various kinds of scepticism. Strawson starts by saying:

(1) We think of the world as containing objective particulars in a single spatiotemporal system.

He emphasizes that this is a remark about the way we think of the world, about 'our conceptual scheme' (p. 15), and he wants to discover some of the necessary conditions of our thinking in this way. In discovering these conditions Strawson claims to have demonstrated that the sceptic's doubts are illegitimate, since they amount to a rejection of some of the necessary conditions of the existence

---

[4] See J. O. Urmson, 'Some Questions Concerning Validity', in A. Flew (ed.), *Essays in Conceptual Analysis* (London, 1956), 120. According to the still fashionable view that all mathematical truths are true by virtue of the meanings of their constituent words, this assumption would also render 'absurd' all questions of the form 'Does 3695 times 1583 really equal 5748785?'. Given the meanings of the constituent words and numerals, it *follows* that the answer is 'Yes'. Has the question therefore been 'exposed' as 'absurd'?

[5] P. F. Strawson, *Individuals, An Essay in Descriptive Metaphysics* (New York, 1959).

of the conceptual scheme within which alone such doubts make sense (p. 35). This can be understood in two ways, depending on what the sceptic is thought to doubt.

Strawson sometimes takes the sceptic to doubt or deny:

(6) Objects continue to exist unperceived.

Only on this understanding of the sceptic is there any plausibility in the claim that he is merely a 'revisionary' metaphysician who rejects our conceptual scheme and offers a new one in its place (pp. 35–6). But if the sceptic doubts or denies (6) and if the truth of what the sceptic doubts or denies is to be a necessary condition of those doubts' making sense, then Strawson would have to show that (6), a statement about the way things are, follows from (1), a statement about how we think of the world, or what makes sense to us. How could such an inference ever be justified?

Strawson's argument is this. The sceptic's doubts about the continued existence of objects make sense only if (1) is true. But it is a necessary truth that:

(2) If we think of the world as containing objective particulars in a single spatiotemporal system, then we are able to identify and reidentify particulars.

And again, necessarily:

(3) If we can reidentify particulars, then we have satisfiable criteria on the basis of which we can make reidentifications.

Strawson's argument actually stops here, thus showing that he regards what has been established as sufficient to imply his diagnosis of scepticism, but it is clear that it does not follow from (1)–(3) alone that objects continue to exist unperceived. The most that has been explicitly established is that if the sceptic's statement makes sense then we must have satisfiable criteria on the basis of which we can reidentify a presently observed object as numerically the same as one observed earlier, before a discontinuity in our perception of it. And this does not imply that objects continue to exist unperceived if it is possible for all reidentification statements to be false even though they are asserted on the basis of the best criteria we ever have for reidentification. Only if this is not possible will Strawson's argument be successful.

A principle that would explicitly rule out this alleged possibility would be:

(4) If we know that the best criteria we have for the reidentification of particulars have been satisfied, then we know that objects continue to exist unperceived.

Either this is a suppressed premiss of Strawson's argument or it is what he means by 'criteria for reidentification of particulars'—in either case it is required for the success of his attack on scepticism. But the argument now comes down to the claim that if we think of the world as containing objective particulars, then it must be possible for us to know whether objects continue to exist unperceived. We could not make sense of the notion of unperceived continued existence without having criteria of reidentification, and if we have such criteria then we can sometimes know whether objects continue to exist unperceived. I shall call this result, which is the conclusion of the argument from (1) to (4), the *verification principle*. If this principle is not true Strawson's argument is unsound.

It does not follow from (1)–(4) that we actually *do* know that objects continue to exist unperceived and, hence, that (6) is true; but that conclusion will follow if we add to the verification principle one more premiss to the effect that:

(5) We sometimes know that the best criteria we have for the reidentification of particulars have been satisfied.

The fact that (5) is needed shows that it was wrong to interpret Strawson as making a purely deductive step from how we think, or what makes sense to us, to the way things are. (6) is not a consequence of (1) alone, but only of the conjunction of (1) and (5), and so there is an additional factual premiss which enables Strawson to make the otherwise questionable transition. And this in turn shows that Strawson was wrong to take the sceptic to be denying (6). If the truth of what the sceptic denies is a necessary condition of that denial's making sense, and if, as we have seen, it is not the case that the truth of (6) is a necessary condition of the sceptic's making sense, then the sceptic cannot be denying (6). On his grounds, to deny this would be just as unjustified as our asserting it—he argues only that our belief that objects continue to exist unperceived can never be justified.

If this is so, then the factual premiss that warrants the inference to (6) is obviously superfluous. The verification principle that the argument rests on is: if the notion of objective particulars makes sense to us, then we can sometimes know certain conditions to be fulfilled, the fulfilment of which logically implies either that objects continue to exist unperceived or that they do not. The sceptic says that we can never justify our acceptance of the proposition that objects continue to exist unperceived, but now there is a direct and conclusive answer to him. If the sceptic's claim makes sense it must be false, since if that proposition could not be known to be true or known to be false it would make no sense. This follows from the truth of the verification principle. Without this principle Strawson's argument would have no force; but with this principle the sceptic is directly and conclusively refuted, and there is no further need to go through an indirect or transcendental argument to expose his mistakes.

Strawson's apparently more complicated account of scepticism about other minds is essentially the same as this. In order for me to understand, or make sense of, talk of *my* experiences, I must at least understand the ascription of experiences to others. But it is a necessary condition of my understanding this that I be able to iden- tify different individuals as the subjects of such ascriptions. And this in turn is possible only if the individuals in question are such that both states of consciousness and corporeal characteristics are ascribable to them. But talk of identifiable individuals of this special or unique type makes sense only if we have 'logically ade- quate kinds of criteria' for ascriptions of such predicates to them. Hence 'the sceptical problem does not arise'—its very statement 'involves the pretended acceptance of a conceptual scheme and at the same time the silent repudiation of one of the conditions of its existence' (p. 106). But what the sceptic 'repudiates' is the possi- bility of my knowing that there are any states of consciousness other than mine, and so Strawson's characterization of the sceptic is correct only if my possession of 'logically adequate criteria' for the other-ascription of a particular psychological state implies that it is possible for me to know certain conditions to be fulfilled, the fulfilment of which logically implies either that some particular person other than myself is in that state or that he is not. This must be either a suppressed premiss of Strawson's argument or an explanation of 'logically adequate criteria'.

As before, then, the sceptic is seen as maintaining both that (i) a particular class of propositions makes sense and that (ii) we can never know whether or not any of them are true. For Strawson the falsity of (ii) is a necessary condition for the truth of (i), and the truth of (i) is in turn required for the sceptic's claim itself to make sense. Therefore the success of Strawson's attack on both forms of scepticism depends on the truth of some version of what I have called the 'verification principle'.

In *Self-Knowledge and Self-Identity* Shoemaker[6] argues against the other-minds sceptic as follows (pp. 168–9). A person who understands 'I am in pain' cannot utter those words sincerely and without a slip of the tongue unless he is in pain. Therefore, if it is possible to know whether another person understands the word "pain" it must be possible to know whether another person is in pain. But the word "pain" could not have an established meaning if it were not possible for people to be taught its meaning and possible for us to determine whether a person is using it correctly. Therefore to assert, as the sceptic does, that it is logically impossible for one person to know of another that he is in pain is to imply that the word "pain" has no established meaning. But if the word "pain" has no established meaning, then the putative statement that it is logically impossible for one person to know of another that he is in pain has no established meaning either. Therefore, either what the sceptic says has no established meaning, or it is false.

This conclusion is the same as Strawson's, but in summarizing the argument Shoemaker makes a further claim for it which appears to be mistaken. He says:

Of any sentence that appears to say that it is logically impossible to know that another person is in pain we must say either that it actually expresses no statement at all or that it expresses a statement that is necessarily false. (p. 170)

But it does not follow from the necessity of the conditional 'if the sceptic's statement makes sense, then it is false' that the sceptic's statement is a necessary falsehood. Although Shoemaker does not go on to draw any conclusions from this summary of the argument that do not follow from the argument itself, later on he does claim that:

---

[6] Sydney Shoemaker, *Self-Knowledge and Self-Identity* (Ithaca, NY, 1963).

It is a necessary (logical, or conceptual) truth, not a contingent one, that when perceptual and memory statements are sincerely and confidently asserted, i.e., express confident beliefs, they are generally true.   (p. 229)

One argument he gives for this starts out as follows:

(I) A primary criterion for determining whether a person understands such terms as "see" and "remember" is whether under optimum conditions the confident claims that he makes by the use of these words are generally true.   (p. 231)

It is essential for anyone's using the words "see" and "remember" correctly—and hence for their having the established meanings they have—that statements made by the use of those words be generally true. Therefore, if perceptual and memory statements were not generally true, then "see" and "remember" would not have the meanings they appear to have, and there would be no perceptual or memory statements.

To say that the words "see" and "remember" would not have the meanings they do have unless the statements people made by the use of those words were generally true is explicitly to rule out the possiility of our understanding those statements when they are, unknown to us, always false, or false most of the time, although they appear to be true and hence we *believe* them. Therefore this argument too depends on the truth of the verification principle. But more is needed in order to prove that it is a necessary truth that perceptual and memory statements are generally true. The most that has been established is that the putative statement that it is not the case that perceptual and memory statements are generally true is either false or meaningless. But this alone does not imply that it is a necessary falsehood, and so does not imply that it is a necessary truth that perceptual and memory statements are generally true.

The rest of the argument is:

(II) So to suppose that (*a*) it is a contingent fact, which could be otherwise, that confident perceptual and memory statements are generally true is to suppose that (*b*) we have no way of telling whether a person understands the use of words like "see" and "remember", or means by them what others mean by them, that (*c*) we can never have any good reason for regarding any utterance made by another person as a perceptual or memory statement, and that (*d*) we could therefore never discover the supposedly contingent fact that perceptual and memory statements are generally true. And this is a logically absurd supposition.[7]

But the conclusion that it is a necessary truth that perceptual and memory statements are generally true does not follow from this alone, because (*b*), (*c*), and (*d*) do not follow from (I) and (*a*). All that follows is that it is a contingent fact that any person understands "see" and "remember". And that this is a contingent fact does not itself imply that (*b*) we can have no way of telling whether it obtains or that (*c*) we can never have any good reason for regarding any utterance as a perceptual or memory statement, since the contingency of "*p*" does not in general imply that we can never find out that *p*. Without some independent support for this last step the argument would fail. Given (1), (*c*) and (*d*) do follow from the assumption that perceptual and memory statements *are not* generally true, but they do not follow from the quite different assumption that it is a contingent fact that perceptual and memory statements are generally true.

Shoemaker's independent argument is that, in trying to discover by inductive means the allegedly contingent fact that perceptual and memory statements are generally true, I could not rely on anything that I believe on the basis of observation or memory. But there is no other way in which I could come to know it; therefore I could never know it. From the assumption (shared by the sceptic) that if it is a contingent fact that *p* then our acceptance of "*p*" can be supported only by experience or by inductive means, and the fact that we could not rely on perception or memory in order to establish that our perceptual and memory beliefs are generally true, Shoemaker concludes that it is a necessary truth that those beliefs are generally true. But this does not follow, and the most that he has shown, as he himself sometimes points out (cf. p. 238), is that a conditional statement to the effect that 'if . . . , then perceptual and memory beliefs are generally true' is a necessary truth.

What should the antecedent of such a conditional be? Shoemaker says that 'it follows from the logical possibility of anyone's knowing anything about the world that perceptual and memory beliefs are generally true' (p. 235), but this alone raises no

[7] Ibid. 231–2. In this and the previous quotation I have inserted numerals and letters into Shoemaker's text.

difficulties for the sceptic who denies that we can know anything about the world. He too insists on the truth of that conditional. It is no accident that those concerned with all of our knowledge of the world have concentrated on perception and, to a lesser degree, on memory.

Rather than dealing with the conditions of *knowledge*, then, those conditionals must assert that the truth of what the sceptic doubts or denies is a necessary condition of the *meaningfulness* of that doubt or denial. But even this could fail to be a conclusive refutation of the sceptic. If only a restricted class of propositions is in question, it is always open to the sceptic to accept the argument and conclude that talk about, say, the continued existence of unperceived objects really doesn't make sense to us. Although he wouldn't, and needn't, say this at the outset, he would be forced into it by an argument that relied on the truth of the verification principle. Far from refuting scepticism, this would make it stronger. Not only would we be unable to know whether the proposition allegedly expressed by a certain form of words is true; we would not even understand those words.[8] A successful anti-sceptical argument will therefore have to be completely general, and deal with the necessary conditions of anything's making sense, not just with the meaningfulness of this or that restricted class of propositions.

Furthermore, it won't be enough to deal simply with all of language *as it now is*. David Pears described the conclusions of Strawson's arguments as 'conditional necessities' to the effect that such-and-such is necessary if we are to think and speak as we now do.[9] But even if such conditionals are true, it is still open to the conventionalist to claim that no 'theoretical' justification has been given for our acceptance of the propositions the sceptic doubts or denies, since we could simply give up our present ways of thinking and speaking (of which they are the necessary conditions) and adopt others (of which they are not). Transcendental arguments must yield more than 'conditional necessities' in this sense—they must make these sceptical and conventionalist replies impossible.

---

[8] That this result follows from an application of the verification principle seems to me more an argument against the verification principle than against scepticism. A. J. Ayer expresses a somewhat similar belief in discussing Strawson; see *The Concept of a Person and Other Essays* (New York, 1963).

[9] *Philosophical Quarterly*, 11: 43 (Apr. 1961), 172.

Kant thought that his transcendental proofs counted in a unique way against both scepticism and conventionalism because their conclusions were synthetic and could be known a priori. They are shown to have this status by a transcendental argument which proves that the truth of its conclusion is a necessary condition of there being any experience or thought at all. If the conclusion were not true, there could be no experience to falsify it. For Kant, proofs that such-and-such is a necessary condition of thought or experience in general, therefore, have a special feature which is not shared by other proofs that one thing is a necessary condition of another,[10] and because they have this feature they can answer the 'question of justification'.

Suppose we have a proof that the truth of a particular proposition *S* is a necessary condition of there being any meaningful language, or of anything's making sense to anyone. For brevity, I will say that the truth of *S* is a necessary condition of there being some language. If we had such a proof we would know that *S* cannot be denied truly, because it cannot be denied truly that there is some language. The existence of a language is a necessary condition of anyone's ever asserting or denying anything at all, and so if anyone denies in particular the proposition that there is some language it follows that it is true. Similarly, it is impossible to assert truly that there is no language. This suggests that there is a genuine class of propositions each member of which must be true in order for there to be any language, and which consequently cannot be denied truly by anyone, and whose negations cannot be asserted truly by anyone. Let us call this the 'privileged class'.

There are some propositions which it is impossible for one

---

[10] 'Through concepts of understanding pure reason does, indeed, establish secure principles, not however directly from concepts alone, but always only indirectly through relation of these concepts to something altogether contingent, namely, *possible experience*. When such experience (that is, something as object of possible experiences) is presupposed, these principles are indeed apodeictically certain; but in themselves, directly, they can never be known a priori. Thus no one can acquire insight into the proposition that everything which happens has its cause, merely from the concepts involved. It is not, therefore, a dogma, although from another point of view, namely from that of the sole field of its possible employment, that is, experience, it can be proved with complete apodeictic certainty. But though it needs proof, it should be entitled a *principle*, not a *theorem*, because it has the peculiar character that it makes possible the very experience which is its own ground of proof, and that in this experience it must always itself be presupposed.' Kant, *Critique of Pure Reason*, A737.

particular person ever to assert truly. For example, Descartes cannot assert truly that Descartes does not exist—his asserting it guarantees that it is false. Also, there are some propositions which it is impossible for a particular person to assert truly in a certain way, or in a particular language. I can never truly say (aloud) 'I am not now speaking', but everyone else can sometimes say this of me without falsity, and I myself can write it or think it without thereby demonstrating that it is false. Similarly, DeGaulle cannot truly say 'DeGaulle cannot construct an English sentence', but anyone else can truly say this of DeGaulle, and he himself can truly say in French that he cannot construct an English sentence. Furthermore, there are some propositions which it is impossible, not just for one person, but for any member of a particular class of people to assert truly. A Cretan cannot assert truly that every statement made by a Cretan is false—if he does assert this it must be false—but of course any non-Cretan can assert this without thereby guaranteeing its falsity. But the 'self-guaranteeing' character of the members of the privileged class is more general than that of any of these. There is no one, whoever he might be, whatever language he might speak, or whatever class of people he might belong to, who could truly deny any of the members of the privileged class of propositions.

Now no *true* proposition could be denied truly by anyone. But for any proposition *S* that is a member of the privileged class, the truth of *S* follows from the fact that somebody asserted it, or denied it, or said anything at all; and this does not hold for all true propositions generally. It might also be argued that, since a necessary truth could not be false under any circumstances, it could not be denied truly under any circumstances either, and hence that all necessary truths belong to this class. This might be so, but from the fact that a proposition is a member of the privileged class it does not *follow* that it is a necessary truth, and so it seems that there are some propositions, such as 'There is some language', the truth of which is necessary for anyone's ever asserting or denying anything, but which are not themselves necessary truths.[11] It could have been,

---

[11] The tendency to confuse these two different kinds of necessity has seemed an almost inevitable occupational hazard in transcendental philosophy, with its claims to establish necessary or 'conceptual' truths (cf. Shoemaker). If to say that a proposition is 'necessary' or 'conceptual' is only to say that it must be true in order for us to have certain concepts or for certain parts of our language to have the meanings they have, then it does not follow that 'necessary' or 'conceptual' truths are not contingent. Perhaps my privileged class will provide a way of keeping these different kinds of necessity distinct.

and undoubtedly was, the case at one time that there was no language, and it probably will be again. Although it could not be truly denied, still it might have been, and might yet become false.

The existence of the privileged class is obviously important, since if it could be proved that those propositions which the sceptic claims can never be adequately justified on the basis of experience are themselves members, then from the fact that what the sceptic says makes sense it would follow that those propositions are true. This would be a way of replying to the sceptic while still acknowledging the contingency of the things he questions. If those propositions could be shown to belong to the privileged class, there would appear to be no more sceptical questions left open, as there are at every point when we try to answer his questions directly. In general, given an answer to the question 'What are the necessary conditions of X?' does not tell one way or the other about the answer to the question 'Do those conditions obtain?' But in the special case of asking for the necessary conditions of there being some language, giving an answer to the first implies an affirmative answer to the second. One's asserting truly that the truth of S is a necessary condition for there being some language implies that S is true. Therefore there is no other question about the truth value of S yet to be answered, and anyone who denied that we know S and still demanded empirical evidence for its truth would have failed either to understand or to be convinced by the argument. In either case the proper reply would be to go through the argument again.

The question now arises whether there is anything special, and perhaps unique, about transcendental arguments even when they deal with the necessary conditions of language in general, or of anything's making sense. Is it only because Strawson's and Shoemaker's arguments are limited in scope that they depend on an appeal to the verification principle? There are some general reasons for being pessimistic on this question. Although it seems to me unlikely that there should be no members of the privileged class, we have yet to find a way of proving, of any particular member, that it is a member. More specifically, we have yet to show that those very propositions which the epistemological sceptic questions are themselves members of this class. It is obviously extremely difficult to prove this, and not just because talk about 'language in general' or 'the possibility of anything's making sense' is so vague that there seems to be no convincing way of deciding what it covers and what it excludes. That is certainly a difficulty, but there are others. In particular, for any candidate *S*, proposed as a member of the privileged class, the sceptic can always very plausibly insist that it is enough to make language possible if we *believe* that *S* is true, or if it looks for all the world as if it is, but that *S* needn't actually be true. Our having this belief would enable us to give sense to what we say, but some additional justification would still have to be given for our claim to *know* that *S* is true. The sceptic distinguishes between the conditions necessary for a paradigmatic or warranted (and therefore meaningful) use of an expression or statement and the conditions under which it is true.

Any opposition to scepticism on this point would have to rely on the principle that it is not possible for anything to make sense unless it is possible for us to establish whether *S* is true, or, alternatively, that it isn't possible for us to understand anything at all if we know only what conditions make it look for all the world as if *S* is true, but which are still compatible with *S*'s falsity. The conditions for anything's making sense would have to be strong enough to include not only our beliefs about what is the case, but also the possibility of our knowing whether those beliefs are true; hence the meaning of a statement would have to be determined by what we can *know*. But to prove this would be to prove some version of the verification principle, and then the sceptic will have been directly and conclusively refuted. Therefore, even when we deal in general with the necessary conditions of there being any language at all, it looks as if the use of a so-called 'transcendental argument' to demonstrate the self-defeating character of scepticism would amount to nothing more and nothing less than an application of some version of the verification principle,[12] and if this is what a transcendental argument is then there is nothing special or unique, and certainly nothing new, about this way of attacking scepticism.

[12] This suspicion is strongly confirmed by Judith Jarvis Thomson's excellent account of the verificationism in Malcolm's argument against the possibility of a private language, in 'Private Languages'. *American Philosophical Quarterly*, I: I (Jan. 1964), 20–1.

Stuart Hampshire's discussion of the necessary conditions for any language in which a distinction can be made between truth and falsity, while of the required generality, will have force against scepticism only if it is interpreted as resting on a verification principle (i.e. if in order for us to 'successfully identify' an *X*, *X*'s must actually exist). Hampshire himself does not directly apply the argument to scepticism; see *Thought and Action* (New York, 1960), ch. I.

What we need to know at this point is whether or not some version of the verification principle is true. It is not my intention to discuss that issue now, but I do want to insist that it is precisely what must be discussed by many of those who look with favour on the much-heralded 'Kantian' turn in recent philosophy. It could be that we are not so far as we might think from Vienna in the 1920s.

For Kant a transcendental argument is supposed to answer the question of 'justification', and in so doing it demonstrates the 'objective validity' of certain concepts. I have taken this to mean that the concept "*X*" has objective validity only if there are *X*s and that demonstrating the objective validity of the concept is tantamount to demonstrating that *X*s actually exist. Kant thought that he could argue from the necessary conditions of thought and experience to the falsity of 'problematic idealism' and so to the actual existence of the external world of material objects, and not merely to the fact that we believe there is such a world, or that as far as we can tell there is.

An examination of some recent attempts to argue in analogous fashion suggests that, without invoking a verification principle which automatically renders superfluous any indirect argument, the most that could be proved by a consideration of the necessary conditions of language is that, for example, we must *believe* that there are material objects and other minds if we are to be able to speak meaningfully at all. Those propositions about what we believe or about how things seem would thereby have been shown to belong to the privileged class. Although demonstrating their membership in this class would not prove that scepticism is self-defeating, it would refute a radical conventionalism of the kind outlined earlier. It would then be demonstrably false that, for every one of our present concepts, we could dispense with it and still find our experience intelligible. But until this much has been shown, not even part of the justification Kant sought for our ways of thinking will have been given.

3

Doubts about the Legacy of Scepticism

There might never have been such a thing as philosophy. And, just possibly, there might never have been such a thing as philosophy even though everything else in the world had gone on just as it has. People could have claimed to know things, they could have doubted or challenged or denied what others claimed to know, and they could have asked whether certain things were the case, or whether anyone ever does or can know whether they are the case. In short, the very forms of words used by philosophers might have been used in that non-philosophical world. They are so used by millions of people every day right now, without those people having a philosophical thought in their heads.

It is difficult, but not impossible, to imagine situations in which questions and remarks that sound just like those of the philosopher would naturally arise in that non-philosophical world. Thompson Clarke offers us some specimens (pp. 756, 758). A physiologist lecturing to his audience might say:

Unlike each of *us*, who know that we are awake, not dreaming, and that there is a real world of three-dimensional bodies that we are now perceiving, those suffering from certain mental abnormalities believe that what we know to be the real, public world is nothing but their own imaginative construction.

He is asserting that we do know certain things, and the words he uses are the very words a philosopher might use in summing up his defence of common sense against the attacks of the philosophical sceptic: 'We *do* know that there is a real world of three-dimensional bodies that we are now perceiving.'

Leaving the speculation aside, we must face the fact that in our

This paper was presented in an APA symposium on Epistemological Skepticism on 28 December 1972 as a commentary on Thompson Clarke's 'The Legacy of Skepticism', which appeared in the *Journal of Philosophy*, 69: 20 (9 Nov. 1972), 754–9. All page references in parentheses in the text are to that paper.

world there *is* such a thing as philosophy, and ask what it is. What is going on when the *philosophical* question is raised and answered in that way? This problem is more difficult and important than it has seemed to most people. I think we sense that the philosophical question of whether we do know that there is a real world of three-dimensional bodies, even if it is to be answered in the very words used by the lecturing physiologist, is not being settled once and for all by him in his lecture. What he says, as Clarke points out, is a 'verbal twin' of what is said by the philosophical defender of common sense, but each of them, in saying what he says, *means* something different, although it can scarcely be said that the *words* each of them uses mean something different. How then do their remarks differ? What is going on when a philosopher 'defends common sense'?

It is Clarke's general strategy to argue that only the views expressed by the philosophical defender of common sense are touched by the efforts of the philosophical sceptic who denies or questions those views, and that what is said by the lecturing physiologist (or by the experimenter on soporifics in another example) or by anyone else in everyday life is completely immune to attack by those philosophical arguments. So although philosophical scepticism in a sense 'refutes' *something*, it has no tendency to undermine what might be called our 'epistemic position' in the common affairs of ordinary and scientific life. The claims we make there are what Clarke calls 'plain'. The sceptical denial of the claims of philosophical common sense is irrelevant to them.

This optimistic conclusion rests on a certain conception of what the philosophical sceptic and the philosophical defender of common sense are, and perhaps even must be, doing. It can be illustrated by the fable of Clarke's airplane-spotters (p. 759). When one of them says of an airplane 'That's an *F*' on the basis of the features he has been taught to take as sufficient for an airplane's being an *F*, he is making what Clarke calls a 'restricted' claim. In that situation, given his training, it is still possible for the airplane to be of one of the antiquated types, but the urgency of the war effort makes that not worth worrying about, so perhaps he has not even been told about it. In saying 'That's an *F*' he commits himself to less than would his words alone, considered outside the practical context of identifying the kinds of airplanes we care about. This is what might be called only 'knowledge for practical purposes'; for practical purposes he can say he knows it's an *F*. According to the philosophical sceptic (according to Clarke) this is strictly analogous to what goes on in non-philosophical ordinary life; this is what 'plain' questions and claims are like.

Philosophizing, on the other hand, is analogous to asking 'pure', as opposed to 'restricted', questions, and making 'pure', as opposed to 'restricted', claims. We ask: 'Is that really an *F*?', and we mean not 'Has he followed his instructions to the letter?', or 'Is there something else we should take into account to help with the war effort?', but simply 'Is it true that that airplane is an *F*?' We want to ask whether what he is committed to by his words alone, independent of the restrictions of the identification practice, is true. So philosophizing is stepping outside the ordinary practices of common life; it is standing back and asking whether any of the things we say within those practices are literally true, and whether we know that they are, or whether they are only 'taken as true for all practical purposes'.

This conception of philosophy as a stepping outside the practical contexts in which ordinary claims are made in everyday life, and asking just *how things are* 'objectively', 'absolutely', is one that many have found attractive. It is implicit, I think, in Descartes's distinction between 'moral' certainty and what he called 'metaphysical' or 'true' knowledge, and perhaps also in Hume's recognition that what one can say and get away with while merrily playing backgammon with one's friends will not stand up to the cool, detached scrutiny of the philosopher. But Hume also saw with characteristic shrewdness that the philosopher's detached 'results' do not stand up when one is conversing and is merry with one's friends, either, and so some further account of the exact nature of those alleged 'results' is needed. How can they be such important 'discoveries' when all their plausibility and relevance is dissipated with one roll of the dice? Do we *forget* that scepticism is true, and that we can never know anything?

It might be thought that this problem is avoided by those who think that scepticism is *not* true, and that we *do* know that there is a world of three-dimensional objects that we are perceiving. There would then be nothing to 'forget' when we move from our philosophical studies into the world. Clarke has two things to say about this. I definitely agree with the first point, and will not say much about it, and the second I will discuss at greater length. It is one of the main points of his paper.

First, to say that philosophical scepticism, the view that we do not know whether there is a world of three-dimensional objects that we are now perceiving, is false, and that we *do* know such things, is to make a remark belonging to what Clarke calls 'philosophical common sense'. But if it is designed to answer the *philosophical* question, it seems nothing more than sheer dogmatism. It is just shouting or gesticulating in the face of philosophical argument. This does not necessarily imply that, for example, what G. E. Moore said in his defence of common sense was simply outrageous or absurd. But it does mean that in so far as Moore's remarks are perfectly legitimate and acceptable, they cannot be taken as a straightforward answer to the philosophical question of the possibility of knowledge. So I agree with Clarke that, on the philosophical question to which scepticism and philosophical common sense are competing answers, scepticism wins hands down, or at least that the mere assertion of philosophical common sense is just a kind of uncomprehending dogmatism—*considered as an answer to that question.*

But secondly, and more importantly, Clarke is concerned with the nature of that philosophical question itself. And he argues that both 'answers'—both philosophical common sense and its sceptical denial—would be fully legitimate and full-bodied in meaning only if a certain conception of concepts, or what might be called 'concept-use', were correct. This conception of what Clarke calls 'our conceptual-human constitution' is the 'standard' one in philosophy; it lies behind the traditional account of philosophizing as the raising of 'pure', detached questions and the giving of equally 'pure' and detached answers to them. But, according to Clarke, this conception must be wrong; our 'conceptual-human constitution' cannot be of the 'standard' type. So it follows that both philosophical common sense and its sceptical denial are spurious fictions, illegitimate, or in some way not fully meaningful, forms of words that 'should both be erased from the books' (p. 762).

What, then, is a 'conceptual-human constitution' of the 'standard' type? Clarke characterizes it this way. We understand and make sense of the world and ourselves by means of a set of concepts for sorting out and distinguishing items in the world. Our concepts either have things falling under them or they do not. Whether they do or not depends solely on the conditions defining the concepts in question, and so whether or not something falls under a given concept depends solely on the concept (or the conditions) in question and the item. It is a purely 'objective' matter; it is in no way 'up to us'; it is, as he says, 'an issue to be settled solely by the concepts and the item' (p. 761). Of course we can and do try to *ascertain* whether items fall under our concepts, but in doing so we are purely 'observers' standing apart both from the items and from the concepts and asking simply whether in fact the former fall under the latter. This is true even when the items in question are aspects of ourselves, for example our own experiences.

For instance, on this view, in asking 'Am I awake now, or dreaming?' as a philosophical question I am standing back as an 'observer' and asking simply under which concept, 'awake' or 'dreaming', my present experience does in fact fall. Of course, I might not be able to ascertain which it falls under, but it does fall under one or the other whether I or anyone else can ever know it or not. One or the other is 'objectively' the case.

This conception of what it is like to possess concepts, and to philosophize, expresses the traditional philosopher's goal of complete or absolute objectivity. He wants to ask just *how things are*, not how we all think they are, or even how we in some sense must think they are. He wants to escape the restrictions and limitations of ordinary practical and scientific life and ask a question, so to speak 'from outside', about even those practical and scientific goings-on themselves. That is why Moore's mere assertions are so unsatisfying philosophically. They are legitimate and acceptable only as 'plain' remarks—as a mere list, drawn up perhaps for its own sake, of some of the things we know. But the philosopher wants to ask whether all the assertions made by plain and scientific men, including Moore's, even if they continue to be said as legitimately and as adamantly as ever, might not still all be wrong or unjustified. That is not a question that can be asked 'from within' the world.

I find the 'conceptual-human constitution of the standard type' immensely plausible. That seems to me to be just how things are with respect to our thought about the world, and it seems to me to express precisely what true objectivity is. I think most people find the view extremely plausible. But I think we cannot be satisfied with this extremely plausible view, because if it were correct and unproblematic, then scepticism would be true. That is, it would follow that what we have in ordinary and scientific life is at most just 'knowledge for all practical purposes'—we would be in a position analogous to that of Clarke's airplane spotters. In short, it would follow that we would be epistemically much worse off in everyday life than we thought we were before we began philosophizing. We wouldn't know what we thought we did. With this consequence of the 'constitution of the standard type' Clarke would agree.

His objections to it, however, go beyond this point. Most people who believe that the 'constitution of the standard type' accurately expresses the way things are do not take scepticism seriously. For various reasons they think it is no threat, and so they simply assert its negation. We *do* know that there is a world of three-dimensional objects that we are now perceiving, and so we can forget about, or ignore, the alleged sceptical challenge. But if Clarke is right this view is just as unacceptable as scepticism, since it too rests on a 'conceptual-human constitution of the standard type', and he argues that that conception of how things are *cannot* be correct. Furthermore, if it were, there would be no way to repel the sceptical attack. Both philosophical common sense and its sceptical denial must be rejected.

The support for this conclusion is very complicated. When the sceptic cross-examines the claims of philosophical common sense he does so by raising a possibility designed to undermine our claim to know some current matter of empirical fact. For example, I think I am sitting comfortably by the fire, but surely I must admit that it is possible that I will wake up in a few minutes and find that all of this has been a dream. But according to Clarke, when we grant that this is a possibility and that it does undermine my present claim to know, we are taking it as perfectly 'plain', and not as having any relevance to the general philosophical question of the possibility of knowledge.

What this means, I think, is that when I allow that it *is* possible that I will wake up in a few minutes and discover that all this has been a dream, I am imagining that the remark I might make later, when I do wake up—a remark to the effect that I know I'm awake and that a few minutes ago I dreamt about sitting by a fire—is a perfectly 'plain', non-'philosophical' remark. That is, it would be just like the remark made by the experimenter on soporifics in

Clarke's example (p. 758). It cannot be taken by itself as answering in the affirmative the philosophical question of whether we can ever know we're awake, and not dreaming. In order for the possibility I envisage to be realized I must later discover, i.e. come to *know*, something. But the knowledge must be perfectly 'plain' knowledge. It cannot be knowledge of the sort such that if I know that *p* then I know the non-actuality of all those possibilities incompatible with my knowing that *p*.

Of course, the sceptic is not unaware of this. He realizes that in order to answer the philosophical question I would have to be able to show how I could know *later*, when I apparently 'woke up', that I was awake *then*, and not dreaming. Only if I could know that then could I discover that earlier I had been dreaming about sitting by a fire. So it is obvious that the mere possibility that I will wake up in a few minutes and *discover* that all this has been a dream will not do the job demanded of it by the philosophical sceptic. By itself it cannot serve his purposes, so according to Clarke he 'throws it in the trash can'. This does not mean that it is not a genuine possibility after all. It is. But what the sceptic says describes a genuine possibility only if it is taken as involving at some point some 'plain', non-'philosophical' knowing, so it cannot serve to undermine *all* of knowledge at one fell swoop. If the knowledge required for the realization of the possibility were 'philosophical'—if it were such that, in order for me to discover later that I am dreaming now, I would have to know *then* that I am not dreaming—the alleged possibility would vanish. 'It calls in question (negates) the very knowing it presupposes' (p. 765), Clarke says. So far, then, although the sceptic cross-examines common sense for philosophical purposes, the possibility he raises in that cross-examination is genuine only if we understand it in a way that renders it irrelevant to the establishment of any *philosophical* theses.

It might seem fairly easy to avoid this initial difficulty by raising for the sceptic a slightly different possibility, one that mentions nothing about our ever finding out or discovering anything—for example, the simple possibility that I am now dreaming, not the possibility that later I will discover that I am. Even if I am never able to find it out, it seems possible that I am dreaming nevertheless, and if I am, then I don't now know that I'm sitting by the fire. Unlike the earlier one, there appears to be no knowledge required for the realization of this possibility at all, so the sceptical philosophical conclusion to which the raising of this possibility is supposed to lead does not seem to call in question or negate any knowing that is presupposed in the very possibility itself. There seems to *be* no knowing involved or presupposed in the possibility at all.

Clarke denies this. He says that this apparently 'non-epistemic' possibility is genuine only if certain things are at least knowable, if not actually known, in a 'plain', non-'philosophical' way. If I am dreaming, he says, then what state I am actually in must at least be *knowable* by someone, if not by me. And he suggests that this is a condition of our using the very concept of dreams that we possess. He says:

> Dream can conceivably be true of an *x* only if the real environs of *x* are *knowable* (plain) as real ... Thus it is integral to Dream's being a concept that its antithesis, the real or portions of the real, be knowable (plain) as real, not just part of a dream. For our concept Dream, if not conceivably true of any *x*, would be bankrupt.   (p. 768)

This claim plays a central role in Clarke's argument, and I want to question its truth in a moment, but let me first sketch the role it does play.

Suppose that it *is* a condition of the concept of a dream's being truly applicable to an item (presumably to a stretch of someone's experience) that the real state or environs of that person be at least knowable by someone in a 'plain' way. That is, suppose that if 'dream' is truly applicable to an item then it could not be the case that *no* being could ever tell whether that concept is true of that item or not because he could never know whether or not *he* is dreaming. Then according to Clarke both philosophical common sense and its sceptical denial would be spurious, for the following reason.

Let us call the question 'Can we ever know that we're awake, not dreaming?' the Philosophical Question. How is it to be answered? Suppose it is answered 'Yes, we *can* know that we're awake, not dreaming.' If we *can* know that, then surely we must admit now that we could wake up and discover later that what is going on now is a dream. But if that is a genuine possibility, if we might wake up in a few minutes and find we've been dreaming, then we must admit that we can't know *now* that we're awake, not dreaming. So the Philosophical Question must be answered in the negative. There is a certain possibility which, if always genuine, always precludes our knowing that we're not dreaming. So suppose the Philosophical Question is answered negatively—we *cannot* ever know that we're awake, not dreaming. But if we *can't ever* know that, then it is not possible for us to wake up later and discover that what is going on now is a dream. That was the possibility that earlier precluded our knowing that we're awake now; but that 'possibility' has just been seen not to be a possibility after all, so no possibility has yet been raised which precludes our knowing that we're awake. Therefore, the Philosophical Question can be answered: 'Yes, we *can* know that we're awake, not dreaming.'

So the Philosophical Question, to which scepticism and philosophical common sense are competing answers, cannot be answered either way, either negatively or affirmatively, without paradox. So the Philosophical Question is in some way phoney or illegitimate. That is the central point of Clarke's rejection of philosophical scepticism and of the philosophical search for absolute objectivity.

That such a search rests on a faulty conception of the nature of our concepts, or of our use of concepts, is shown by another conclusion derived from Clarke's strong claim about the knowability requirement built into the concept of a dream. Since it clearly makes sense to suggest that I might wake up later and discover that all this has been a dream, then on any particular occasion on which I consider the question I cannot then say that I *know* that possibility will not come about. This shows that Descartes was right in saying that 'there are no certain marks (or tests) by which waking life can be distinguished from sleep', and if our 'conceptual-human constitution is of the standard type' it follows that no one could ever know whether he is awake or dreaming. But that is incompatible with what Clarke claims is built into the very concept of dreams, namely, that if 'dream' is truly applicable to an item, then it must be the case that someone could know what is really true about the surroundings of the person involved. So the concept of a dream that we actually possess 'cannot be fitted into a conceptual-human constitution of the standard type'. That 'standard' account of what it is like to have and use concepts must be wrong, since if it were correct we could not have one of the concepts that we actually possess at the moment. So we need a new understanding of what it is to have and use concepts, and to seek and claim knowledge expressed in terms of them. In short, we need a new and unproblematic conception of the only sort of objectivity that could be available to us.

These are the most exciting, most original, and also the most ambitious legacies of Mr Clarke's account of philosophical scepticism, and they all depend to a very large degree on the claim that 'it is inconceivable that I could not be asleep, dreaming, *if* no outsider could know my real environs because . . . he, too, could not know he was not asleep, dreaming' (p. 766).

Clarke is aware that what he says in his paper hardly settles the issue of whether or not that is conceivable. As he says, we have no satisfactory techniques for settling such questions except, perhaps, trying to conceive of it and seeing what happens. When I try it I find very little difficulty at all—but of course I might be smuggling in many things I'm not aware of. Could it be that I am now dreaming? Is it possible that I am now only dreaming of sitting by the fire? To me the answer seems clearly 'Yes' and, more importantly, it seems to remain 'Yes' even if I go on to imagine that no one on the face of the earth, or anywhere else, could ever know whether I *am* dreaming or not because each of them could never know whether they were awake or dreaming. I simply say I find no difficulty in this, but so far it looks as if I am merely asserting what Clarke denies. Is there anything more to be said?

Clarke is impressed by the fact—which *is* interesting and has not usually been noticed—that when we accept as possible the kinds of possibilities usually raised by the sceptic we do not explicitly build in this further condition of unknowability. That is, when we are asked to imagine an evil demon out to deceive us, or an evil physiologist who has us deceptively wired, we do not immediately ask how the evil demon knows someone isn't fooling *him*, or how the physiologist knows that *he* isn't cleverly wired as well. We just take the situation as described and go on to worry about its implications for *us*, for what *we* can or cannot know.

I agree that usually we do not think of that question, but is it *essential* to our acknowledging the possibilities as genuine that we forget it? *Must* we suppose that the evil demon, or some being lurking somewhere in the wings, knows, or even could know, what is really going on? Again, it seems to me the answer is 'No'. And that is because, when the question arises of how or whether the demon or the physiologist does know what's really going on, I think

I can concede that he does not, or even could not know, without in any way threatening the intelligibility of the possibility I am trying to conceive of. If *I* could be in such a situation then I don't know now that I'm not being fooled by a demon or a physiologist, and if *they* could be in a similar situation (as they could) then they don't know either. So we are all in the same boat.

In raising his possibilities the sceptic tells us what would actually be the case if the possibilities were realized, and he perhaps makes use of some plausible explanation of how things might have come to be that way, e.g. we're dreaming, or we're cleverly wired, or whatever. Such stories serve to make the possibilities dramatically real, especially to the more recalcitrant, but it does not seem essential that the demon or the physiologist (or anyone) be thought to be actually immune to the kinds of doubts we manage to raise about our own position. In fact, granting that the possibilities, and therefore, the doubts, are relevant to oneself seems enough to give the whole game away. There then seems to be no way of stopping short of completely universal scepticism.

For example, Descartes's *Meditations* are written in the first person. But when I read the *First Meditation* I do not say simply, 'How interesting. *Descartes* can't tell whether he's awake or not. What a curious man.' If I find what he says at all convincing or plausible, I recognize that his first-person utterances can also be uttered by me, and so I see immediately that I am in the same boat as he is. But I don't think this is just a curious deficiency which only Descartes and I share. I immediately recognize that those same words can be used by anyone, and everyone, and so granting that if it is possible that *I'm* now dreaming then *I* can never know which state I'm actually in leads to the conclusion that since everyone else is just like me in that respect, then *no one* can ever know which state he is in.

That is one reason, then, why I'm not convinced by Clarke's claim that if I *am* really dreaming then it must be possible for some being, somehow, to know that I am. Whatever that being, or possible being, would have to be like, I cannot see why the words of Descartes's *First Meditation* would not be just as applicable by him to himself as I find them to be to myself. And if they were, then not just Descartes and I, but all other actual and even possible knowing subjects would be in the same boat. And once again, I don't find that this thought even suggests that therefore none of us really *could* dream. The possibility that *I* am dreaming, for example, seems as real as ever.

It is what Clarke says about the concept of a dream that is supposed to preclude its being 'fitted into' a 'conceptual-human constitution of the standard type'. My initial devotion to that 'standard' account of concepts is unshaken by what Clarke has said in his paper, but I recognize its unpalatable sceptical consequences, and so I would be willing to jettison it if I could. But how can it be rejected? Isn't everything said in characterizing the 'standard' conception obviously true? 'Our concepts either have things falling under them or they do not.' 'Whether they do or not is a purely objective matter to be settled solely by the concept and the item.' 'If an item falls under a concept it does so whether anyone could ever know that it does or not.' And so on. These remarks seem to express the very heart of objectivity, and to deny the slightest hint of psychologism or anthropocentrism. But what then is wrong? Is it the split between what we mean and what we could ever know? Or is it the apparently unrestricted use of the law of excluded middle that leads us astray? Or is there really nothing wrong with such remarks after all? Can't they be taken to express truths? Perhaps I find them convincing, only because I make them, so to speak, 'from inside' our system of concepts and practices, where it would seem that realism must always look like the truth. Taken this way, taken, in Clarke's phrase, as 'plain', the remarks can seem perfectly true. And for that very reason they do not manage to express the traditional *philosophical* conception of what it is like to have concepts and to use them in our attempts to understand the world.

Clarke apparently understands, even if he does not endorse, that philosophical conception. But can it be understood, if Clarke's account of 'philosophical' claims is correct? It is perhaps not surprising to find that Clarke has joined what is by now an impressive group of his predecessors in falling back on pure and detached 'philosophical' utterances in his attempt to expose the spurious and illegitimate character of all purely 'philosophical' remarks.

4

Taking Scepticism Seriously

Those familiar considerations about knowledge and perception which have traditionally been thought to lead to philosophical scepticism have not occupied as central a place in the philosophy of the last twenty years or so as in the forty of fifty years before that. It is not that the best philosophers used to believe or advocate scepticism and that they no longer do so, but that, in the past, scepticism was seen as a constant and profound threat, and the urge to understand precisely how it is to be avoided was a motivating force in philosophy. Generally speaking, that is no longer so. With a few notable exceptions, contemporary philosophers do not take scepticism seriously, or seriously enough.

There are no doubt many reasons for the present state of affairs. One is the rise of 'linguistic' philosophy in the 1950s, as a result of which scepticism and the arguments thought to lead to it came to be regarded as little more than a mess of false analogies, definite errors, and even identifiable fallacies which had bewitched the intelligence of earlier philosophers through insufficient attention to the complexities of language and to the general conditions for the significant functioning of our actual conceptual scheme. In particular, the influence of Austin on the epistemological views and interests of a whole generation of philosophers can scarcely be overemphasized.

But the heyday of 'linguistic' philosophy is behind us, and although we are no longer so optimistic about the direct philosophical significance of the facts of language discoverable by its best techniques, the generally unsympathetic attitude towards philosophical scepticism remains widespread. That is perhaps partly because of the roughly 'scientific' character attributed to phi-

This essay first appeared as a review of Peter Unger's *Ignorance: A Case for Scepticism* (Oxford, 1975), in the *Journal of Philosophy* (1977). Page numbers in parentheses in the text refer to that book. I would like to thank Thompson Clarke for helpful discussions of an earlier version of this paper.

losophy by many of its most recent practitioners. Scepticism is now more likely to be seen not as an incoherent product of error and confusion, but as a perfectly meaningful, albeit very implausible, 'theory' that easily loses out in competition with other 'hypotheses' that better explain the nature of our experience. This apparently liberal approach completely blunts the force of traditional scepticism by claiming to absorb it; it takes it seriously only to the extent of weighing it in the scales of theoretical plausibility, fully on a par with a series of alleged competitors. And, on that assessment, not surprisingly, philosophical scepticism is felt to be even less worthy of serious consideration than, say, Ptolemaic astronomy or the account of creation in the book of Genesis.

It is perhaps to be expected that radical scepticism should not be taken seriously in a subject that becomes increasingly professionalized. Peter Unger is one of the few who write out of a dissatisfaction with that state of affairs. He deplores the superficiality of fashionable 'refutations' of what one quite naturally regards as some of the most important and most profound arguments in philosophy, and he hopes to get philosophers to take them seriously. He wants to explain precisely how and why those traditional arguments are so deep and compelling, and why the putative refutations of recent years look shallow by comparison and seem invariably to miss the main point. These are admirable aims, and are apparently not widely shared in recent epistemology. It is very encouraging to find a serious work devoted to leading us to 'demand from ourselves a reasonable explanation of those feelings and intuitions which certain sceptical arguments so forcefully and so perennially arouse' (p. 10).

Unger says that is his aim, and he does pursue it in an honestly straightforward, even personal way, but from the explanation he offers one begins to doubt that he is primarily engaged on such a diplomatic mission. Struck by the weakness of attempted refutations of scepticism, he tells us, he reasoned that their failure might be explained by the fact that scepticism cannot be refuted:

And, then, I thought, of all the reasons why scepticism might be impossible to refute, one stands out as the simplest: scepticism isn't wrong, it's right. The reason that sceptical arguments are so compelling, always able to rise again to demand our thought, would then also be a simple one: These arguments, unlike the attempts to refute them, served the truth. (p. 2)

Unger is not one who finds things unduly complex. Not only is the force of sceptical arguments simply explained; so too is their apparent depth. Scepticism finds its source in our language, and sceptical arguments can be seen to reveal the 'real meanings' of key terms like "know", "certain", and "reasonable".

With this diagnosis Unger would undermine the liberal 'scientific' attitude to scepticism by in effect adopting it and arguing that scepticism is indeed the 'hypothesis' that best explains all the facts. And he would undermine 'linguistic' attacks by arguing that scepticism is a 'theory' embodied in the very meanings of our words and so, given our language, we must regard it as correct.

If this is a strategy for getting from philosophers a fair and patient examination of the source of the appeal of scepticism, it can only be described as a case of undiplomatic overkill. Unger sees the issue as a matter of adopting the correct 'theory', and he thinks there is philosophical profit to be derived from taking scepticism seriously just as there is much to be learned from asking how and why the heliocentric astronomy is superior to the geocentric. But he is not in the position of one who would focus attention on that issue by exposing the complexities and the profound current misunderstandings of the real reasons for the success of the heliocentric theory. He is rather like someone who hopes to get us to take that issue seriously by arguing that the geocentric theory is true. The philosophers Unger hopes to persuade are likely to give his defence of scepticism about as sympathetic a hearing and about as much credence as astronomers would give to a present-day supporter of Ptolemy. And that is unfortunate. Unger's outrageous view will not encourage the kind of discussion I agree with him in thinking is needed.

The view really is outrageous—in the literal sense, at least, of being immoderate, extravagant, and extraordinary. Unger himself acknowledges that it will probably be regarded as 'crazy'. But he is undaunted—even, I suspect, slightly encouraged—by that. He thinks that nobody knows anything at all about anything, and that, as a consequence, nobody is ever to the slightest degree reasonable or justified in believing anything or in doing anything. Furthermore, it follows that every attribution to a person of an attitude or state of mind that implies that something is known to that person is false; so, for example, nobody ever notices anything, or regrets anything, or is ever angry or happy or gratified that something or other is so.

In fact, Unger in his zeal even devotes a chapter to showing that there is no truth, on the grounds that if something is true it is in agreement with 'the whole truth about everything', but that there is no such thing as 'the whole truth about everything'. He concludes that nothing whatsoever is true, and that consequently nobody ever believes or thinks that anything is so, or asserts or says that anything is so.

This depletion of our intellectual resources makes it difficult for a sympathetic reader even to describe, let alone endorse, what Unger does in this book. He appears to accept scepticism, he certainly asserts that it is right, and he tells us many of the things he thinks or has thought about it. But, if we go along with him, we cannot take any of this seriously. We cannot ascribe any views, or thoughts, or feelings to him at all. Certainly to do so requires at least that we know what he wrote in this book.

What is odd is perhaps not that Peter Unger is a sceptic, but that he should write a book about it if he really means it. And there is an interesting discussion in the book of why we find that strange. We feel that a sceptic ought, in consistency, to remain silent. He has no reason to believe his view and no reason to assert it. But on his view he has no more reason to be silent than to speak, so that alone cannot be the source of our feeling of inconsistency. Unger suggests that it derives from the fact that in asserting or stating something one represents oneself as knowing that something is so, and so in asserting that nobody knows anything a sceptic is representing something that is actually inconsistent.

That is unfortunate, to say the least, but for Unger it is inevitable. Paradoxes and contradictions are no more than the price he thinks a sceptic can be expected to have to pay in order to express his point of view in the only language now available. That shows nothing wrong with his point of view, he thinks, but only something wrong with the language in which he is at present forced to express it.

Unger finds himself a captive of an inherited 'theory' that our early ancestors gradually deposited in our language (although he never says what it is a 'theory' about), and he presents his work as a heroic declaration of his captivity in the hopes that the 'theory' can eventually be jettisoned by 'reconstructing' the language in terms of which we now think. Unger personally finds his own inclinations and aptitudes unequal to that formidable task, and he confesses that contemporary English is the only language in which he can think, but he recommends the job to those more creative and constructive than himself—to 'dextrous logicians' with 'a subtle appreciation of the function and workings of a natural language' (p. 317). But that process of 'reconstruction' itself will presumably involve careful, serious thinking on the part of those constructive thinkers, and quite understandably Unger provides no hint of where or how they will be able to find or forge trouble-free forms of thought that will take them and us entirely outside the allegedly myth-eaten resources of the present.

Something—in fact, a great deal—has clearly gone wrong, but it is not easy to say exactly how Unger's original intuitions and concerns came to be so ill served. If we ask what really convinces him of his scepticism and thereby leads him to these outrageous consequences of it, Unger himself would undoubtedly point to his theory of 'absolute terms' in English. He sees that as his most novel contribution to the subject and as providing the basis for the claim that scepticism is a 'theory' built into the very meanings of terms like "know" and "certain".

An 'absolute' term purports to denote an absolute limit which can be approached more or less closely but which is itself either totally present or totally absent without degrees. Thus "flat" is said to be an absolute term because something is flat only if it is absolutely or perfectly flat. For Unger, that means that 'if it is logically possible that there be a surface that is flatter than a given one, then that given surface is not really a flat one' (p. 66). This makes it extremely unlikely that there is or ever has been anything in existence that is flat. Of course, we can speak of relative flatness, but for Unger to say that one surface is flatter than another is to say that it approaches more nearly than that other to (probably uninstantiated) absolute flatness.

The same kind of 'syntactico-semantic evidence' that indicates to Unger that "flat" is an absolute term is also available, he thinks, in the case of "certain", and he draws the parallel conclusion that 'if it is logically possible that there be something of which any person might be more certain than [a given person] is of a given thing, then [that given person] is not actually certain of that given thing' (p. 67). This is intended to make us correspondingly pessimistic about finding many cases in which someone can truly be said to be certain of something. And with the premiss that lack of certainty implies lack of knowledge Unger concludes that, at best, knowledge is in fact extremely rare.

But the most powerful conclusion he draws from this conception of certainty is that it is *never* 'all right' to be certain—that the attitude of certainty is always 'dogmatic' or 'irrational'. That is the main thesis of his book and it is used both to establish his own completely general scepticism and to explain the persuasiveness of the traditional sceptical arguments found in Descartes and elsewhere. The argument for scepticism is brief, given this strong thesis: if someone knows something to be so, then it is 'all right' for him to be certain that it is so; but it is never 'all right' for anyone to be certain of anything; therefore no one ever knows anything. And the thesis would account for the force of Descartes's argument by explaining exactly why Descartes (and, *mutatis mutandis*, each of the rest of us) could never know that he is sitting by the fire in his dressing gown; he would be 'dogmatic' or 'irrational' to claim that he knew it, since knowledge implies certainty and certainty is always 'dogmatic'.

It is very difficult to identify the reasons that convince Unger of his strong thesis about certainty. He thinks 'any reflection at all makes it pretty plain' that it is true. That is because, by the theory of absolute terms, being certain involves being absolutely certain, and for Unger that implies that 'I will not allow *anything at all* to count as evidence against my present view in the matter' (pp. 122–3), or that 'no new information, evidence, or experience will now be seriously considered by one to be *at all* relevant to any possible change in how certain one should be in the matter' (p. 105). And since it is clearly dogmatic to 'count nothing as even appearing to speak against one's position' (p. 109), certainty is always dogmatic and never "all right".

Unger seems to think this closed-mindedness is required by certainty because it is impossible to be absolutely certain while acknowledging that one might change one's mind if certain other evidence comes along. The statement 'He is absolutely *certain* that there are automobiles, but *his attitude* is that he really *may* change his mind should certain evidence come up', he says, is 'inconsistent' (p. 110). That, or something like it, seems to me to be right, but Unger does not show how it supports the strong thesis that certainty is always dogmatic. And that thesis, on the face of it, does not seem to be true.

In looking over my books on the shelf before me, I find that I am not certain that I have read the one by Updike, but I am absolutely certain I have read the one by Unger. I simply couldn't be wrong about it; I have been reading it, thinking about it, and writing all over it for the past several weeks. And I am equally certain that nothing can refute the claim that I have read it. Of course, I know that others might come to infer quite reasonably from certain considerations that I did not read the book, but that does nothing to shake my present certainty. And I must concede that those same or other considerations might in fact lead me in the future to believe that I did not read it—I might simply forget that I read it and come to believe that I did not. But that implies nothing about my present attitude towards the question of whether or not I read that book. I am now certain that I read it, and certain that no such considerations will be enough to show that I did not.

So my present attitude is one of certainty, but I have not resolved or determined to shut my eyes and ears in the face of such putative counterevidence. It is true that my attitude is that such considerations will not affect my own certainty in the matter, but that is because I am already certain that I read the book, and not because I simply will not allow them to count as relevant or as even appearing to speak against my position. Any such 'resolution' or 'determination' on my part would be completely idle anyway; it is not up to *me* to determine what does or does not appear to show that I did not read Unger's book, or what counts as relevant to the question. So I do not see how my certainty implies that 'without any further thought or consideration' I will simply reject as misleading or irrelevant any putative counterevidence that comes up. It is just that I am confident that it all can be explained away without implying that I did not read Unger's book.

Since I am now certain that I read the book, I do not think that if I were to explain away more and more bits of putative counterevidence put up to show that I did not, I should then be described as being *more certain* that I read it than I am now. On Unger's account of 'certain' as an absolute term, if I would be more certain after successful rebuttal of counterevidence then I am not (absolutely) certain right now. But my present attitude is one of certainty that I read the book and certainty that all such counterevidence is spurious; so demonstrating its spuriousness should not be expected to render me more certain than I am now. I am already certain.

Correspondingly, since I am now certain that I read the book, my attitude now is that my certainty will not be diminished if I am in fact unable to explain away some of the counterevidence advanced to show that I did not. There are many mysteries, tricks, and other puzzling phenomena in this world that I cannot explain. Magic shows are interesting to me only because I know at the outset that rabbits do not materialize out of handkerchiefs or silk hats. My admitted inability to explain the sudden appearance of the rabbit before me does nothing to undermine that conviction, and it will not be undermined even if (as is likely) I go to my grave without being able to explain the appearance of any rabbits out of any silk hats.

Unger's view that it is not 'all right' for me to be certain, or in general that it is *never* 'all right' for anyone to be certain of anything, because an unacceptable dogmatism is *intrinsic* to certainty, does not seem to me to follow from anything said so far about the attitude of certainty I actually have in the matter of whether or not I have read Unger's book. Of course it hardly needs proving that people are often certain when they should not be—they are often hasty, careless, and prejudiced, and that is not 'all right'—but that no more shows that the attitude of certainty is intrinsically 'not all right' than the unfortunate fact that people sometimes drive when drunk shows that the activity of driving is intrinsically 'not all right'.

The most Unger does to establish the completely general truth of his strong thesis—although he says such considerations are not strictly required—is to suggest that, for anything one claims to be certain of, there are always possibilities which one is not undogmatically certain will not be realized and which are such that, if one of them were realized, one ought to be less certain than one now is. In discussing particular examples he presents some of these bizarre and fantastic possibilities, in the spirit of Descartes 'but in a more modern and scientific vein'.

For example, if you now claim to be certain that there are rocks in the world, then consider the possibility that a physiologist has you wired in such a way as to induce in you the belief that there are rocks. Or if you are now as certain that there are automobiles as that 10 and 10 are 20, then consider the possibility of a disembodied voice, coming from nowhere, denying the first and affirming the second. Unger thinks in this case that your attitude should now be that you would be at least slightly less certain of the first than of the second if that possibility were to be realized. If your present attitude is that the voice 'will not be counted as having any weight at all', then you are dogmatic. And if you allow that it would have some weight, and so would make you slightly less certain, then you are not absolutely certain now.

On this line of reasoning, I cannot now be undogmatically certain that I read Unger's book if I acknowledge that it is possible for me to have the experience in a few hours of waking up and realizing that I have been asleep with an unopened package containing Unger's book on the bedside table. I confess that when I said I was certain that I read Unger's book I had no attitude at all towards the possibility of such an experience. If I remain certain once the possibility is raised, Unger maintains, I am being dogmatic.

Now I do think it must be conceded that the 'possibilities' Unger envisages are possible states of affairs. It is also possible for me to have the experience of waking up that I have described. And since I had no attitude at all towards that possibility when I said I was certain that I read Unger's book, I must admit that I did not even consider it. It was not that I did not consider it because I was certain that I would not have it; in fact, if pressed in the way Unger would undoubtedly press the question, I must now concede that I am not absolutely certain that I will not have that experience. Does that imply that I am not now certain that I read Unger's book, or that if I am certain then I am being dogmatic? It seems to me that that conclusion would follow only if the possibility of that experience's occurring is one that I *ought to* consider, or *ought to* have considered, and did not. But is that true? Unger takes it for granted that it is, but, if it is not, then he does not come close to establishing his general sceptical conclusion. If it is not true that I ought to have considered that possibility—along with countless others just like it—then Unger will not have made it plausible that, for anything one claims to be certain about, there will *always* be possibilities which one is not undogmatically certain will not be realized and which are such that, if one of them is realized, one ought to be less certain than one is at present. And only then will he have shown that there is never any undogmatic certainty.

This seems to me to point to the fundamental question about the source of the persuasiveness of traditional sceptical arguments. Why do we find it so natural when philosophizing to hold that in order to know or to be certain of something we must know or be certain that *no* conceivable possibilities obtain which are such that, if they obtain then we do not know what we thought we did, or ought not to be certain of it? We do not in fact insist on that in everyday life, even in important scientific or legal matters; so why do we find it so obvious when we think philosophically about human knowledge? The answer, whatever it might be, should not be expected to be simple. Unger does not raise the question, perhaps because he believes that that principle is true. It is in effect what he relies on to establish that certainty is always dogmatic, and thereby to establish his scepticism. In making this latter inference, at least, he is probably correct. It seems to me highly likely that, if that principle were straightforwardly true, then scepticism would be true.

It is for just this reason that I find completely implausible Unger's additional claim to have provided an *explanation* of the effectiveness of the traditional arguments in Descartes and elsewhere. He suggests that, once we imagine the possibility of an evil scientist artificially inducing in us the belief that there are rocks, we come to agree that no one can ever know there are any rocks (or anything else about an 'external world') *because* we recognize that dogmatism is intrinsic to all claims to certainty or knowledge. Once we see the dogmatism or irrationality of any such belief, we must acknowledge the truth of general scepticism. In fact I found quite unconvincing the examples Unger uses to convince us that it is the dogmatism or irrationality involved in certainty that is responsible for the admitted lack of knowledge or certainty in such cases, and, if I am right about the source of his strong thesis, there is a good reason why they are unconvincing. Given the fundamental principle he assumes, Descartes's argument for scepticism does not rest on any appeal to the alleged dogmatism intrinsic to certainty at all. And, since Unger shares that principle, he could have reached his scepticism directly, without his strong thesis about certainty.

If, for everything I claim to know (or everything about an 'external world'), it is true that in order to know it I must at least know that there is no evil scientist artificially inducing in me the beliefs on the basis of which I claim to know it, then, in particular, in order to know that no evil scientist is doing that to me, I must know that there is no evil scientist artificially inducing in me the beliefs that lead me to believe that no evil scientist is doing that to me. And then there is nowhere to stop. Without some independent way of establishing that that possibility does not obtain, I find there is a necessary condition of knowledge that I can never fulfil. That is what seems to me to make the prospect of knowledge hopeless once that possibility is taken seriously. If it is assumed to be relevant to *every* knowledge claim, including the claim to know that that possibility itself is not realized, then as Unger himself puts it at one point, 'no matter how involved the going gets, it may always get still more involved' (p. 27). That is the heart of the matter, and it is strictly parallel to Descartes's reasons for concluding that there are no certain indications by which waking can be distinguished from sleeping. In both cases it is assumed that a certain possibility is relevant to every knowledge claim (or to every one of a certain kind), and from that, in conjunction with the conclusion that that possibility cannot be known not to obtain, scepticism can be derived directly, quite independently of any strong thesis about the alleged dogmatism of certainty.

What needs to be examined, then, by anyone seeking an explanation of the force of traditional sceptical arguments, is the attractiveness of the idea that *all* conceivable counterpossibilities must be ruled out if one is to know something, despite the fact that we do not actually behave according to that principle in real life. Unger does not go very far into that complicated question, perhaps because he thinks his theory of absolute terms makes it superfluous. But I do not think the fundamental principle he and Descartes rely on can be shown to follow even if it is conceded that "know" and "certain" are absolute terms, and that no one is certain of a particular thing if it is 'logically possible' for someone to be more certain of something. It still remains to be shown, and explained, how my certainty that I read Unger's book must be dogmatic if I retain it even when I am not certain that I will not have the experience of waking up and realizing that it lies unread on the table beside me. Certainly no such possibilities are canvassed or taken seriously in real life unless there is some special reason to suppose they might obtain; and in this case, there is no such reason.

That is not to say that Unger's scepticism owes nothing to his theory of absolute terms. In offering that view as an account of what he calls the 'real meanings' of certain terms in English, he tries to explain how absolute terms can be useful to us in everyday speech even though they never truly apply to anything. We call Holland flat and Switzerland not flat although, given what Unger thinks "flat" really means, it is not, strictly speaking, true that Holland is flat. But in discussing the merits of the two countries for a cycling trip, for example, the literal falsity of what we say does not matter; our words serve their purpose without having to state what is true. Similarly, Unger thinks that nothing about our actual use of words like "know" and "certain", our saying on certain occasions that we know and on others that we do not, will itself imply that we know or are certain of anything, since the practical point of speaking in those ways can be well served without our words' having to mean something that is true. Saying we know, for example, could indicate that we take our epistemic position to be considerably further along the spectrum towards knowledge than we indicate it to be when we say we do not know, even though in neither case do we know. So our linguistic practice can be perfectly compatible with the literal falsity of every assertion of knowledge or certainty in whatever circumstances, and so everything that happens would be compatible with the truth of scepticism.

This does not really constitute a positive argument in favour of scepticism, but insisting as Unger does on the complete independence of the 'real meanings' of words from all facts about the ways those words are used or the situations in which they are justifiably applied does provide an extremely strong defence against those who would claim that scepticism simply conflicts with the facts. Unger's view of what we are doing in ordinary life when we say we know or are certain of something would seem to account for all the 'data' while leaving the literal truth of scepticism intact. In particular, it could be used to explain why we do not normally check, or even feel we ought to check, to see whether we have been wired up by an evil scientist before we claim to know something in ordinary life. Unger's view would attempt to make our behaviour intelligible and perhaps even reasonable while retaining the idea that we really must have dismissed that possibility if it is to be true that we know or are undogmatically certain of something.

I suspect that the philosophical attractiveness of the principle that knowledge requires that *all* conceivable counterpossibilities be ruled out is of a piece with the attractiveness of that conception of meaning and of the uses of language which Unger and many other philosophers rely on. If the meaning of what is said on a particular occasion is to be explained completely in terms of the conditions under which it would be true, and independently of the epistemic position of those who could say it or understand it, then it will always seem possible for all our knowledge claims to be false even though some of them are made in the best position human beings could ever achieve. Even if Unger does not provide us with anything true that has not been said before in support of scepticism, it is one of the distinctive merits of his work that it draws attention to the strong but generally disregarded pressures toward scepticism inherent in that conception of meaning.

And it must be admitted that the conception is a very powerful one. It seems to embody the very idea of true objectivity which we aspire to as seekers of knowledge and which, if scepticism is right, we could never attain. If the very possibility of our grasp and employment of that notion is what is really at stake in discussions of human knowledge, that would help explain the depth of the subject. And it would help explain why a careful study of the real sources of philosophical scepticism would undoubtedly have within it the prospects of something profound and revealing. For that very reason one expects the prize to be something more—and something less—than the truth of scepticism.

5

Reasonable Claims: Cavell and the Tradition

So many of the numerous topics and themes of Stanley Cavell's *The Claim of Reason*[1] are so important and (to judge from the way things have gone so far) so likely to go unappreciated that the welcome task even of elaborating and endorsing them, let alone criticizing some of them, in a brief space is truly daunting. Even without straying beyond the subtitle we find 'Wittgenstein, Skepticism, Morality, and Tragedy'. Before concentrating on one of those topics I want to connect what I will say with some general themes which go unmentioned in that subtitle but which permeate the book and are to my mind largely responsible for its importance. And also responsible, perhaps, for what I think is, or will be, the difficulty of its reception.

   Central to Cavell's writing in these pages and elsewhere is his conception of what he calls 'modernism' and the correspondingly 'modernist' character of his own work. He is fully aware that that feature is itself one obstacle to the easy acceptance of his ideas by the tradition he takes as his subject-matter. 'Modernism' finds problematic the relation between the present practice of an enterprise and the history of that enterprise; it cannot take for granted the traditional procedures or purposes thought to be definitive in the past, and so the very enterprise itself becomes a problem. In so far as it remains alive, it therefore tends to become its own subject-matter. Cavell thinks modern philosophy shares this condition with the modern arts. That is not to say that most of our contemporaries who would describe what they are doing as philosophy (especially

This essay was my contribution to an American Philosophical Association symposium on Stanley Cavell's *The Claim of Reason*. A shorter version was published in the *Journal of Philosophy* (1980). I am grateful to Thompson Clarke and Samuel Scheffler for their help.

[1] *The Claim of Reason: Wittgenstein, Skepticism, Morality and Tragedy* (New York and Oxford, 1979). Unless otherwise indicated, page numbers alone in parentheses refer to this book.

'professional philosophy') would agree with this verdict or would admit to any qualms. They know what they are doing, and they are busy (one might feel all too busy) doing it. For Cavell this indicates that 'the reception of Wittgenstein and of Austin has yet to have its public or historical effect on this philosophical culture' (p. xvi).

I would say that that seems undeniably true to me—were it not for a sudden uneasiness that I don't really know what public or historical effects work as radical as Wittgenstein's can reasonably be expected to have on a philosophical culture like this. Maybe it has had as much real effect as it possibly could have had, beyond that dissemination of a certain jargon that Wittgenstein accurately predicted for it. But, for whatever reason, there seems to me no doubt that, as Cavell puts it, 'Wittgenstein is still to be received' by our philosophical culture (p. xvi).

It is out of a recognition of that state of affairs, and of what he perceives as the 'modernist' crisis of philosophy, and not, as it has seemed to some, simply out of nostalgia for the 1950s, that Cavell writes. *The Claim of Reason* is dedicated to Thompson Clarke and to the memory of J. L. Austin, and in its remarkable foreword Cavell tells us that it was Austin and ordinary language philosophy that knocked him off his horse as he was on his way to a 'proper dissertation' on the concept of human action. The shocking revolutionary effects of linguistic philosophy were 'doubled' by Thompson Clarke who showed Cavell how everything that can be said 'in defense of the appeal to ordinary language could also be said in defense, rather than in criticism, of the claims of traditional philosophy'.[2] Ordinary language philosophical procedures were not directly destructive of the enterprise of traditional epistemology, as their most fervent propagandists had supposed.

This important lesson grew for Cavell into an 'ideal of criticism' that has remained central to all his work, and especially, he says, to *The Claim of Reason*. The ordinary language philosopher's concentration on the context in which things are said, on the conditions which must obtain in order for even the apparently simplest linguistic acts to succeed, his emphasis on the fact that expressions are used by human beings in specific situations and directed towards other human beings who share a common language and

---

[2] Cavell, *Must We Mean What We Say?* (New York and Cambridge, 1976), pp. xii–xiii.

much else besides—all this reinforces the idea that philosophical criticism, if it is to escape irrelevance or obtuseness, must proceed by seeking to discover what Cavell calls 'the specific plight of mind and circumstance within which a human being gives voice'[3] to whatever it is he is trying to say or do.

That is not something it had to be left to ordinary language philosophy to teach us, one might think, but I agree with Cavell in his assessment of the alienating and philosophically disastrous, not to mention just plain boring, effects of philosophy's earlier concentration on something it was pleased to call *the meanings* of words and sentences apparently established and analysed in isolation from their application or their use. The new philosophy's desire to, in Cavell's words, 'put the human animal back into language and therewith back into philosophy' (p. 207) provided him with his 'ideal of criticism'—that of understanding a position or a programme or a plight or a person, or even a philosophy, from the inside: to see what the person or text in question is really doing, or really manages to mean, and not just to impose some construction that could be said to fit the words used. That is always sound practice, no doubt, but 'in the philosophy which proceeds from ordinary language', Cavell claims, 'understanding from inside is methodologically fundamental'.[4]

Now this 'ideal of criticism', this insistence on getting inside the concrete and 'specific plight of mind and circumstance', is a high ideal. For that reason alone it is not often fully achieved in philosophy. I will be interested in a moment in the extent to which Cavell himself achieves it. But more often than not that ideal is not reached because it is not even aspired to. That alone makes *The Claim of Reason* a special, and an important, book.

In Cavell's explanation and application of the philosophy he rightly thinks has not been properly acknowledged or fully absorbed in current philosophical practice, the famous passage with which Kant begins *The Critique of Pure Reason* is never far from view. It is alluded to in Cavell's title, it serves as a motto to Part II of the book, it is specifically applied and developed in the text of that part called 'Skepticism and the Existence of the World', and is a central idea or insight out of which the whole book is written.

---

[3] Ibid. 240.   [4] Ibid. 239.

Human reason has this peculiar fact [Kant wrote] that in one species of its knowledge it is burdened by questions which, as prescribed by the very nature of reason itself, it is not able to ignore, but which, as transcending all its powers, it is also not able to answer.[5]

It is worth trying to imagine what it would be like if that were true—if human reason or the human mind were consigned to that fate. It is perhaps not so easy to imagine how such a thing might be known to be true; not simply true so far (which seems easy enough), but true, true of human reason or the human condition itself. Kant thought he knew it, and he even thought he cold explain it and thereby reconcile us to our fate. But it is also important for understanding Cavell to ask what *philosophy* would be like if it were true; what the unavoidable questions, and that activity in which they are inevitably asked, would really be like for those who knew or believed that something like Kant's conception of the human condition was essentially correct. Philosophy would certainly be an enterprise whose very credentials or possibility were constantly in question, despite its undeniable source in human reason or human nature itself. Our greatest hope under those conditions would be to identify and to come to understand the *source* of reason's apparently undeniable claim, presumably by demonstrating and perhaps eventually even by explaining in some illuminating way the impossibility of our ever satisfying its demand.

These ideals and inspirations of Cavell's work lead me to Part II of *The Claim of Reason*, called 'Skepticism and the Existence of the World'. I want to see how the Kantian idea is put to work there, how it is exemplified in the diagnosis of the traditional philosophical investigation of our knowledge of the world, and how Cavell fulfils his own 'ideal of criticism' in explaining the way that investigation does and must fail to show what we think we have discovered when we conclude from it that none of us can know anything about the existence of any of the things around us.

I therefore will say nothing about morality or tragedy. And I have already learned so much from Cavell about Wittgenstein, most of it from these very pages, and I learned it so long ago—lessons that few commentators on Wittgenstein seem to have taken in even

---

[5] Immanuel Kant, *Critique of Pure Reason*, tr. N. Kemp Smith (London, 1953), Avii (7).

today—that I can no longer document my indebtedness to him. I find what he says about the need for a proper understanding of the problem of the external world so important and so little appreciated, especially in what now goes under the name of epistemology, that I want to concentrate on that. What I have to say about it might perhaps turn out to have wider implications, not only for epistemology, but also for the understanding of Wittgenstein and for the significance of Cavell's own philosophizing about other minds and about tragedy and perhaps about other things as well.

Cavell sees no prospects of intellectual progress in responding to philosophical scepticism about the external world either by simply denying it in the name of a robust common sense or by attempting to refute it by abstract philosophical argument. Scepticism says, or appears to say, that we can never know with certainty of the existence of any of the things around us, and for Cavell a truly 'formidable criticism' of the philosophy that leads to that verdict, or expresses itself in that way, would be to discover and exhibit how anyone engaging in the traditional investigation could come to think or want to say that *that* is what he has discovered. We might then be in a position to provide an altered understanding of what goes on in traditional philosophizing, one that does not simply deny or accept its conclusion as is, but rather absorbs it and makes accessible what it can genuinely teach us, however far that might be from the flat and uncompromising, if sometimes exhilarating, pronouncement that we know nothing.

It is worth stressing once again just how rare and how valuable this philosophical ideal or aspiration of Cavell's really is among present-day responses to scepticism. In discussing the problem of other minds Cavell refers to all the more-or-less standard 'answers' which rely on 'the argument from analogy' or other 'theoretical' inferences as themselves 'skeptical' and therefore all of a piece with the conclusion they are specifically designed to avoid. All these 'solutions', he says, 'can seem to make good sense only on the basis of ideas of behavior and of sentience that are invented and sustained by skepticism itself' (p. 47), and so they remain 'skeptical' despite the contrary protestations of their defenders. In the same way, Cavell would surely agree, all current so-called 'theories' of our knowledge of the world are themselves fundamentally 'skeptical'. The kinds of 'inferences' or 'hypotheses' we are said to rely on, the 'data' from which those inferences are said to begin, the very

'belief' we are said to have in the external world—all this, and
more, which makes up the common coin of so much epistemology,
can be explained or motivated only by accepting the very ideas that
the sceptical challenge rests on or exploits or invents. No wonder
familiar epistemological theories can all seem unsatisfactory to
anyone who understands the sceptical challenge and takes it
seriously.

But, judging from the way traditional epistemology in one form
or another goes sturdily on even today, there are very few who
acknowledge what seems to me to be true, that the worst thing to
do with the traditional question about our knowledge of the world
is to try to answer it. If you get that far, it's already too late. I believe
that most people who concern themselves at all philosophically
with human knowledge fall into that trap, even those who protest
that everything is different nowadays, much more enlightened and
scientific, and then go on to say that their own enlightened theory
really *is* the explanation of how all our knowledge of the world is
possible. Cavell's attitude towards scepticism stands opposed to all
that—and rightly so—and it is remarkable to me that responses like
his are as rare as they are.

The insight from which Cavell's treatment begins—and it is the
same insight that the traditional epistemologist also had, or never
managed to escape—is that once the question which the traditional
philosopher asks about our knowledge is allowed to stand as legitimate and intelligible in the way he understands it, we are easily
but inevitably forced to the negative or sceptical answer. Finding
the best bases for all our knowledge-claims inadequate, and
thereby finding that we must or should abandon them, seems like
nothing more than a dictate of reason, something that any careful,
conscientious, reasonable person would find himself forced to do if
he considered his position objectively in the way the traditional
philosopher intends. This appreciation of the philosopher's plight
is discovered by accepting as sympathetically as possible Cavell's
'ideal of criticism'. It requires, as he puts it, 'that we take the
philosopher's original—and originating—question with the same
seriousness that the ordinary language philosopher wishes us to
take any statement a human being utters' (p. 138).

What do we find when we take the question seriously in that
way? There is first a rehearsal of or a reflection on our familiar
beliefs or knowledge about the world, and the general recognition

that they are based on seeing, touching, hearing, and so on. The reliability of that basis is then tested by selecting an instance—a 'best case' of knowledge of the world—and assessing the adequacy of its sensory basis. By following the same procedures we all ordinarily follow in assessing knowledge-claims in everyday life we find that there are reasonable doubts that can be raised about the adequacy of the sensory basis even in what we had taken to be the best kind of case of knowledge. Not only are the doubts of the right sort to bring the putative knowledge into question (if I *were* dreaming or hallucinating, then I certainly wouldn't know that I am sitting by the fire), but they are also reasonably raised, given the epistemologist's question or project. But if the only basis we can have even in the best kind of case is inadequate, as we have found it to be, then we can safely generalize to all knowledge; we cannot know of the existence of any of the things around us.

This familiar story has of course been criticized at many points— probably at every point at some time or other—but Cavell is right, I think, that those attempts we are all familiar with to show that the best philosophical investigations of knowledge deviate radically in one way or another from our ordinary procedures for assessing knowledge-claims are not really convincing. Of course, the philosophical *conclusion* is taken to deviate from what we all believe, but that alone does not show that the procedures used to reach it are deviant, and I agree with Cavell that the attempt to confront that conclusion with 'what we would say' or 'what we do' seems intellectually less impressive—less deep—than the thinking that led the philosopher to it in the first place. As he puts it, the force of traditional philosophical investigations of knowledge 'depends upon their proceeding in terms of our ordinary investigations of claims to knowledge' (p. 191). 'If the philosopher's request for a basis is accepted as a real question, then the bases he offers are the right, or anyway the only, bases which would seem natural.' And we can see that his grounds for doubting those bases 'are forced by the nature of the investigation itself'; 'any competent speaker of the language will know that they are relevant and know what their implications are' (p. 191). These remarks conflict with a great deal of recent philosophizing, and cannot be expected to carry conviction in the abstract, without detailed application to the philosophical investigation. I do not have time to go into Cavell's good reasons for his judgements of the force of the traditional

investigation. It is enough for present purposes to say that I regard
them as fully correct.

What then can be our response to the philosophical investigation if we concede so much to it in this way? If we grant its conditional correctness—that given its starting-point, the conclusion it
reaches is inevitable, and fully naturally and reasonably arrived
at—how good are the prospects of deflecting it and absorbing its
'lessons' but not its literal truth? Obviously they are only as good
as the chances that its very starting-point is defective or ill-formed
or not fully intelligible. But what *is* its very starting-point? It is not
easy to say. And it is not easy to say what is wrong with it, once you
have identified it. And it is more difficult still to do both of these
things while remaining faithful to Cavell's 'ideal of criticism'.

He pushes his scrutiny of the philosophical investigation back to
its first step, and he tries to show that the investigation at that point
does not 'fully follow an ordinary investigation of a claim of knowledge' (p. 165). Of course it seems to do so; it must have seemed to
the traditional philosopher to do so. But for Cavell the philosopher
does not or cannot mean what he thinks he means by his words.
Since those are words whose meaning is shared by all masters of
the language, including himself, any convincing explanation or diagnosis of the philosopher's investigation will have to explain how a
careful, intelligent master of a language may not know that he has
not managed to mean what he thinks he means, or is somehow 'pre-
vented' from meaning what he wishes to mean—what he *must*
mean if his conclusion is to mean what it says (p. 193).

To show that something as delicate, and as devastating, as that is
true of the traditional philosophical investigation is presumably not
an easy task. And it is not one that has even been undertaken by
those who have 'refuted' or denied philosophical scepticism or
those who have wittingly or unwittingly embraced it. But the pay-
off of such a subtle and sympathetic exposure is high. For Cavell it
promises the discovery of what he refers to as 'some critical fact
about the mind, and one which neither side has been able, or
willing, to articulate' (p. 159).

Now I eventually want to ask what that 'critical fact about the
mind' is, or even whether there could be any such fact. But first we
must look at the account of what is deviant or defective in the
philosopher's first step. That is Cavell's own special contribution to
a programme he takes himself to have shared with Thompson

Clarke, who would agree with most of what I have outlined so far. Cavell contributes the idea that, in the concrete case that the philosopher offers as the 'best' kind of case by which the adequacy of the sensory basis of our knowledge can be tested, no actual *claim* is being made. 'The philosopher's context is non-claim,' Cavell says; 'no concrete claim is ever entered as part of the traditional investigation' (p. 217). The philosopher *imagines* a claim to have been made in a context he specifies (e.g. sitting by the fire with a piece of paper in his hand) and he then goes on to examine the grounds for that imagined claim in that context. But that is not to imagine a real situation in which a real knowledge-claim is made. Since the examples considered and subjected to assessment as best cases of knowledge are not really examples in which a claim is made, there is nothing for the philosopher's bases to be the bases of. So the philosopher has not discovered anything when he thinks he has discovered that sense-experience is an inadequate basis for knowledge as a whole.

That discovery, once made, would leave us with the plaintive question: 'Then how *do* we know anything about the world?' The question, if accepted, seems to demand an answer. But since what produced that request for a basis of our knowledge was 'a non-claim situation', 'there is no claim which can provide the relevance of a basis' (p. 239). 'The conditions under which a request for a basis can be answered have been removed'; 'we have deprived ourselves of the conditions for saying anything in particular' (p. 239). That is why we cannot possibly answer what we feel we must answer. This is Cavell's version of the Kantian idea of our being forced by reason to answer questions which it is beyond the power of reason to answer (p. 239).

I think many will feel, as I felt, a distinct disappointment, a feeling of high hopes suddenly dashed, at this climax of Cavell's story. He says it is 'no more than a schema for a potential overthrowing or undercutting of skepticism' (p. 220), but its schematic character contrasts so sharply with the rich delineation in earlier pages of the undeniable persuasiveness of traditional philosophical investigations, and the briskness and ease with which it is delivered contrast so sharply with the admirable earlier insistence on the high diagnostic standards any successful 'overthrow' would have to meet, that we cannot avoid a certain let-down or frustration if we have endorsed or even applauded those earlier pages, as

I have done. The tasks and procedures Cavell recommends go against a great deal of contemporary philosophizing. But I fear his admirable recommendations might not be accepted with the seriousness they deserve if his own way of fulfilling them is taken as sufficient for their successful implementation.

It is not that I find Cavell's final diagnosis untrue, or unilluminating if true. I find, first of all, that he has given very little of what I would regard as reasons for believing his specific account of what goes wrong. He offers what he acknowledges is only a 'glimpse' of 'the grammar (conditions) of saying (claiming) something' and hopes that that is enough to support his charge that no concrete claim is made in the context the philosopher imagines. But the section in which these conditions are glimpsed does not contain a description, or even a sketch, of the conditions that must be present in order for a claim to have been made. It illustrates only the general point, insisted on again and again by Austin and ordinary language philosophers, that saying something, stating something, asking something, claiming something, and so on, all have their conditions (pp. 204–17). A series of vocables tumbling from a human mouth does not in itself amount to a remark, or a statement, or a claim, unless certain other conditions are fulfilled. Even if we know what the words in the utterance mean we do not thereby know what the person means, or what the person is doing, or even whether he has managed to mean or to say anything at all. But this is only the point that claims, like everything else, have certain conditions that make them what they are. Cavell does not identify those conditions.

Even if he had, he would still have to show that nothing fulfilling those conditions—no claim—is present in the philosopher's context. And for the kind of understanding of traditional philosophy we aspire to we would like to know which particular conditions of claiming the philosopher violates, and how and why he comes to do so. Cavell thinks that what he says about no claim being present in the philosopher's context 'ought to explain why he imagines himself to be saying something when he is not' (p. 221). But I do not find that it does. I do not yet understand how a careful, intelligent master of a language—C. I. Lewis, for example—got to the point of simply 'hallucinating what he . . . means, or . . . having the illusion of meaning something' (p. 221).

Cavell elsewhere disparages the work of those ordinary language philosophers who directly confront the philosopher with the oddness of what he is saying or point out somewhat abusively that he cannot mean what he says. But here Cavell himself appears simply to assert that the philosopher has not managed to say or mean anything. I do not think that the admirable ideal of making a successful undercutting diagnosis fully comprehensible from inside, perhaps even to the person himself, is well served here. How is the philosopher understanding what he is doing, or trying to do? Has Cavell really identified correctly the very first step of his enquiry? It is difficult to feel that the philosopher's remarks have been taken with the same seriousness as that with which the ordinary language philosopher wishes us to take any statement a human being utters.

My difficulty does not result merely from Cavell's neglect of the specific conditions of *claiming* as opposed to asserting, judging, contending, believing, and other ways of putting something forward as true. His diagnosis does not, or should not, turn on the special features of claims in particular. Assertions, judgements, beliefs,—any of these could serve equally well for the philosopher. Even assumptions, or taking something for granted, would be enough. It can come as a revelation to a detective, and the reader of detective fiction, as well as to a careful philosopher, that he has been simply assuming something or taking for granted something which he can now subject to scrutiny and perhaps even find wanting. He does not have to imagine that he was actually claiming it all along.

What the philosopher subjects to scrutiny is what he takes to be his knowledge that, say, there is a fire before him as he sits by the fire with a piece of paper in his hand. And whether he takes himself to assert that there is a fire, or to judge that there is, or to believe or assume or to claim that there is, is irrelevant to his task. As long as there is some 'attitude' or some 'relation' or other—some way in which the philosopher can subject to assessment what he takes to be his knowledge or his position—then his investigation will get off the ground. Any attitude, claim, or belief which could possibly be wrong, or could be found on examination to go beyond what is strictly speaking justified or strictly speaking true, would be enough to give the philosopher the subject-matter he needs. He thinks the examples he gives are examples of knowledge—in fact, best cases of knowledge—and Cavell has to show that they are no such thing. He has to show that the examples or the imagined situations do not contain any knowledge, or putative knowledge, or whatever else it might be that can be subjected to the kind of assessment that the philosopher directs to the objects of his investigation.

How is that to be shown? Certainly not by examining the conditions of *claiming* alone. Cavell points out that the philosopher imagines a context (e.g. sitting by the fire), but that that is not to imagine a context in which a claim is made. Certainly it is not to imagine that a claim is made aloud to someone else who hears it. And perhaps it is also not to imagine that any claim at all has been made. But I don't think that is enough to give Cavell his conclusion. Perhaps it is even true that in asking us to imagine that we are sitting by a fire, fully conscious, unanaesthetized, with eyes and ears open, and so on, the philosopher has not thereby managed to ask us to imagine that we are sitting by a fire and know or believe or assume that there is a fire there. But that is quite independent of whether the example is also an example of claiming something. Perhaps Cavell is right that the philosopher does not, and cannot, give an example of knowing that there is a fire before him that will serve his philosophical purposes in the way he needs. I suspect that something like that *is* right. And if it is right it would be extremely illuminating to see how and why it is right. But I do not see that Cavell's use of the notion of claiming gives us good reason to think it is right.

Consider the application of his point about claiming to G. E. Moore's example of seeing an envelope. That was put forward as a case of seeing rather than knowing, but presumably the point applies to both. At least, Cavell takes it that it does. Moore wanted to investigate seeing—to consider what happens when we see a material object—and he took a specific, concrete example. He held up an envelope in good light before a number of people, and to stress that it was really an example of what he wanted, he said 'We should certainly say (if you have looked at it) that we all *saw* that envelope . . .'[6] and then he goes on to ask what happened in that case. Cavell interprets Moore's 'we should certainly say' to be asserting that he and his audience in that situation would all *say* or *claim* that they saw the envelope. And that, as Cavell says, taken literally, 'is mad: it suggests that whenever any of us sees anything we claim to see it' (p. 219).

---

[6] G. E. Moore, *Some Main Problems of Philosophy* (London, 1953), 30.

I agree that that suggestion is mad. But I do not agree that that is what Moore is saying. Moore began, characteristically, with a single concrete instance, 'so that there may be no mistake as to exactly what it is that is being talked about'.[7] He wanted to be sure that everyone would agree that it was a case of seeing, and then to ask '*what* this occurrence, which we call the *seeing* of it, *is*'.[8] And he was making explicit the equally uncontroversial fact that it is a case of everyone's seeing the envelope; that too is something everyone in the audience who looked at the envelope would immediately agree to. It was not even an imagined case at the time. Moore was right there, with his audience and his envelope, doing it.

Now I for one certainly want to concede that that really is a case of seeing; anyone interested in what happens in cases of seeing would do well to investigate a case like that. But in conceding that to the philosopher (it is hardly a *concession*) I do not see that I must be imagining the case as one in which Moore and those people at that time were also *claiming* that they saw an envelope. The fact that they *saw* it, and that we all agree that they *saw* it, is all that the philosopher of perception needs in order to get going. Cavell speculates that perhaps Moore meant only that he and his audience are all *in a position* to claim to see the envelope; and he rightly points out that being in a position to claim it is not the same as claiming it. But I am suggesting that Moore was simply getting his audience to see the envelope, and to agree that it is a case of seeing an envelope, and when we read about it we immediately recognize it as an example of seeing, just as they did.

If the case does not have to be imagined from the outset as one in which a claim is made or is in the offing, then I do not see how Cavell's point that the philosopher's context is 'non-claim' can itself stop the philosophical investigation from getting off the ground. His point in the case of knowledge is that since no concrete claim is entered in the philosophical case, it is not really a case of knowing. But would he say the same thing about this case of seeing? Is it at all plausible to say that since no concrete claim is entered, it is not really a case of *seeing*? I think we are all strongly inclined to say, as I am, that if that's not seeing an envelope then I don't know what is, and if I want to understand seeing, that is just the sort of thing I want to understand.

[7] Ibid. 29.   [8] Ibid. 30.

The philosopher concerned with knowledge regards his example as an example of knowledge just as we regard this case as an example of seeing. Cavell claims that he is wrong in so regarding it. Or, more accurately, Cavell's view is that either he is wrong, and it is not really a case of knowing or, if he were to examine a real case of knowledge and subject it to a convincing assessment following recognized procedures for evaluating putative knowledge in everyday life, then any conclusion he reached about the particular example could not have the kind of generality he seeks. The traditional philosopher is therefore confronted with a dilemma. If there is no concrete claim under scrutiny, his enquiry will not be persuasive since it will not fully follow our ordinary procedures for evaluating concrete claims; but if there is a concrete claim under scrutiny, the conclusion that the evaluation reaches cannot be general.

In order to make out this charge it would obviously not be necessary to prove that 'no concrete claim is ever entered as part of the traditional investigation' (p. 217). It would be enough to show that no verdict arrived at about any claim that *is* entered in the kinds of examples the philosopher considers could be, or could support, a general conclusion of the sort the philosopher seeks about our knowledge as a whole. But that immediately raises the question of what 'a general conclusion of the sort the philosopher seeks about our knowledge as a whole' is like. The question is more difficult than it looks. Cavell, in his emphasis on his 'non-claim context', suggests that it is simply any *general* conclusion about our knowledge. Because claims have their conditions, and each concrete claim is made in specific conditions and for particular reasons, he suggests that no *general* verdict is derivable from our procedures of assessing actual claims. But I do not think the mere notion of generality itself is enough to capture the special character of the philosopher's concern with our knowledge.

It is quite possible to assert, perfectly legitimately and unproblematically in everyday situations, what sound like the very thing the philosopher is concerned to assert or to deny—for instance, 'We all know that there is a world of enduring physical bodies existing independently of us.' A psychologist might say some such thing in speaking to a normal audience about a very disturbed group of people who by contrast are said not to know even that much of

what the rest of us know.[9] Or, at the beginning of a set of intro-
ductory lectures, a physicist might say 'Many things are known
about the world around us.' These are both general remarks, and
they are about our knowledge of the world.

I think G. E. Moore is to be interpreted as making assertions of
just this sort about our knowledge—general assertions supported
by particular instances of knowledge of the world. They all imply
that somebody knows something about the world around us. That
is a general proposition, and it might appear to be something that
the negative conclusion of the philosophical investigation denies. I
think most of us feel that the unremarkable assertions that Moore
and the rest of us make every day do not *refute* the philosophical
conclusion that nobody knows anything about the physical world.
But if we nevertheless regard those assertions as fully legitimate in
their own way, as things that can be said, or even claimed, in just
the way Moore and the rest of us do or could say them, then it
cannot be that their difference from the philosopher's remarks, and
their legitimacy, consists in their lack of generality.

Those mundane assertions about our knowledge are *general*
enough—they are about all our knowledge of the physical world—
but I think we agree that they are not 'general conclusions of the
sort the philosopher seeks about our knowledge as a whole.' Not
simply because they happen to say that we *do* know, whereas the
sceptical philosophical conclusion appears to say we do not; but
because they are not the kind of general conclusion a traditional
philosopher would be seeking even if he wanted to avoid scepticism and give a positive general answer to the problem of our
knowledge of the physical world. Kant, for example, did not
suppose that the mundane or 'empirical' general truth that the
objects we perceive exist independently of us conflicted with his
philosophical or 'transcendental' view that the objects we perceive
are all appearances and dependent upon us.

Obviously I can do no more than rely on what I hope is your
sense of the philosophical irrelevance of scientific or ordinary or
Moore-like general assertions about our knowledge of the world.
I would hate to have to explain precisely how they differ from the
exciting philosophical conclusions expressed in the same words

[9] For this example, and an elaboration of the point and some of its consequences,
see Thompson Clarke, 'The Legacy of Skepticism', *Journal of Philosophy*, 69: 20
(1972), 654–769.

(especially since I do not see that the words *mean* anything different in the two cases).

I do not raise the possibility of the mundane assertion of philosophical-sounding general remarks because I think Cavell would deny it or because I think it is in any way incompatible with his final diagnosis of traditional philosophizing. On the contrary, I think it is fully in accord with the dilemma at the heart of his diagnosis. But it does show that, for that diagnosis to succeed, it need not be the case that *no claim at all* is made in any context the philosopher considers. We could allow that a concrete claim about the existence of a familiar object *is* or *can be* made in that context, as long as it could also be shown that what was true of that claim in that context could not possibly be taken as a conclusion that is representative of our knowledge as a whole in the way the philosopher intends. That does not imply that no conclusion we reached could be *general* in form; it could be as general as any of the mundane remarks I mentioned a moment ago. So its lack of the appropriate kind of representativeness for the philosopher would not be the same as its lack of generality. To establish Cavell's dilemma it would therefore have to be demonstrated, in a way Cavell does not attempt, exactly why and how the verdict arrived at in the philosopher's example cannot be representative in the way the philosopher needs, even though it is general or could be generalized.

This in turn raises some doubts about that so-far unarticulated 'critical fact about the mind' that Cavell promises as the pay-off from a successful diagnosis of philosophical scepticism. I will be able to offer only some brief, half-formed thoughts and questions about it by way of conclusion.

For Cavell, what we learn from a demonstration of the traditional sceptical philosopher's failure to give sense, or the right kind of sense, to his words, is that 'the human creature's basis in the world as a whole, its relation to the world as such, is not that of knowing, anyway not what we think of as knowing' (p. 241). This 'moral of scepticism' is something both Wittgenstein and Heidegger would 'affirm' or assent to; they differ from most recent philosophers in taking seriously a problem or mystery about the existence or the being of the world. If the human creature's 'relation to the world as such' is not that of knowing, what is it? In *The Claim of Reason*, as far as I can see, Cavell does not say. But in his earlier essay 'The Avoidance of Love' he says that the world is not to be known, but 'accepted', just as 'the presentness of other minds is not to be known, but acknowledged'.[10] A great deal of *The Claim of Reason* is about that acknowledgment, and about what tragedy reveals about it, and about its absence. But our 'acceptance' of the world is not further characterized or explored.

My difficulty with this idea is not with the specific candidate Cavell offers as the key to understanding our relation to the world as a whole. I would be equally puzzled by any other candidate he might offer in its place. My difficulty is that I do not understand how there could be any such 'critical fact' to be articulated, or how or why Cavell could talk illuminatingly of any such 'relation' to 'the world as such', if his dilemma had been reached in the way I sketched. It is something on which I wish Cavell had said a lot more.

First, I do not see how any such 'thesis'[11] or 'moral' can avoid being 'sceptical' in just that sense of the term in which Cavell rightly applied it to all those views which make good sense only on the basis of ideas that are invented and sustained by scepticism itself. What is 'the world as a whole' or 'the world as such,' and what is a creature's 'basis' in that world, or its 'relation' to it? And why is there thought to be only *one* such 'relation', or anyway one basic 'relation'? These ideas can perhaps be given content with the help of Descartes's *First Meditation* or some other traditional investigation of our relation to what comes to be called 'the world around us'. But if I agree that that investigation cannot get off the ground, and for the reasons that Cavell has in mind, then I am no longer sure that I can fill those ideas with the sense they must have if the

---

[10] Cavell, *Must We Mean?*, 324.

[11] Cavell says that Wittgenstein's appeal to criteria 'does not negate the concluding thesis of scepticism, that we do not know with certainty of the existence of the external world (or of other minds). On the contrary, Wittgenstein, as I read him, rather affirms that thesis, or rather takes it as *undeniable*, and so shifts its weight. What the thesis now means is something like: Our relation to the world as a whole, or to others in general, is not one of knowing, where knowing construes itself as being certain' (p. 45). Cavell sees a bond here with Heidegger. 'An admission of some question as to the mystery of the existence, or the being, of the world is a serious bond between the teaching of Wittgenstein and that of Heidegger. The bond is one, in particular, that implies a shared view of what I have called the truth of scepticism, or what I might call the moral of scepticism, namely, that the human creature's basis in the world as a whole, its relation to the world as such, is not that of knowing, anyway not what we think of as knowing' (p. 241). [Footnote added in 1999.]

'moral' Cavell wants to draw from scepticism is to be intelligible. So one question I would ask Cavell is: why is his 'moral' not still 'sceptical' in that sense?

Furthermore, it seems to me that Cavell should find his 'moral' or 'thesis' unacceptable because it remains too close to traditional philosophy. It implies that, although the traditional philosopher was wrong, he was not very far wrong. He had the right conception of 'us,' and of 'the world as a whole,' and of there being one, or one basic, 'relation' between them, but he happened to pick on the wrong 'relation'. He thought it was knowledge, but it isn't—it is 'acceptance'. And he thought we knew other minds in general; but we don't, we 'acknowledge' them. But it appears that the traditional philosopher was right about everything else.

This must also be unacceptable in seeming to leave open the possibility of a more or less traditional investigation or assessment of the specific 'relation' now chosen to represent our 'relation' to 'the world as a whole'. Cavell himself mentions the difficulty, but then drops it, when he introduces the notion of 'acceptance' of the world as a whole. 'What is this "acceptance",' he asks, 'which caves in at a doubt?'[12]—presumably doubt of the Cartesian or sceptical kind. The trouble, it seems to me, is not simply that 'acceptance' caves in, but that *if* it caves in at a doubt it must be because it was subject to assessment or examination. Is it possible for us to 'accept' something that is not in fact as we 'accept' it to be? Can we come to wonder whether our 'acceptance' is properly or securely based and then go on to try to rule out the disturbing possibility that it might not be? If so, then we will not have left traditional philosophy far behind in the move from 'knowing' to 'accepting'. Similar questions arise about acknowledgment. Are 'acceptance' and 'acknowledgment' as susceptible of scrutiny and assessment by traditional philosophical procedures as knowledge was? If not, why not? If so, and if the traditional investigation, once started, is as internally persuasive as Cavell and I agree that it is, won't we be forced once again to a sceptical conclusion?

The point is quite general. It would have to be shown why the same, or a similar, quandary would not be reached with respect to any 'relation' chosen to represent our 'relation' to 'the world as a whole' as was reached in the case of knowledge. Any 'relation',

---

[12] Cavell, *Must We Mean?*, 324.

whether it be acceptance or acknowledgment or something else, will just be one 'relation' among many—one among many ways in which we can be 'related' to something or to somebody in specific contexts in real life, and each one of which has its own particular conditions, just as Cavell insists that knowing or seeing or claiming does. Knowing, with its contextual conditions, could not be generalized into *the* relation in which we stand to 'the world as a whole', according to Cavell's diagnosis. So another question I would ask Cavell is: why does he think acceptance or acknowledgment or whatever else it might be can be freed from its specific contextual conditions and generalized into *the* relation in which we stand to 'the world as a whole' or to 'others in general' if knowledge cannot?

Resisting the philosophical or metaphysical employment of what, after all, must be ordinary notions like knowledge or acceptance or acknowledgment seems to me to be more in the spirit of Wittgenstein than does the 'affirming' of 'theses' of the sort Cavell attributes to him. That is not to deny what I think is Cavell's valid point that Wittgenstein philosophized from a strong sense of the inescapable urge towards a metaphysical understanding of our 'relation' to 'the world as a whole' or 'others in general.' I think he saw that urge as essential to philosophy. It is what gives the description of how our words are actually used its power of illumination.[13] And in that respect he certainly differed from Austin, as Cavell points out. But I do not see that honouring that distinction requires attributing to Wittgenstein, or accepting as our own, 'theses' that would articulate metaphysical or 'absolute' (p. 226) or context-free answers to expressible metaphysical questions.

I do not at all mean to suggest that it is not *true*, or that there is something wrong in saying, that 'the world is accepted' or that 'we acknowledge others'. I suggest only that, when we make or endorse such remarks, we cannot be sure that we have stated anything that a philosopher interested in what he calls our 'relation' to 'the world as a whole' wants to say. We cannot even be sure that there *is* anything that such a philosopher wants to say, or manages to say, in those words—something philosophical, and not just mundane. That is precisely the insight behind the kind of diagnosis of philosophical scepticism that Cavell offers. Why would we be any better off with the 'moral' that he wants to draw from his diagnosis? Can we

[13] Ludwig Wittgenstein, *Philosophical Investigations*, tr. G. E. M. Anscombe, Oxford, 1953, §109.

be sure that we do not get whatever intellectual satisfaction we might derive from that 'moral' only because we press into metaphysical or 'transcendental' service one or another ordinary notion which requires particular contexts and conditions for the 'empirical' employment that gives it its sense? That would be to fall victim to a species of the very illusion which Kant exposed and warned against in his own response to the fate of human reason.

6

Transcendental Arguments and 'Epistemological Naturalism'

It is not easy to incorporate the depth and power of Kant's transcendental deduction into present-day philosophical attitudes and preconceptions. Partly because of a still-dominant picture of the nature of necessary truth, and no doubt partly for other reasons even less well understood, it is difficult to assimilate or appreciate significant ideas and arguments that remain reasonably faithful to the spirit of Kant. In this paper I first examine one recent attempt to explain and to save the most important and most profound Kantian ideas, and then make some general remarks about the special nature of transcendental arguments and the conditions for their success.

I

In his 'Transcendental Arguments Revisited'[1] Jay Rosenberg finds the task of Kant's transcendental deduction to be that of 'justifying' or 'legitimizing' our use of certain concepts and our corresponding acceptance of certain principles or truths. That is indeed Kant's aim, but to say only that is not to say much, since there are any number of ways in which our use of something might be said to be 'legitimate', and correspondingly numerous ways in which that 'legitimacy' might be established. Kant has a legal model at least partly in mind, and the 'deduction' he envisages is to be

This essay was my contribution to an American Philosophical Association symposium on transcendental arguments. It was first published in *Philosophical Studies*, 31 (1977) © 1977. Reprinted with kind permission of Kluwer Academic Publishers.

[1] *Journal of Philosophy* (23 Oct. 1975). Page numbers alone in parentheses in the text refer to that article.

contrasted with what he calls a merely 'empirical deduction' of concepts which concerns only their '*de facto* mode of origination.'[2] A special 'transcendental' kind of 'deduction' is required for that core of concepts, central to our thinking, which are not and could not be derived from experience. These non-empirical or a priori concepts are to be 'legitimized' by a demonstration of what Kant calls their 'objective validity'. For Kant there is what Rosenberg calls 'one conceptual core'—an interrelated set of concepts or principles the possession of which is necessary for the possibility of thought and experience—and this set of concepts comes as a 'package deal' that cannot be added to or subtracted from piecemeal. I think it would not be too much to say that the presence of one such indivisible core is precisely what is established once and for all by the transcendental deduction (along with the Principles).

Although Rosenberg sees Kant as trying to legitimize the employment of a certain set of concepts, he finds an adherence to a *single* core to betray a certain narrowness of vision on Kant's part—a failure of imagination or perspective which, however understandable historically and therefore forgivable, had the unfortunate consequence of 'limiting' Kant to asking how he can justify his employment of these fundamental concepts only '*from within*' (p. 618). It is difficult to understand why Rosenberg sees this as a limitation, since this special feature would seem to be the very mark of the 'transcendental' method. If there are certain ways in which we must think if thought and experience are to be possible at all, it will not be surprising to find that we can think about those ways of thinking only from 'within' them. We could stand 'outside' them only by violating the very conditions that make thought possible. So if we also manage to 'legitimize' those ways of thinking we will have to do so 'from within' as well. It is perhaps true that, in some moods, we might come to see this situation as a 'limitation' or 'constraint' on us, but that is no reason to attribute the alleged limitation to the scope of Kant's vision.

Indeed, it would seem that it is only because of this special feature of the transcendental method that Rosenberg is right in attributing great importance to Kant's point that corresponding to the core concepts there are 'principles' which 'make possible the very experience which is [their] own ground of proof'.[3] That

[2] Kant, *Critique of Pure Reason*, tr. N. Kemp Smith (New York 1963), A85–B117.
[3] Ibid., A737–B765.

is presumably what their being 'justified' or 'legitimized' only *from within* comes to. And the other side of this same coin is, as Rosenberg puts it, that we cannot justify our employment of the set of fundamental concepts by showing that they give us a good, or a better, or the best 'fit between our system of representations and how things-in-themselves stand' (p. 621). So a transcendental deduction will differ from ordinary theoretical arguments or justifications which it is perfectly appropriate to describe in just that way. It is often possible to say of a theory or hypothesis that it 'fits the facts' better, or 'fits more of the facts', than its competitors. But the possession of those concepts Kant is interested in is what makes it possible for us even to have so much as a conception of there being 'facts' which our theories either do or do not 'fit'.

But it is not Rosenberg's general description of Kant's aims that causes most of the difficulty. It is when he enters into his own positive programme of saving and assimilating what he repeatedly calls the 'brilliant' and 'deepest insights', the marks of the 'special genius', of that 'giant' Immanuel Kant, that it becomes difficult to see how anything reasonably close to Kant's leading ideas would be saved.

Rosenberg claims to be justifying ways of thinking, or 'conceptual cores', in the spirit of Kant's transcendental deduction. That spirit for him is embodied in a piece of what he calls 'practical reasoning' to a 'normative' conclusion to the effect that we have a right or permission to employ certain concepts. Whatever its merits for Rosenberg's own projects, I think there are at least two serious difficulties in attributing such a mode of reasoning to Kant. First, it is difficult to see how he *could* argue in such a way for the kind of conclusion he wants. He is concerned with how it is possible for us to think and experience anything at all, and I don't see how one could deliberate or reason about how best to achieve human thought and experience, or what means to adopt in order to achieve it. If you could engage in the deliberative thinking at all it would already be too late. You would have achieved your 'desired end'.

Secondly, Rosenberg moves directly from the observation that Kant distinguishes the *quid facti* from the *quid juris* (or question of right) and wants only to answer the latter, to the conclusion that his answer to that question is secured by a 'practical syllogism' with a 'practical' or 'normative' conclusion. But that does not seem to

me to follow, even in the legal case. For example, I could establish
that I now have a right to use a certain thing by showing that I
legally bought it and have legally retained possession of it since
then, and none of that reasoning need be 'practical reasoning' at
all. The actual 'deduction' or bit of reasoning I would go through
to answer the question of right with respect to the particular thing
could be any kind of reasoning that would establish that a certain
state of affairs holds, e.g. that I bought the thing. It need not be part
of that 'deduction' or reasoning itself to prove, for example, that
anyone who legally possesses something has a right to employ it.
Only because that principle is true does my 'deduction' succeed,
but to establish my 'right' in a particular case I do not have to
'prove' the principles or laws themselves (whatever that would be).
I need show only that my present case falls under this or that law
or statement of right or permission.

So from the fact that Kant's transcendental deduction seeks to
justify or legitimize our employment of certain concepts nothing
much follows about precisely what form that argument or bit of
reasoning will take—and in particular it does not follow that it is
a species of 'practical' or 'means-end' reasoning. Kant in fact tries
to establish, of certain concepts, that they are indispensable for
thought and experience—that possession and employment of them
is a necessary condition of the possibility of thought. And it would
seem to me very natural for someone who thought he had established that to think that he had thereby 'justified' or 'legitimized'
our employment of those concepts in a fairly solid and profound
way. If showing that our not being able to think at all—of anything—without those concepts is equivalent to showing that those
concepts could not lack what Kant calls 'objective validity', then
the justificatory aim of the transcendental deduction would have
been achieved, and solely by a demonstration of the necessity or
absolute indispensability of certain concepts. There is nothing especially 'deliberative', 'practical' or 'normative' about that part of it.
It has much more the character of a *discovery* than of a resolution
or a policy.

Rosenberg on the contrary does not see the task of a transcendental deduction as that of revealing to us the necessary conditions
of the possibility of any thought or experience, but rather that of
justifying or legitimizing a transition from one particular set of concepts (one 'core') to another (p. 618). He thinks this is the most that

'epistemological naturalists', with their wider 'evolutionary' perspective and their greater understanding of 'theory succession in the natural sciences' can and should hope for in a Kantian direction (p. 618). For him, 'a transcendental deduction is no different from a Peircean abduction' aimed at 'the fixation of belief' (p. 623). It shows in effect that one 'conceptual scheme' provides increased explanatory power and coherence over another and accounts for some of the anomalies and limitations of that earlier scheme, and thus wins out over its predecessor.

My question is whether there is anything especially Kantian or 'transcendental' about this kind of reasoning. It appears to be nothing more than ordinary empirical, theoretical inference, perhaps on a very large scale. I wish not to malign such reasoning, but only to ask whether, if it were the only way a 'conceptual core' could be justified or legitimized, anything would remain of what was important to Kant.

Rosenberg thinks that in 'transposing' the transcendental deduction into his 'naturalistic key' very little that is essential is lost. He thinks he even retains the important 'ostensive' character of transcendental justification, according to which certain principles are established by making possible 'the very experience which is [their] own ground of proof' (p. 620). But I don't think Rosenberg really saves that fundamental Kantian insight, but only something much weaker that does not do the job he wants.

The kind of argument he describes and recommends would justify a way of thinking, or give us 'licence and title to engage in it', only after we have the system of concepts into whose legitimacy we wish to enquire (p. 620). That, of course, parallels Kant. And for Rosenberg, that the adoption of the new set of concepts makes possible the very experiences in which they are employed is what is supposed to justify or legitimize our use of that set of concepts. He would say, for example, that when we move from the apparently minimal conception of an object as merely something distinguished from its contemporary environment to the employment of a richer conception of objects as 'per during physical substances', our employment of that richer conception is legitimized in the having of certain particular experiences that were not available before, namely, those experiences which we can have only because we employ that richer conceptual structure. He says that:

where our adoption of a certain, successor conceptual core makes possible the reconceptualization of the experienced world under a new
categorial characterization, that it makes this possible is supposed to be
what gives us the right actually to so reconceptualize the world.   (p. 620)

By this he must mean that our employment of a new concept, or
set of concepts, F, is legitimized relative to an earlier set G in that
the employment of F, but not that of G, makes possible experiences
of Fs—experiences of things as Fs. So the point he 'saves' is that
one cannot experience Fs unless one has the concept of an F; and
he goes on to say that in certain cases the having of an experience
of an F legitimizes the employment of the concept of an F.

But this first point is much weaker than the 'insight' of Kant.
Kant claims that there are certain concepts the employment of
which is necessary for any experience whatever, so what contributes in the special 'ostensive' way to the legitimization of such
concepts is *any experience at all*. The particular character of the
experience is irrelevant. Rosenberg retains only the weaker principle that a certain experience, say an experience of an F, is made
possible by, and hence legitimizes, our employment of the concept
of an F. Putting the difference in most general terms, Rosenberg
holds that for every experience there is some concept or set of
concepts without which that particular experience would be impossible or would not be had. Kant's stronger principle is that there
are certain concepts which are such that, for any experience whatever, that experience would be impossible or would not be had
unless we possessed those concepts. That, of course, is a consequence of the fact that certain specific concepts are required for
experience or thought to be possible at all, and that is a Kantian
'insight' that Rosenberg explicitly says he wants to abandon in his
'naturalism' (p. 618).

Furthermore, the fact that possessing and employing the concept
of an F makes it possible to have experiences of Fs, in this weaker
sense, is surely not in itself a justification or legitimization of our
employment of the concept of an F. There could be *no* concepts
whose employment was illegitimate if that were so, since every
concept is such that possession of it makes possible experiences of
things as falling under that concept. No one could be afraid of
ghosts, or have what he took to be an experience of seeing one,
without the concept of a ghost. But that is not enough to answer
Kant's question of right. Rosenberg realizes that our different

conceptual repertoire and corresponding new experiences after a change to a new 'conceptual core' would not themselves alone legitimize our employment of that 'core'. He says the transition would be justified only if 'there is some overriding epistemic end-in-view—call it "E"—better served by thus reconceptualizing the world' (p. 620). That is what leads him back to 'practical reasoning', and to the idea that historically successive 'transcendental deductions' adduce better and better means for achieving this desired 'end-in-view'. But then it is not the fact that it makes possible a certain experience that legitimizes our employment of a certain set of concepts, but simply that it is a better instrument for achieving our 'end-in-view' E. And so the Kantian 'insight' about the special character of transcendental proof has vanished.

Rosenberg's emphasis on the transcendental deduction's being a species of 'practical reasoning' then takes on many of the characteristics of a red herring as well. Whatever that reasoning is like, it certainly is not deliberation about what to do. It takes place only after we have introduced and employed the new concepts and found that their use provides greater explanatory power and coherence over that of their predecessor. Rosenberg might be tempted to argue that in a way that still leaves room for deliberation about a future goal, since at each stage we still have not achieved our final end E, but have only taken one more step towards it, and so we can deliberate about how to get closer. But that requires that there be some independent or non-relational specification of what that end E is, and there is no such thing. Rosenberg says that we seek 'more and more thoroughly unified, structured, and integrated systems' (p. 622), and we presumably recognize on particular occasions whether what we have now is better than its predecessor in those combined respects. But that does not imply that we have any independent conception of some 'final stage' of this process. As far as I can see, it does not even imply that the relation of 'better than' thought to hold between successive stages is transitive. The fact is that when we find a scheme or theory superior to its predecessor on the score of explanatory power, coherence, and comprehensiveness, we regard it as better and therefore, to that relative degree, justified. There is no real objection to calling this reasoning 'practical', as long as one realizes that probably *all* reasoning—including the most 'theoretical'—will be 'practical' in precisely the same sense. And a transcendental deduction will not thereby have been distinguished from any other instance of theoretical reasoning.

II

It has not been my aim to object to Rosenberg's 'naturalism', with its concern for the self-conscious evolution and development of new and better-adapted cognitive resources. I want only to suggest how much of Kant and the special character of transcendental philosophizing is given up in Rosenberg's conception of that move. To better understand that special character I think we must try to identify and explain the unique depth and universal scope of Kantian philosophy and of transcendental proof generally.

In searching for the essential characteristics of the transcendental deduction or of transcendental arguments generally, it should not be supposed that we seek some unique and heretofore undiscovered form of argument or pattern of inference, understood fairly strictly as a certain formal or logical structure. The term 'transcendental' is not to be thought of as naming another form to be put alongside *modus ponens, modus tollens,* and the others. Rather, we understand what is special or unique about a transcendental argument when we appreciate the special status of the 'principles' that would be established by a successful transcendental proof.

For Kant the categories are to be shown to be necessary for thought of an object.

If we can prove that by their means alone an object can be thought, this will be a sufficient deduction of them, and will justify their objective validity.[4]

And in concentrating on the conditions under which thought or experience can have an 'object', Kant is certainly concentrating on one of its fundamental and ineradicable characteristics. He is not saying that we can think only of physical or spatial things, but rather that any thought or experience must be 'of' something, it must have 'content', or a 'target', or an 'objective'. Our thinkings and experiencings must have accusatives, and so in at least that sense must have 'objects'. They must be 'about' something. It is difficult to see that as a 'time-bound' and therefore possibly changeable feature of

---

[4] Kant, *Critique of Pure Reason*, tr. N. Kemp Smith (New York 1963), A96-7.

thought and experience. Whatever the conditions might be that make thought and experience of objects possible, then, they will be conditions of the possibility of any thought or experience at all.

It is from this minimal but indispensable condition of human thought that Kant hopes to get his rich results. He does so by focusing on something that he sees to be required for thoughts or experiences to have 'objects' in this minimal sense. The constituents of thought and experience (our 'representations') must be unified in certain ways. They get their sense or content only through their relations or connections with others. In particular, all 'representations' must belong to someone. 'Representations' belong to me only if it is possible for me to think of them as mine. And that in turn is possible only if they are unified or connected in another way, as 'representations' of something that is not myself—a single world through which I move and which my 'representations' reflect from a certain point of view. And such a world, to be thought of in that way, must for example be seen as subject to causal laws, so that everything that happens in that world follows upon something else that happens in accord with a rule or law.

My concern here is not with the details of this argument, but with its conclusion. If the general strategy is successful, certain truths or 'principles' will have been shown to have a very special status. Concentrating on such 'principles', or on their status, rather than looking for some unique form of argument used to arrive at them, seems to me the best way to determine what is special or unique about transcendental arguments. That would be to ask, in effect, what position one would be in *vis à vis* those truths or 'principles' if one had successfully completed a transcendental deduction. That is the point at which recent discussions most fully overlap with Kant. Some recent philosophers have wanted to show that, with respect to various concepts or general 'principles', we are actually in a position like the one Kant tried to reach.

If there were 'principles' or propositions whose truth is required for us to be able to think of, or experience, anything at all, then doubts about the truth of such 'principles' would have to be unreal or philosophically unthreatening. Any denial of such 'principles', in order to be true, would have to violate the necessary conditions of that very denial's making sense. That would show that the 'principles' have a special status in our thought. They are not to be thought of as contingent hypotheses supported inductively by the findings of sense-experience, nor are they necessary truths guaranteed by the meanings of their constituent concepts alone. For Kant they are to express what are ultimately the necessary conditions of our being able to think of or experience anything at all—conditions of our having thoughts or experiences that are *of* or *about* something, or that have 'objects'.

Now the problem, obviously, is whether any such rich and interesting 'principles' can ever be shown to have this exalted status, and if so, how. Can any substantial results be spun out of nothing more than the minimal conditions of thought? It is here that the arguments of many recent scaled-down Kantians have seemed to me weak, or at best incomplete, and not sufficiently Kantian.[5] Kant tries to reach his interesting results by showing that the possession and applicability of certain concepts are necessarily involved in the possession and applicability of certain others—that the capacity to think in certain ways carries within it the capacity to think in certain other ways—and so the indispensable core of concepts is an interrelated package. But he does not achieve that result merely by showing that the content or meaning of one concept is itself 'contained' or 'included' in that of another. Unlike most recent philosophers, he is not restricted by a view of all necessary truths as 'analytic', or as guaranteed by concepts alone. If all we could show were that certain concepts 'contained' certain others, we could arrive at nothing more than conditional necessities and hence could not get into the unique position that a successful transcendental deduction would provide. We must therefore concentrate, not just on the concepts themselves, or on their content, but on the conditions of our possessing and applying them. Kant saw that the conditions of our being able to think in certain ways are what must be understood, and not just the contents of what we think, or the relations of meaning holding among them.

It is true that Kant's much-maligned transcendental psychology tends to come into play at this point in his own theory, but I think philosophers who have wished to avoid such doctrines while still arriving at interesting transcendental results have not really provided much to put in its place. An ungrounded appeal to a general principle of meaning or significance, according to which concepts

---

[5] I have discussed some recent arguments of this sort in Ch. 2, above, 'Transcendental Arguments'.

are intelligible to us only if we know the empirical conditions under which they could be truly and knowingly applied,[6] seems to me implausible in fact as an account of the intelligibility or significance of particular propositions, and, more importantly, it would deny or render superfluous the very special project Kant set himself. Armed at the outset with a general principle to the effect that, for every proposition that is intelligible to us it must be possible under some conditions for us to determine that that proposition is true, or that it is false, we would be in a position to regard all doubts about the knowability of anything as philosophically unthreatening. A sceptical denial of the knowability of any particular proposition would, if true, violate the necessary conditions of that very proposition's making sense to us. The general principle of significance alone would endow *every* intelligible proposition with this privileged epistemic status, and so there would be no need to discover a special central core or a fundamental set of 'principles' which are necessary for all thought and experience. If this more direct strategy were to work, there would not have to be any substantial 'principles' or any specific concepts necessary for the possibility of thought and experience at all.

Of course, it might well be that what recommends this more direct strategy is precisely the suspicion that there really are no interesting or substantial conditions which are absolutely necessary for the possibility of any thought or experience whatever—that all putative necessities, however firm they might seem to us now, are really contingent and 'time-bound'. That, I think, is Rosenberg's suspicion, and it is widely shared. But that suspicion would certainly have to be confirmed; the absence of any interesting necessary conditions of thought and experience must be established, and not simply asserted as likely on general historical or 'evolutionary'

---

[6] Strawson in *The Bounds of Sense* (London, 1966) attributes to Kant some such principle as 'there can be no legitimate, or even meaningful employment of ideas or concepts which does not relate them to empirical or experiential conditions of their application' (p. 16). The question is not whether Kant would accept some such principle, but whether he could do so at the outset as a way of securing his transcendental results, or only subsequently, and therefore legitimately, as a consequence of them. Strawson agrees that the principle was required if philosophy was to be set 'on the sure path of a science', and that that was something Kant wanted to prove, and not simply assume, but since the only support he can find in Kant for the principle comes from the doctrines of transcendental idealism, he prefers to treat it as 'autonomous' and therefore as independent of that (and apparently any other) putative support.

grounds. Even the most uncompromising 'evolutionary' attitude would not preclude us from asking what it is that makes thought or experience possible—how it is possible for thought and experience to have 'objects', or be 'of' or 'about' something. It remains to be seen that that very general question itself must be given an historical or 'evolutionary' answer, even if an historical or 'evolutionary' answer must be given to the quite different question of how and why in the development of *homo sapiens* those conditions ever in fact came to be fulfilled.

7

The Allure of Idealism

We all know that, for the most part, thinking something does not make it so, and that, in general, something's being so does not require that it be thought to be so—or that anything else be thought to be so either. Many of the things we think—in astronomy, geology, and biology, for example—were so (or were not) long before there were any people or other beings who could have thought anything. Even most of what has actually been thought to be so has not depended on being thought in order to be so. The eruption of Vesuvius in AD 79, for example, was in fact perceived and since then has been thought about by many people, but no one supposes that that eruption occurred only because it was seen or thought about, or that it would not have occurred if no one had ever thought of it, or even that its occurrence required that something or other be thought by someone.

I begin with these commonplaces because I think there is a strong tendency to ignore or even to deny them (or something like them) in philosophy. Frege was well aware of the tendency, and in his own work resolved 'always to separate sharply the psychological from the logical, the subjective from the objective'.[1] He insisted on distinguishing *what* is thought from someone's thinking it. Any questions about how human beings come to know or think what they do—any questions not solely about the logical relations among the things we think—are for Frege irrelevant to *what* we think. They concern our *taking* something to be so, not its being so.

It is when we become interested in our thinking or knowing itself—our ways of thinking and knowing and not just what we think and know—that we seem especially prone to run together

This essay was my contribution to a Joint Session Symposium with Jonathan Lear on 'The Disappearing "We" '. It was first published in the *Proceedings of the Aristotelian Society: Supplementary Volume*, 58 (1984). Reprinted by courtesy of the Editor of the Aristotelian Society: © 1984.

[1] G. Frege, *The Foundations of Arithmetic*, tr. J. L. Austin (Oxford, 1953), p. x.

what Frege resolved to keep apart. Why should that be? Is there
something in the very concern with the 'psychological' itself that
forces or even inclines us to ignore or deny the distinction between
something's being so and its being thought to be so? I don't see
that there is. Just as we can distinguish the question whether Vesuvius erupted in AD 79 from the further 'psychological' question
whether anyone thinks Vesuvius erupted in AD 79, so we can distinguish that 'psychological' question from the further 'psychological' question whether anyone thinks that anyone thinks that
Vesuvius erupted in AD 79.

But I think it cannot be denied that there *is* a tendency to ignore
or deny the distinction between what Frege called the 'subjective'
and the 'objective' when we get interested in our knowledge and
our ways of thinking in that special way we get interested in ourselves *in philosophy*. That seems a fair comment on philosophy
since 1781, if not earlier. I cannot identify that special philosophical interest unequivocally, but I think we all have enough of a sense
of it to recognize it and be attracted by it. We want to understand
not just how it is possible for us to think or know this or that particular thing, given that we already think or know something else;
we want to understand how human thought or knowledge in
general is possible. That certainly was Kant's interest in our ways
of thinking. But that is not enough to identify uniquely the special
philosophical project Kant had in mind. It is possible to reach
general conclusions about all human thought or knowledge that
would find no place in a Kantian or philosophical investigation.

Kant sought what he called a 'critique' of human reason; he
wanted to establish and to identify the limits of what he called the
'objective validity' of our thinking. For him there was a question
about the 'legitimacy' of our ways of thinking that would not have
been answered even if every question about what we think and
every question about how we came to think in those ways had been
settled. What is that question of 'legitimacy'? I think its presence
in some form or other, and the felt need to answer it, is what is
characteristic of the special philosophical concern with our ways
of thinking. It is also, I believe, what leads us to conflate what we
otherwise have no trouble keeping apart—the 'subjective' and the
'objective', or our thinking something to be so and its being so.

Jonathan Lear describes Kant's project as that of showing how
subjective conditions of thought can have *objective validity*', how

the ways in which we must think ('the categories') 'legitimately apply to objects given in intuition'.[2] It might be thought that we could show that our concepts apply to objects presented to us in our sensory experience simply by being presented with objects in our sensory experience and correctly applying to those objects concepts that are true of them. But that for Kant would not show that that application was 'legitimate' in the required sense. It might be thought that the 'categories' we employ could not fail to be legitimate since (as Kant believes) we simply could not think at all without them. But again that is not enough to secure the 'legitimacy' Kant is concerned with. Even Hume could insist that for us there is no alternative to our thinking in terms of cause and effect, say; we cannot help thinking that way. But Hume's is precisely the sort of view Kant thinks does not establish the 'objective validity' of the concept of causation, among others. So there is a very special question at the heart of the Kantian project. So far we know something about what would *not* be an adequate answer to it, even if we do not yet know why, or what an adequate answer would be.

One approach is to ask how things would stand if Kant's question had not been answered satisfactorily—if the 'objective validity' of our ways of thinking had not been secured. If it were possible for us to think at all under such conditions, as it would be on the Humean view, we would nevertheless have to acknowledge the possibility of a gap, in general, between our thinking things to be so and their being so. The 'subjective conditions of thought', for all we know, might just fail to match up with any 'objective' conditions in the way things are. Our concepts would in that way fail to be 'objectively valid'. Our thinking things to be so about the objective world would have come apart from their being so, in general—or at least it would not have been shown that the two do not come apart.

Of course, Kant thinks they cannot come apart in that way. He thinks the 'objective validity' of our ways of thinking is a condition of our being able to have the thought of an object—of our being able to think about or experience anything at all. But that view is what is meant to *answer* Kant's question of 'legitimacy'. Only because that view is true is the 'legitimacy' secured. To establish that result—as Kant thinks he does—is to establish the 'objective validity' of our ways of thinking, and hence to eliminate the

[2] Lear, 'The Disappearing "We" ', 221. Page numbers in parentheses in the text refer to this paper.

possibility of such a gap. But short of having established that result, the spectre of that gap—of the 'subjective conditions of thought' possibly not corresponding in any way with what we can understand to be 'objectively' the case—would still be before us.

Kant thinks his question of 'legitimacy' requires a 'transcendental' and not merely 'empirical' demonstration to answer it. In my own attempts to understand what is special about a 'transcendental' demonstration, and why no 'empirical' legitimation of our ways of thinking could succeed, I have resorted to the spectre of philosophical scepticism—the threat of our not knowing whether any of the things we think (or even must think) about the objective world are in fact true. I think I can see a kind of 'illegitimacy', or at least a lack of 'legitimacy', that would infect our thinking if scepticism were correct, and why no appeal to what we find in our experience could ever succeed in removing the threat. Perhaps dwelling on the threat of scepticism is not the only, or even the best, way to try to understand Kant's problem. Lear thinks it is not. He thinks an 'overarching concern for "refuting the sceptic"' (p. 223) will naturally lead one to misconstrue what Kant's 'legitimation' amounts to (p. 220). One will then understand the project too narrowly or shallowly, as simply that of giving a *tu quoque* or an *ad hominem* argument against some character called 'the sceptic'. He thinks such skirmishes cannot be expected to reveal, as Kant wants to reveal, the objective validity of any thought that is about anything at all.

I do not understand why Lear thinks disarming the threat of what I call scepticism cannot go as deeply as that. Nor do I see that one must, or naturally will, misconstrue Kant's project if one understands it that way. I don't think Kant himself misconstrued the nature of his own project, but he was certainly concerned to 'refute the sceptic'. Perhaps his was not an 'overarching' concern, but he does tell us that someone who presses the sceptical threat upon us, as Descartes does, is really 'a benefactor of human reason' in forcing us 'to keep on the watch, lest we consider as a well-earned possession what we perhaps obtain only illegitimately' (A378–9).[3] Scepticism for Kant represents a way of posing the threat of 'illegitimacy'. A condition of adequacy for any 'legitimizing' project is that the threat of scepticism be completely disarmed. That does not mean that the sole value of the transcendental deduction consists

---

[3] References to Kant are to *Critique of Pure Reason*, tr. N. Kemp Smith (London, 1953).

in its ability to combat scepticism, but it does mean that if scepticism is still possible the right sort of 'legitimacy' or 'validity' has not been established. That is why, if scepticism is worth taking seriously at all, disarming it can be expected to involve something deeper than an invented dialogue with some cantankerous misfit who surreptitiously contradicts himself or is able to say what he says only because it is false. So I do not see that a concern with scepticism cannot bring out the true dimensions of Kant's project. Perhaps it has come to look that way because some recent defenders or interpreters of 'transcendental arguments' have not really taken scepticism seriously or have not thought it takes much to 'refute' it. But that is not my view, nor is it my view of Kant.

I agree with Lear, then, that giving a 'transcendental argument for X', and hence establishing its 'legitimacy', is not a matter merely of forcing someone into some form of self-refutation. It is a matter of revealing 'in its broadest and deepest context what it is to be X' (p. 223). How is that to be done? Kant begins by 'deducing' what our concepts or categories are or must be and exploring the conditions of our thinking in those ways. He finds that they are the conditions of our thinking of anything at all. Now how could such an investigation of how we think, or of how it is possible for us to think at all, reveal to us (in Lear's words) 'what it is to be X', as opposed to what it is to think about X, or what makes it possible (and perhaps also necessary) for us to think about X? I do not mean this to be a rhetorical question. I think Lear is quite right to say that Kant's investigation is meant to reveal what it is to *be X*, not merely what it is to think about X. That is how it is meant to answer the question of 'legitimacy'. To understand more and more only about the conditions of our thinking about X would be to understand only 'psychological' or 'subjective' facts about us. It would leave it open that the categories could be (in Lear's words) no more than 'an artefact of our subjective constitution' (p. 221). We would not have connected our thinking of things in a certain way with their being that way, so we would not have understood or established the 'objective validity' of our ways of thinking. The 'transcendental' investigation brings the two together by establishing the necessary accord or harmony between them. It shows how the *'subjective conditions of thought* can have *objective validity*, that is, can furnish conditions of the possibility of all knowledge of objects' (A90 = B122).

It does so by showing that what makes it possible for us to think about or perceive objects at all makes it true that there are objects of the sorts we think about and perceive. There being such objects is a condition of our being able to think about or perceive any objects at all. The short answer to how that is established is to say that the objects we think about or perceive are in some way dependent on our faculty of thinking or perceiving. That is because the things we think about and perceive and have knowledge about are *constituted* by the fulfilment of the conditions of our thinking and perceiving as we do. The objects we think about and perceive just are whatever it is that are united in our thought and experience. So the formal conditions for thought or experience of an object require that the objects we think about or perceive are themselves 'representations' which, as representations, are not independent of being thought or perceived. Kant's view is that all the things we think about and perceive 'are in all their configurations and alterations nothing but mere appearances, that is, representations in us, of the reality of which we are immediately conscious' (A371–2). That is why the 'subjective conditions' of thought and experience could not come apart, in general, from the 'objective' conditions in what we think about or perceive. There is at least a most general and most formal level at which what we think to be so must be so if we are able to think it. At that level, our thinking or perceiving such-and-such to be so and its being so could not come apart. For Kant there is a necessary accord or harmony, in general, between our thought and experience and the 'objective' domain they are about. That is because those 'objective' states of affairs are 'constituted' by the conditions of thought and experience.

This is a bald and crude description of Kant's view, but I think it is enough to show that it is to be understood as a form of idealism. He calls it 'formal' or 'transcendental' idealism. Because the harmony between what we think and our thinking it must be a *necessary* harmony if it is to answer the question of 'legitimacy', that harmony cannot be established 'empirically', but only a priori. That is what makes the idealism 'transcendental'. It is the result of an a priori investigation of the conditions that must be fulfilled a priori, independently of experience, if any thought or perception of objects is to be possible at all. The truth of this transcendental idealism is what shows the impossibility of 'empirical', or what Kant also calls 'problematic' or 'sceptical', idealism. But its incompatibility with those forms of idealism does not show that it is not itself a form of idealism.

What is important about this idealism for Kant is that it is the *only* way the 'objective validity' of our ways of thinking could be secured. It is easy to see why that is so, given Kant's question of 'legitimacy'. He thinks that if the things we think about were completely independent of us and of our ways of thinking, there would be no explaining how we could ever perceive them or come to know of them. That would be 'transcendental realism', and it would leave open the possibility of a gap, in general, between our thinking things to be so and their being so. As Kant puts it, the 'transcendental realist' easily comes to play the part of the 'empirical' or 'sceptical idealist'. 'After wrongly supposing that objects of the senses, if they are to be external, must have an existence by themselves and independent of the senses, he finds that, judged from this point of view, all our sensuous representations are inadequate to establish their reality' (A369). So for Kant the only way to avoid this conclusion is to reject the 'wrong' supposition of the 'transcendental realist' and occupy 'the only refuge still open'. We must view 'all our perceptions, whether we call them inner or outer, as a consciousness only of what is dependent on our sensibility', and thus view 'the outer objects of those perceptions not as things in themselves, but only as representations' (A378). Idealism is the only answer.

I think it is easy to feel the force of Kant's reasoning here. Once our ways of thinking, or all the 'psychological' or 'subjective' facts about our thinking as we do, have been isolated in general from the way things are in the 'objective' domain we think about, Kant's question about the 'legitimacy' or 'objective validity' of those ways of thinking seems real and pressing. And then it seems that the *only* way the question could be answered satisfactorily, the *only* way the necessary harmony between the two could be secured, is through the truth of idealism. If at even the most formal and most abstract level the things we think to be so could possibly all fail to be true even though we nevertheless think them, or perhaps even must think them, our ways of thinking in general would not have been shown to be 'objectively valid'. So I think I understand the allure of idealism once Kant's question about the 'legitimacy' or 'validity' of our ways of thinking has been taken seriously. The only alternative would seem to be scepticism.

One feature of idealism is that, at any level at which it were true, an explicit reference to our ways of thinking would be superfluous. Or, in Jonathan Lear's words, the 'we' would disappear. If idealism is correct and our ways of thinking 'constitute' the way things are, there will be no difference between examining our ways of thinking and examining the way things are. The most general and most formal features of our ways of thinking will be none other than the most general and most formal features of the objective states of affairs we think about and know, so an investigation of those features could be indifferently described as an investigation of our ways of thinking or an investigation of the way things are. That is why a 'transcendental argument' for X, which establishes the 'legitimacy' of the concept of X or of our thinking in terms of X, simultaneously reveals 'in its broadest and deepest context *what it is to be X*'. Once idealism has been established, the factors we began by separating—our thinking of X and X's being so—will have been shown to merge. The 'we' will have disappeared; it will play no essential role in the formulation of what we know. We will no longer be stuck with thinking only about our ways of thinking as opposed to the reality we think about. We will not be restricted to saying things like 'We think (or must think) there are objects' or 'We think (or must think) every event has a cause'. We can say simply 'There are objects' or 'Every event has a cause'.

In fact on Kant's view we can even say 'There must be objects' or 'Every event must have a cause'. That is his idea of the synthetic a priori, which goes hand in hand with transcendental idealism. Something that must be so if we can think or say anything at all can be thought or said to hold necessarily. Not necessarily in the sense that its negation implies a contradiction, but in the sense that it could not be otherwise if anything is thought. It is thus 'synthetic', but it cannot be thought to be otherwise, so it is known a priori. Such knowledge is possible only because our forms of thinking 'constitute' the states of affairs we think about. That is why, as Lear puts it, 'the reflective understanding of the contribution of our mindedness to the necessity we find in the world is not meant to undermine the necessity, but to give us insight into it' (p. 238). The insight we get in Kant is the insight of transcendental idealism.

Now how seriously can we really take transcendental idealism in trying to understand ourselves and our relation to the world? It involves the idea of the things we think about being in some way dependent on their being thought about by us. If we apply that idea directly to some particular thing we think about we end up with the absurd conclusion that, for example, the eruption of Vesuvius was in some way dependent upon its being thought about by us. The only reason that is not enough in itself to dismiss idealism once and for all is that the thesis is supposed to be understood 'transcendentally', and not 'empirically'. Of course it is false as an 'empirical' thesis about the relation between our thoughts and the eruption of Vesuvius, but it is nevertheless true 'transcendentally'. Now do we really understand what it is to take something 'transcendentally', or to give a 'transcendental' and not merely 'empirical' reading to what, after all, is the English sentence 'All the things we think about and perceive are in some way dependent upon us, or are nothing more than representations in us'?

I think we should not try to persuade ourselves that we do understand transcendental idealism solely because we see that it is our 'only refuge' for answering Kant's question of 'legitimacy'. Even if we grant that it must be both intelligible and true if that question is to be answered satisfactorily, it might be at least as productive for us to examine more carefully what is thought to generate that question in the first place. Do we really understand what forces us to seek any 'refuge' at all?

Jonathan Lear wants to press as far as he can a certain parallel between Kant and the later work of Wittgenstein. That is partly because he wants to cast Wittgenstein in a 'post-Kantian' role rather than as the sceptical 'neo-Humean' he thinks Saul Kripke has described.[4] I don't see that the two roles are incompatible, any more than I see that attributing to Kant a concern with scepticism must lead to misconstruing the special character of his philosophy, so I do not want to enter that particular dispute between Lear and Kripke. But I do not want to resist the idea that Wittgenstein is a post-Kantian. The question is *in what respects* is Wittgenstein a post-Kantian? How far can the parallel be pressed?

Lear thinks that pressing it is the best way to explain the effects of reading Wittgenstein seriously. We find our attention drawn to facts about us—what Wittgenstein calls 'facts of our natural

---

[4] See Saul A. Kripke, *Wittgenstein on Rules and Private Language* (Cambridge, Mass., 1982).

history'.[5] He points out that if we were not in accord in our judgements (of sameness, say) there would be no such thing as language,[6]
or that a word or a signpost's meaning what it does depends only
on our all naturally responding to it in a certain way, on there being
a certain 'use and custom among us'.[7] These reminders of the
importance of our shared perceptions of salience, routes of interest, and feelings of naturalness are what I think lead Lear to say
that 'as we study the *Investigations* we come to assert, "We are so
minded as to assert: 7 + 5 must equal 12"' (p. 238). We are struck
by the fact that there is nothing to guarantee our understanding, or
even the existence of language, beyond the facts of how *we* happen
to be. But it is equally important that we are not left with some
form of subjectivism or conventionalism either. It is not that
'human agreement decides what is true and what is false'.[8] Lear
finds that we come back to where we started, to the 'objective'
assertion that 7 + 5 must equal 12. As in Kant, 'the reflective understanding of the contribution of our mindedness to the necessity we
find in the world is not meant to undermine the necessity, but to
give us insight into it' (p. 238).

The questions Lear is asking seem to me just the sorts of questions to raise about Wittgenstein's philosophy. What exactly do we
get from it? How is it meant to work on us? Do we get insight from
it, and what form does such insight take? How closely can its results
be assimilated to the justly famous philosophies of the past, and to
which ones?

Lear thinks Wittgenstein's work is Kantian in more than its
effects. He even finds something like the transcendental deduction
in *Philosophical Investigations*. He thinks, first, that 'Wittgenstein
argues, roughly, that it must be possible for the "I understand" to
accompany each of my representations' (pp. 227–8)—that is, each
of my acts of using an expression meaningfully or with understanding. That analogue of Kant's 'analytic unity of apperception'
carries with it the requirement that there be 'a certain synthetic
unity among my representations', and in Wittgenstein that
requirement is to be fulfilled by the 'agreement in judgements' or

---

[5] L. Wittgenstein, *Philosophical Investigations*, tr. G. E. M. Anscombe (Oxford,
1953), §415; *Remarks on the Foundation of Mathematics*, tr. G. E. M. Anscombe
(Oxford, 1956), I, 63.

[6] Wittgenstein, *Phil. Inv.* §242.   [7] Wittgenstein, *Remarks*, I, 63.

[8] Wittgenstein, *Phil. Inv.* §241.

in 'form of life' that is needed for language to be possible. Lear therefore finds Wittgenstein arguing in addition that it must be possible for the 'We are so minded:' to accompany each of our acts of speaking a language meaningfully or with understanding (p. 229). Language could not be a means of communication if that were not so. But that does not leave us with mere subjective necessities about how *we* happen to speak or think, or about what makes it possible *for us* to speak meaningfully or with understanding. Wittgenstein is said to bring us to see, thirdly, that 'there is no concept of being "other minded". The concept of being minded in any way at all is that of being minded as we are' (p. 233). 'We cannot make sense of the possibility of being "other minded"' (p. 232). This provides us with what Lear calls a 'groundless legitimation' of our representations (p. 233). 'Being one of "our" representations is all there could be to being a representation' (p. 233).

Does Wittgenstein ever argue this way? I find no evidence that he does. Jonathan Lear does not say where those arguments appear in Wittgenstein's text. He gives no references to such proofs, nor does he identify any of the premises of the arguments or the steps by which those Kantian-sounding conclusions are reached. If there is a proof or an argument in there somewhere, we ought to have some idea of where it begins and where it ends, and of how it proceeds. I find no evidence for it.

What is more, I think there is good evidence against it. Consider even the builders and their helpers described near the beginning of *Philosophical Investigations*. Those people understand one another; they speak meaningfully and with understanding. Wittgenstein says in §2 that we are to 'conceive of this as a complete primitive language'. But none of the participants in that form of life can append 'I understand' to any of his acts of speaking meaningfully and with understanding. There is no such expression in their language. They say and understand only things like 'd—slab—there'. They cannot in that sense (in Lear's words) 'take conscious possession' of their acts of speaking (p. 228). But that does not mean that they do not engage in acts of speaking meaningfully and with understanding.

Similarly for the 'We are so minded:'. Those simple builders and their helpers must share certain judgements of sameness and certain natural reactions or they could never have come to share the language they have got. If they did not come to respond in the

same way to the pointings in front of the slab-pile, for example,
there would simply be no such community. That is something
Wittgenstein stresses. But their being 'minded' in a certain way
does not have to be something they themselves can say or think in
order for it to be true. We know they cannot say or think it, given
their linguistic resources, but they can understand the things they
do meaningfully say. So it seems incorrect to attribute to Wittgenstein the thesis that anyone who is unable to append the expressions 'I understand' and 'We are so minded:' to his utterances
simply could not be speaking meaningfully or with understanding.

The third ingredient in Wittgenstein's Kantian 'legitimation'
seems to me equally ruled out by the text, but here things are
admittedly more complicated. Lear thinks that in Wittgenstein we
come to see that 'there is no concept of being "other minded"' (p.
233). Wittgenstein does from time to time invite us to consider
people or cultures different from ourselves. That is an important
part of his philosophical strategy. They needn't be real people; for
his purposes he could invent 'fictitious natural history'.[9] In most
cases, when we try to understand in detail what those imagined
'others' do, and why, I think we do not really succeed. I am not sure
Lear is right to say we lapse into 'nonsense', but I think we do find
ourselves unable fully to understand the people in question; we
cannot domesticate them, so to speak, and so find them intelligible.
As Wittgenstein puts it at one point, 'Wir können uns nicht in sie
finden'.[10]

Does this mean that the point of such thought-experiments is, as
Lear says, to show that 'we cannot make sense of the possibility of
being "other minded"'—that we cannot understand the possibility
of different forms of thinking? I think it cannot be. Wittgenstein
comments as follows on his technique of reminding us in these ways
of the importance of certain facts of our natural history:

I am not saying: if such-and-such facts of nature were different people
would have different concepts (in the sense of a hypothesis). But if anyone
believes that certain concepts are absolutely the correct ones, and that
having different ones would mean not realizing something that we
realize—then let him imagine certain very general facts of nature to be different from what we are used to, and the formation of concepts different
from the usual ones will become intelligible to him.[11]

---

[9] Wittgenstein, *Phil. Inv.* p. 230.   [10] Ibid. p. 223.   [11] Ibid. p. 230.

This seems to me to acknowledge the intelligibility of there being forms of thinking different from ours. Even if we founder when we try to understand in some detail what it would be like to think in one or another of those ways, so that we do not find fully intelligible any particular way of thinking different from ours, Wittgenstein does seem to be suggesting that we can nevertheless be brought to see the contingency of our thinking in the ways we do, or the contingency of anyone's being 'minded' as we are rather than in some other way. It goes too far, then, to say that for Wittgenstein we cannot even make sense of the possibility of there being other ways of being 'minded'—that 'the concept of being minded in any way at all is that of being minded as we are'—even if there is no other way of thinking that we can succeed in understanding.

So I think there is good evidence against attributing to Wittgenstein any of the theses that form the heart of the Kantian-sounding 'legitimation' of our ways of thinking that Lear has in mind. But whether it is to be found in Wittgenstein or not, how is that 'legitimation' supposed to work? The key to the success of a 'legitimation' for Lear is that the "for us" must 'cancel out'. Only then will the 'objective validity of our representations' have been established (p. 233). We must not be able to isolate our ways of thinking, or our simply thinking certain things to be so, in a way that leaves it an open question whether, in general, things are that way.

The central idea of Lear's 'legitimation' is that 'being one of "our" representations is all there could be to being a representation'. Suppose we did come to see that. Suppose we acknowledged that it is not even possible for anyone or anything anywhere to think at all in any way different from the fundamental ways in which we think. Would that mean that we could give no content to the idea that our ways of thinking might still fail to conform, in general, to the way things are? If we can have that thought, our 'representations' will not have been shown to be 'legitimate' or 'objectively valid'. But is there enough in the 'legitimation' Lear describes to rule it out?

We saw that it was not enough, for Kant, to show that discursive thought is possible at all only in terms of the categories—our categories. Even if that were so, in the absence of further argument it would still leave it open that the categories might be no more than 'an artefact of our subjective constitution', with no essential connection with the way things are or must be. We could not then go from saying 'We must think that . . .' to the conclusion that '. . .' or that 'It must be that . . .'. The 'we' or the 'for us' would not have disappeared in the right way. Why would it disappear if we realized with Lear that anyone who thinks at all must think as we do? If what gives rise to the problem of 'legitimacy' is the thought or fear that we might be imprisoned, as it were, in our own inescapable forms of thinking, with no guarantee of their general legitimacy or validity, I do not see that we would be closer to solving the problem or allaying our fears if we found that it is essential to thinking itself that it be conducted as we do it. That would still be something about thought—something on the 'subjective' side—which so far would do nothing to guarantee any one thing rather than another on the 'objective' side—in the way things are.

Of course, we might drop the 'we think' or the 'for us' when we realize there could be no other ways of thinking; we would no longer be picking out our own ways of thinking as one among others. We might also drop the 'we think' or the 'for us' if we realized that that is all we are ever in a position to say. If the 'objective validity' of our ways of thinking had not been established, and we knew we could do no more than append the 'we think' to everything we say, we could just as well leave it off. There would be no point in adding it every time. But its disappearance for that reason would not mean that our ways of thinking had been 'legitimated'. It depends on *why* the 'we think' or the 'for us' disappears. For Kant it disappears because the things we think about and perceive are 'constituted' by our thinking and perceiving as we do. It seems to me that Lear's idea that 'our' representations are the only representations there could be would also have to be supplemented by some such idealist thesis if the 'legitimation' he has in mind is to work. The parallel with Kant will succeed only if it is pressed all the way. Idealism is the only answer to the problem of 'legitimacy'.

Jonathan Lear is understandably ambivalent about attributing idealism to Wittgenstein. He thinks we do get a 'reflective understanding' of ourselves and our position in the world from Wittgenstein, but not one that requires an 'external' or 'detached' point of view on our ways of thinking and the world. Idealism does demand just such a perspective. It is not something we discover to be true from 'inside' our ways of thinking; from there, only 'realism' seems correct. But idealism is supposed to be the truth about our position that would explain how all the thought and experience we are actually capable of are really possible. Even without such a 'detached perspective' Lear thinks we can achieve a 'reflective understanding' of our position by appreciating 'the importance of our being so minded to the form of life which we constitute' without at the same time 'looking down' on our ways of thinking (p. 241). By this I take him to mean that we can see our representations as 'objectively valid', as not *merely* the way we 'take' things to be.

I do not think we would be entitled to that comfortable reflection on the basis of the only grounds Lear gives us, even if it were true—the realization that there are no other ways of thinking. If we understand Kant's question of 'legitimacy' at all, surely it cannot be enough to say, as Lear does, that 'establishing the objective validity of our representations consists in showing that they are all there could be to being a representation' (p. 241). That would not be enough to 'legitimate' our ways of thinking. Once we get ourselves in the position of asking Kant's question about our 'subjective' contribution, or about our ways of thinking, in general, and their relation to the way things are, I think we must inevitably end up with idealism or with the negative conclusion that our ways of thinking cannot be 'legitimated' or 'validated'. I myself would take that to be equivalent to saying that there cannot *be* a satisfactory philosophical account of the relation, in general, between 'our ways of thinking' and 'the way things are'. Once *everything* we take to be true has been isolated, and our thinking it to be so has been identified as something 'subjective' whose 'objective validity' is in question, it will be too late to hope for anything we should recognize as success.

It is in his treatment of what it would take to get that philosophical question off the ground that I would look for evidence about the special character of Wittgenstein's philosophizing—what effects his work is meant to have on someone who believes or even wonders whether, for example, certain concepts are absolutely the correct ones. I do not find those effects to be like those of a lobotomy or the cure of a disease. Something is gained as well as lost in the course of his philosophizing. To insist that what is gained must be expressible in the form of some philosophical doctrine or theory would be, I think, to insist in this case that Wittgenstein is an idealist. That seems to me reason enough to seek some other account of Wittgenstein's philosophy, and indeed of philosophical progress generally.

8

Understanding Human Knowledge in General

The philosophical study of human knowledge seeks to understand what human knowledge is and how it comes to be. A long tradition of reflection on these questions suggests that we can never get the kind of satisfaction we seek. Either we reach the sceptical conclusion that we do not know the things we thought we knew, or we cannot see how the state we find ourselves in is a state of knowledge.

Most philosophers today still deny, or at the very least resist, the force of such reflections. In their efforts to construct a positive theory of knowledge they operate on the not-unreasonable assumption that since human perception, belief, and knowledge are natural phenomena like any other, there is no more reason to think they cannot be understood and explained than there is to think that digestion or photosynthesis cannot be understood and explained. Even if there is still much to be learned about human cognition, it can hardly be denied that we already know a great deal, at least in general, about how it works. Many see it now as just a matter of filling in the details, either from physiology or from something called 'cognitive science'. We might find that we understand much less than we think we do, but even so it would seem absurd simply to deny that there is such a thing as human knowledge at all, or that we can ever understand how it comes to be. Those traditional sceptical considerations, whatever they were, therefore tend to be ignored. They will be refuted in any case by a successful theory that explains how we do in fact know the things we do.

It would be as absurd to cast doubt on the prospects of scientific investigation of human knowledge and perception as it would be to declare limits to our understanding of human digestion. But I

This essay was first published in M. Clay and K. Lehrer (eds.), *Knowledge and Scepticism* (Westview Press, Boulder, Colo., 1989). I would like to thank Janet Broughton, Thompson Clarke, Fred Dretske, Alvin Goldman, Samuel Guttenplan, and Christopher Peacocke for helpful comments on an earlier version.

think that what we seek in epistemology—in the philosophical study of human knowledge—is not just anything we can find about how we know things. We try to understand human knowledge in general, and to do so in a certain special way. If the philosophical investigation of knowledge is something distinctive, or sets itself certain special or unique goals, one might question whether those goals can really be reached without thereby casting any doubt on investigations of human knowledge which lack those distinctive philosophical features. That is what I shall try to do. I want to raise and examine the possibility that, however much we came to learn about this or that aspect of human knowledge, thought, and perception, there might still be nothing that could satisfy us as a philosophical understanding of how human knowledge is possible.

When I say nothing could satisfy us I do not mean that it is a very difficult task and that we will never finish the job. It *is* very difficult, and we *will* never finish the job, but I assume that is true of most of our efforts to understand anything. Rather, the threat I see is that once we really understand what we aspire to in the philosophical study of knowledge, and we do not deviate from the aspiration to understand it in that way, we will be for ever unable to get the kind of understanding that would satisfy us.

That is one reason I think scepticism is so important in epistemology. It is the view that we do not, or perhaps cannot, know anything, and it is important because it seems to be the inevitable consequence of trying to understand human knowledge in a certain way. Almost nobody thinks for a moment that scepticism could be correct. But that does not mean it is not important. If scepticism really is the inevitable outcome of trying to understand human knowledge in a certain way, and we think it simply could not be correct, that should make us look much more critically at that way of trying to understand human knowledge in the first place. But that is not what typically happens in philosophy. The goal itself is scarcely questioned, and for good reason. We feel human knowledge ought to be intelligible in that way. The epistemological project feels like the pursuit of a perfectly comprehensible intellectual goal. We know that scepticism is no good; it is an answer, but it is not satisfactory. But being constitutionally unable to arrive at an answer to a perfectly comprehensible question is not satisfactory either. We therefore continue to acquiesce in the traditional problem and do not acknowledge that there is no satisfactory solution. We proceed as if it must be possible to find an answer, so we deny the force, and even the interest, of scepticism.

What we seek in the philosophical theory of knowledge is an account that is completely general in several respects. We want to understand how any knowledge at all is possible—how anything we currently accept amounts to knowledge. Or, less ambitiously, we want to understand with complete generality how we come to know anything at all in a certain specified domain.

For example, in the traditional question of our knowledge of the material bodies around us we want to understand how we know anything at all about any such bodies. In the philosophical problem of other minds we want to understand how any person ever comes to know anything at all about what is going on in the mind of any other person, or even knows that there are any other minds at all. In the case of induction we want to understand how anyone can ever have any reason at all to believe anything beyond what he himself has so far observed to be true. I take it to be the job of a positive philosophical theory of knowledge to answer these and similarly general questions.

One kind of generality I have in mind is revealed by what we would all regard as no answer at all to the philosophical problem. The question of other minds is how anyone can know what someone else thinks or feels. But it would be ludicrous to reply that someone can know what another person thinks or feels by asking a good friend of that person's. That would be no answer at all, but not because it is not true. I *can* sometimes find out what someone else thinks by asking his best friend. But that would not contribute to the solution to the philosophical problem of other minds. We are not simply looking for a list of all the ways of knowing. If we were, that way of knowing would go on the list. But in fact we seek a more inclusive description of all our ways of knowing that would explain our knowledge in general.

What is wrong with that particular way of knowing the mind of another is not that it is only one way among others. The trouble is that it explains how we know some particular fact in the area we are interested in by appeal to knowledge of some other fact in that same domain. I know what Smith thinks by knowing that Jones told me what Smith thinks. But knowing that Jones told me something is itself a bit of knowledge about the mind of another. So that kind of answer could not serve as, nor could it be generalized into, a satisfactory answer to the question of how we know anything at all about any other minds. Not because it does not mention a legitimate way of knowing something about the mind of another. It does. Coming to know what Smith thinks by asking Jones is a perfectly acceptable way of knowing, and it is a different way of getting that knowledge from having Smith tell me himself, or from reading Smith's mail. There is nothing wrong with it in itself as an explanation. It is only for the general philosophical task that it is felt to be inadequate.

The same holds for everyday knowledge of the objects around us. One way I can know that my neighbour is at home is by seeing her car in front of her house, where she parks it when and only when she is at home. That is a perfectly good explanation of how I know that fact about one of the things around me. It is a different way of knowing where my neighbour is from seeing her through the window or hearing her characteristic fumblings on the piano. But it could not satisfy us as an explanation of how I know anything at all about any objects around me. It explains how I know something about one object around me—my neighbour—by knowing something about another object around me—her car. It could not answer the philosophical question as to how I know anything about any objects around me at all.

The kind of generality at stake in these problems takes its characteristic philosophical form when we come to see, on reflection, that the information available to us for knowing things in a particular domain is systematically less than we might originally have thought. Perhaps the most familiar instance of this is the *First Meditation* of Descartes,[1] in which he asks about knowledge of the material world by means of the senses. It apparently turns out on reflection that the senses give us less than we might have thought; there is no strictly sensory information the possession of which necessarily amounts to knowledge of the material world. We could perceive exactly what we perceive now even if there were no material world at all. The problem then is to see how we ever come to get knowledge of the material world on that sensory basis.

In the case of other minds we find on reflection that the only evidence we can ever have or even imagine for the mental states of other people is their bodily behaviour, including the sounds coming out of their mouths, or even the tears coming out of their eyes. But there is no strictly physical or behavioural information the possession of which necessarily amounts to knowledge of another person's mind or feelings. With induction the general distinction is perhaps even more obvious. The only reason we could ever have for believing anything about what we are not observing at the moment is something we have observed in the past or are observing right now. The problem then is how any knowledge of strictly past or even present fact amounts to knowledge of, or reasonable belief in, some unobserved or future fact.

These apparently simple, problem-generating moves come right at the beginning of epistemology. They are usually taken as so obvious and undeniable that the real problems of epistemology are thought to arise only after they have been made. In this paper I simply assume familiarity with them and with how easily they work. They are the very moves I think we eventually must examine more carefully if we are ever going to understand the real source of the dissatisfaction we are so easily driven to in philosophy. But for now I am concerned with the structure of the plight such reflections appear to leave us in.

If we start by considering a certain domain of facts or truths and ask how anyone could come to know anything at all in that domain, it will seem that any other knowledge that might be relevant could not be allowed to amount to already knowing something in the domain in question. Knowledge of anything at all in that domain is what we want to explain, and if we simply assume from the outset that the person has already got some of that knowledge we will not be explaining all of it. Any knowledge we do grant to the person will be of use to him only if he can somehow get from that knowledge to some knowledge in the domain in question. Some inference or transition would therefore appear to be needed—for example, some way of going from what he is aware of in perception to knowledge of the facts he claims to know. But any such inference will be a good one, and will lead the person to knowledge, only if it is based on something the person also knows or has some reason to believe. He cannot just be making a guess that he has got good evidence. He has to know or at least have reason to believe something that will help get him from his evidential base to some knowledge in the domain in question. That 'something' that he needs to know cannot simply be part of his evidential base, since it has to get him beyond that base. But it cannot go so far beyond that base as to imply something already in the domain in question either, since the knowledge of anything at all in that domain is just what we are trying to explain. So it would seem that on either possibility we cannot explain with the proper generality how the kind of knowledge we want to understand is possible. If the person does know what he needs to know, he has already got some knowledge in the domain in question, and if he does not, he will not be able to get there from his evidential base alone.

This apparent dilemma is a familiar quandary in traditional epistemology. I think it arises from our completely general explanatory goal. We want to explain a certain kind of knowledge, and we feel we must explain it on the basis of another, prior kind of knowledge that does not imply or presuppose any of the knowledge we are trying to explain. Without that, we will not be explaining the knowledge in question in the proper, fully general way. This felt need is what so easily brings into the epistemological project some notion or other of what is usually called 'epistemic priority'—one kind of knowledge being prior to another. I believe it has fatal consequences for our understanding of our knowledge. It is often said that traditional epistemology is generated by nothing more than a misguided 'quest for certainty', or a fruitless search for absolutely secure 'foundations' for knowledge, and that once we abandon such a will-o'-the-wisp we will no longer be threatened by scepticism, or even much interested in it.[2] But that diagnosis seems wrong to me—in fact, completely upside down. What some philosophers see as a poorly motivated demand for 'foundations' of knowledge looks to me to be the natural consequence of seeking a certain intellectual goal, a certain kind of understanding of human knowledge in general.

In the philosophical problem of other minds, for example, we pick out observable physical movements or 'behaviour' and ask how on that basis alone, which is the only basis we have, we can ever know anything about the mind behind the 'behaviour'. Those observable facts of 'behaviour' are held to be 'epistemically prior'

---

[2] This charge has been laid against traditional epistemology at least since Dewey's *The Quest for Certainty* and is by now, I suppose, more or less philosophical orthodoxy. For more recent expressions of it see e.g. Michael Williams, *Groundless Belief* (Oxford, 1977), and Richard Rorty, *Philosophy and the Mirror of Nature* (Princeton, 1979).

to any facts about the mind in the sense that it is possible to know all such facts about others' 'behaviour' without knowing anything about their minds. We insist on that condition for a properly general explanation of our knowledge of other minds. But in doing so we need not suppose that our beliefs about that 'behaviour' are themselves indubitable or incorrigible 'foundations' of anything. Levels of relative epistemic priority are all we need to rely on in pressing the epistemological question in that way.

In the case of our knowledge of the material objects around us we single out epistemically prior 'sensations' or 'sense data' or 'experiences' or whatever it might be, and then ask how on that basis alone, which is the only basis we have, we can know anything of the objects around us. We take it that knowledge of objects comes to us somehow by means of the senses, but if we thought of sensory knowledge as itself knowledge of material objects around us we would not get an appropriately general explanation of how any knowledge of any objects at all is possible by means of the senses. We would be explaining knowledge of some material objects only on the basis of knowledge of some others. 'Data', 'the given', 'experiences', and so on, which traditional epistemologists have always trafficked in, therefore look to me much more like inevitable products of the epistemological enterprise than elusive 'foundations', the unmotivated quest for which somehow throws us into epistemology in the first place.

But once we accept the idea of one kind of knowledge being prior to another as an essential ingredient in the kind of philosophical understanding we seek, it immediately becomes difficult even to imagine, let alone to find, anything that could satisfy us. How *could* we possibly know anything about the minds of other people on the basis only of truths about their 'behaviour' if those truths do not imply anything about any minds? If we really are restricted in perception to 'experiences' or 'sense data' or 'stimulations' which give us information that is prior to any knowledge of objects, how *could* we ever know anything about what goes on beyond such prior 'data'? It would seem to be possible only if we somehow knew of some connection between what we are restricted to in observation and what is true in the wider domain we are interested in. But then knowing even that there was such a connection would be knowing something about that wider domain after all, not just about what we are restricted to in observation. And then we would be left with no satisfactorily general explanation of our knowledge.

In short, it seems that if we really were in the position the traditional account in terms of epistemic priority describes us as being in, scepticism would be correct. We could not know the things we think we know. But if, in order to resist that conclusion, we no longer see ourselves in that traditional way, we will not have a satisfactorily general explanation of all our knowledge in a certain domain.

Theorists of knowledge who accept the traditional picture of our position in the world obviously do not acknowledge what I see as its sceptical or otherwise unsatisfactory consequences. Some philosophers see their task as that of exhibiting the general structure of our knowledge by making explicit what they think are the 'assumptions' or 'postulates' or 'epistemic principles' that are needed to take us from our 'data' or evidence in a particular area to some richer domain of knowledge we want to explain.[3] The fact that certain 'postulates' or 'principles' can be shown to be precisely what is needed for the knowledge in question is somehow taken to count in their favour. Without those 'principles', it is argued, we wouldn't know what we think we know.

However illuminating such 'rational reconstructions' of our knowledge might be, they cannot really satisfy us if we want to understand how we actually do know the things we think we know. If it had been shown that there is a certain 'postulate' or 'principle' which we have to have some reason to accept if we are to know anything about, say, the world around us, we would not thereby have come to understand how we do know anything about the world around us. We would have identified something we need, but its indispensability would not show that we do in fact have good reason to accept it. We would be left with the further question of whether we know that that 'principle' is true, and if so how. And all the rest of the knowledge we wanted to explain would then be hanging in the balance, since it would have been shown to depend

---

[3] Perhaps the best example of this, with a list of metaphysical and epistemological 'postulates' deemed to be necessary, is B. Russell, *Human Knowledge: Its Scope and Limits* (London, 1948). For a more recent version of the same project concentrating only on 'epistemic principles' see the epistemological writings of R. Chisholm, e.g. *Theory of Knowledge* (Englewood Cliffs, NJ, 1977) or *The Foundations of Knowing* (Minneapolis, 1980).

on that 'principle'. Trying to answer the question of its justification would lead right back into the old dilemma. If the 'principle'
involved says or implies something richer than anything to be
found in the prior evidential base—as it seems it must if it is going
to be of any help—there will be nothing in that base alone that
could give us reason to accept it. But if we assume from the outset
that we do know or have some reason to accept that 'principle', we
will be assuming that we already know something that goes beyond
our prior evidential base, and that knowledge itself will not have
been explained. We would therefore have no completely general
explanation of how we get beyond that base to any knowledge of
the kind in question.

The threat of a regress in the support for any such 'principles'
leads naturally to the idea of two distinct sources or types of knowledge. If the 'principles' or presuppositions of knowledge could be
known independently, not on the basis of the prior evidence, but in
some other way, it might seem that the regress could be avoided.
This might be said to be what Kant learned from Hume:[4] if all our
knowledge is derived from experience, we can never know anything. But Kant did not infer from that conditional proposition the
categorical sceptical conclusion he thought Hume drew from it. For
Kant the point was that if we do have knowledge from experience
we must also have some knowledge that is independent of experience. Only in that way is experiential knowledge possible. We must
know some things a priori if we know anything at all.

As a way of explaining how we know the things we do, this
merely postpones or expands the problem. It avoids the sceptical
regress in sensory knowledge of the world by insisting that the basic
'principles' or presuppositions needed for such empirical knowledge do not themselves depend on empirical, sensory support. But
that says only that those 'principles' are *not* known by experience;
it does not explain how they are known. Merely being presupposed
by our empirical knowledge confers no independent support. It has
to be explained how we know anything at all a priori, and how in
particular we know those very things we need for empirical knowledge. And then the old dilemma presents itself again. If our a priori
knowledge of those 'principles' is derived from something prior to
them which serves as their evidential base, it must be shown how

---

[4] See e.g. Kant, *Critique of Pure Reason*, tr. N. Kemp Smith (London, 1953),
B19–20.

the further 'principles' needed to take us from that base to the 'principles' in question could themselves be supported. If we assume from the outset that we do know some 'principles' a priori, not all of our a priori knowledge in general will have been explained. It would seem that a priori knowledge in general could be explained only in terms of something that is not itself a priori knowledge. But empirical knowledge cannot explain a priori knowledge—and it would be no help here even if it could—so either we must simply accept the unexplained fact that we know things a priori or we must try to explain it without appealing to any other knowledge at all.

I do not want to go further into the question of a priori knowledge. Not because it is not difficult and important in its own right, but because many theorists of knowledge would now argue that it is irrelevant to the epistemological project of explaining our knowledge of the world around us. They find they can put their finger precisely on the place where the traditional philosophical enterprise turns inevitably towards scepticism. And they hold that that step is wrong, and that without it there is no obstacle to finding a satisfactory account of our epistemic position that avoids any commitment to scepticism. This claim for a new 'enlightened' theory of knowledge that does not take that allegedly sceptical step is what I want to question.

I have already sketched the hopeless plight I think the old conception leaves us in. The trouble in that conception is now thought to enter at just the point at which the regress I have described apparently gets started. To get from his 'evidence' to any of the knowledge in question the person was said to need some 'principle' or assumption that would take him from that 'evidence' to that conclusion. But he would also need some reason for accepting that 'principle'—he would have to know something else that supports it. And then he would need some reason for accepting that 'something else', and it could not be found either in his evidential base or in the 'principles' he originally needed to take him beyond that base. It must be found in something else in turn—another 'something else'—and so on *ad infinitum*. What is wrong in this, it is now thought, is not the idea that the person cannot find such reasons, or that he can only find them somehow mysteriously a priori. What is wrong is the requirement that he himself has to find such reasons, that he has to be able to support his 'principles', at all. The new 'enlightened' approach to knowledge insists that there is a clear sense in which he does not.

The objection can be put another way. What is wrong with the traditional epistemological project that leads so easily to scepticism, it is said, is that the whole thing assumes that anyone who knows something must know that he knows it. He must himself know that his reasons are good ones, or that his prior 'evidence' is adequate to yield knowledge of the kind in question. And then, by that same assumption, he must know that he knows that, and so on. But that assumption, it is argued, is not correct. It is obviously possible for someone to know something without knowing that he knows it. The theory of knowledge asks simply whether and how people know things. If that can be explained, that is enough. The fact that people sometimes do not know that they know things should not make us deny that they really do know those things—especially if we have a satisfactory theory that explains that knowledge.

Now it certainly seems right to allow that someone can know something even when we recognize that he does not know that he knows it. Think of the simplest ordinary examples. Someone is asked if he knows who won the battle of Hastings, and when it took place, and he tentatively replies 'William the Conqueror, 1066'. He knew the answer. He had learned it in school, perhaps, and had never forgotten it, but at the time he was asked he did not know whether he had really retained that information. He was not sure about the state of his knowledge, but as for the winner and the date of the battle of Hastings, he knew that all along. He knew more than he thought he did. So whether somebody knows something is one thing; whether he knows that he knows it is something else. That seems to be a fact about our everyday assessments of people's knowledge.

The question is not whether that is a fact, but what significance it has for the prospects of the philosophical theory of knowledge. Obviously it turns on what a satisfactory philosophical account is supposed to do. The goal as I have presented it so far is to take ourselves and our ways of knowing on the one hand, and a certain domain of truths that we want to know about on the other, and to understand how we know any of those truths at all on the basis of prior knowledge that does not amount to already knowing something in the domain we are interested in. The question was what support we could find for the bridge that would be needed to get us from that prior basis to the knowledge in question. The present suggestion amounts in effect to saying that no independent or a priori support is needed on the part of the knower. All that is needed is that a certain proposition should be true; the person doesn't have to know that it is true in order to know the thing in question. If he has the appropriate prior knowledge or experience, and there is in fact a truth linking his having that knowledge or experience with his knowing something in the domain in question, then he does in fact know something in that domain, even if he is not aware of the favourable epistemic position he is in.

The truth in question will typically be one expressing the definition of knowledge, or of having reason to believe something. The search for such definitions is what many philosophers regard as the special job of the philosophical theory of knowledge. If knowing something could be defined solely in terms of knowledge or experience in some unproblematic, prior domain, then that definition could be fulfilled even if you didn't know that you knew anything in that domain. You yourself would not have to find a 'bridge' from your evidential basis to the knowledge in question. As long as there actually was a 'bridge' under your feet, whether you knew of it or not, there would be no threat of a sceptical regress.

In one form, this anti-sceptical strategy has been applied to the problem of induction. Hume had argued that if a long positive correlation observed to hold between two sorts of things in the past is going to give you some reason now to expect a thing of the second sort, given an observed instance of the first, you will also have to have some reason to think that what you have observed in the past gives you some reason to believe something about the future. P. F. Strawson replied that you need no such thing. Having observed a long positive correlation between two sorts of things under widely varied circumstances in the past is just what it is—what it means— to have reason to expect a thing of the second sort, given that a thing of the first sort has just appeared.[5] If that is a necessary truth about reasonable belief it will guarantee that you do in fact have a reasonable belief in the future as long as you have had the requisite experience of the past and present. You do not have to find some additional reason for thinking that what you have observed

---

[5] P. F. Strawson, *Introduction to Logical Theory* (London, 1952), 256–7.

in the past gives you good reason to believe something about the future.

This has come to be called an 'externalist' account of knowledge or reasonable belief. It would explain knowledge in terms of conditions that are available from an 'external', third-person point of view, independent of what the knower's own attitude towards the fulfilment of those conditions might be. It is not all smooth sailing. To give us what we need, it has to come up with an account of knowledge or reasonable belief that is actually correct—that distinguishes knowledge from lack of knowledge in the right way. I think the account just given of inductive reasons does not meet that test. As it stands, it does not state a necessary truth about reasons to believe.[6] To come closer to being right, it would have to define the difference between a 'law-like' generalization and a merely 'accidental' correlation which does not give reason to believe it will continue. That task is by no means trivial, and it faces a 'new riddle of induction' all over again.[7] But if we do draw a distinction between having good reasons and not having them it would seem that there must be some account that captures what we do. It is just a matter of finding what it is.

The same goes for definitions of knowledge. One type of view says that knowing that *p* is equivalent to something like having acquired and retained a true belief that *p* as a result of the operation of a properly functioning, reliable belief-forming mechanism.[8] That general schema still leaves many things unexplained or undefined, and it is no trivial task to get it to come out right. But I am not concerned here with the details of 'externalist' definitions of knowledge. My reservations about the philosophical theory of knowledge are not just that it is difficult. I have doubts about the satisfactoriness of what you would have even if you had an 'externalist' account of knowledge which as far as you could tell matched up completely with those cases in which we think other people know things and those in which we think they do not.

Here we come up against another, and perhaps the most

---

[6] I have made the point in more detail in my *Hume* (London, 1977), 64–6.

[7] See N. Goodman, 'The New Riddle of Induction', in *Fact, Fiction, and Forecast* (Cambridge, Mass., 1955).

[8] What the mechanism is, how its reliability is to be defined, and what other conditions are necessary vary from one 'externalist' theory to another. See e.g. F. Dretske, *Knowledge and the Flow of Information* (Cambridge, Mass., 1981), or A. Goldman, *Epistemology and Cognition* (Cambridge, Mass., 1986).

important, dimension of generality I think we seek in the theory of knowledge. We want an account that explains how human knowledge in general is possible, or how anyone can know anything at all in a certain specified domain. The difficulty arises now from the fact that we as human theorists are ourselves part of the subject-matter that we theorists of human knowledge want to understand in a certain way. If we merely study another group and draw conclusions only about them, no such difficulty presents itself. But then our conclusions will not be completely general. They will be known to apply only to those others, and we will be no closer to understanding how our own knowledge is possible. We want to be able to apply what we find out about knowledge to ourselves, and so to explain how our own knowledge is possible.

I have already suggested why I think we cannot get a satisfactory explanation along traditional Cartesian lines. The promise of the new 'externalist' strategy is that it would avoid the regress that seems inevitable in that project. A person who knows something does not himself have to know that what he has got in his prior evidential base amounts to knowledge in the domain in question. As long as he in fact satisfies the conditions of knowing something in the domain we are interested in, there is nothing more he has to do in order to know things in that domain. No regress gets started.

The question now is: can we find such a theory satisfactory when we apply it to ourselves? To illustrate what I find difficult here I return to Descartes, as we so often must do in this subject. Not to his sceptical argument in the *First Meditation*, but to the answer he gives to it throughout the rest of the *Meditations*. He eventually comes to think that he does know many of the things that seemed to be thrown into doubt by his earlier reflections on dreaming and the evil demon. He does so by proving that God exists and is not a deceiver and that everything in us, including our capacity to perceive and think, comes from God. So whatever we clearly and distinctly perceive to be true is true. God would not have it any other way. By knowing what I know about God I can know that He is not a deceiver and therefore that I do know the things I think I know when I clearly and distinctly perceive them. If I am careful, and keep God and his goodness in mind, I can know many things, and the threat of scepticism is overcome.

Many objections have been made to this answer to Descartes's question about his knowledge. One is the 'externalist' complaint that Descartes's whole challenge rests on the assumption that you don't know something unless you know that you know it. Not only do my clear and distinct perceptions need some guarantee, but on Descartes's view I have to know what that guarantee is. That is why he thinks the atheist or the person who denies God in his heart cannot really know those things that we who accept Descartes's proof of God's existence and goodness can know.[9] But according to 'externalism' that requirement is wrong; you don't have to know that you know in order to know something.

Another and perhaps the most famous objection is that Descartes's proof of the guarantee of his knowledge is no good because it is circular. The knowledge he needs in order to reach the conclusion of God's existence and goodness is available to him only if God's existence and goodness have already been proved. What he calls his clear and distinct perception of God's existence will be knowledge of God's existence only if whatever he clearly and distinctly perceives is true. But that is guaranteed only by God, so he can't know that it is guaranteed unless he already knows that God exists.

Taking these two objections together, we can see that if the first is correct, the second is no objection at all. If Descartes is assuming that knowing requires knowing that you know, and if that assumption is wrong, then the charge of circularity has no force against his view. If 'externalism' were correct, Descartes's inability to prove that God exists and guarantees the truth of our clear and distinct perceptions would be no obstacle to his knowing the truth of whatever he clearly and distinctly perceives. He would not have to know that he knows those things. As long as God did in fact exist and did in fact make sure that his clear and distinct perceptions were true, Descartes would have the knowledge he started out thinking he had, even if God's existence and nature remained eternally unknown to him. The soundness of his proof would not matter. All that would matter for the everyday knowledge Descartes is trying to account for is the truth of its conclusion— God's existence and goodness. If that conclusion is in fact true, his inability to know that it is true would be no argument against his account.

[9] R. Descartes, 'Third Set of Objections with the Author's Replies' and 'Author's Replies to the Sixth Set of Objections', in *The Philosophical Writings of Descartes*, i. 137, 289, (Cambridge, 1985).

To develop this thought further we can try to imagine what an 'enlightened' or 'externalist', but still otherwise Cartesian, theory might look like. It would insist that the knowing subject does not have to know the truth of the theory that explains his knowledge in order to have the knowledge that the theory is trying to account for. Otherwise, the theory would retain the full Cartesian story of God and his goodness and his guarantee of the truth of our clear and distinct perceptions. What would be wrong with accepting such an 'enlightened' theory? If we are willing to accept the kind of theory that says that knowing that *p* is having acquired the true belief that *p* by some reliable belief-forming mechanism, why would we not be equally or even more willing to accept a theory that says that knowing that *p* is having acquired the true belief that *p* by clearly and distinctly perceiving it—a method of belief-formation that is reliable because God guarantees that whatever is clearly and distinctly perceived is true? It is actually more specific than a completely general form of 'externalism' or 'reliabilism'. It explains *why* the belief-forming mechanism is reliable. What, then, would be wrong with accepting it?

I think most of us simply don't believe it. We think that God does not in fact exist and is not the guarantor of the reliability of our belief-forming mechanisms. So we think that what this theory says about human knowledge is not true. Now that is certainly a defect in a theory, but is it the only thing standing in the way of our accepting it and finding it satisfactory? It seems to me it is not, and perhaps by examining its other defects, beyond its actual truth-value, we can identify a source of dissatisfaction with other 'externalist' theories as well.

We have to admit that if the imagined 'externalist' Cartesian theory were true, we would know many of the things we think we know. So scepticism would not be correct. But in the philosophical investigation of knowledge we want more than the falsity of scepticism and more than the mere possession of the knowledge we ordinarily think we've got. We want to understand how we know the things we know, how scepticism turns out not to be true. And even if this 'enlightened' Cartesian story were in fact true, if we didn't know that it was, or if we didn't have some reason to believe that it was, we would be no further along towards understanding our knowledge than we would be if the theory were false. So we need some reason to accept a theory of knowledge if we are going to rely on that theory to understand how our knowledge is possible. That is what I think no form of 'externalism' can give a satisfactory account of.

Suppose someone had said to Descartes, as they in effect did, 'Look, you have no reason to accept any of this story about God and his guarantee of the truth of your clear and distinct perceptions. Of course, if what you say were true you would have the knowledge you think you have, but your whole proof of it is circular. You could justify your explanation of knowledge only if you already knew that what you clearly and distinctly perceive is true.' Could an 'enlightened' 'externalist' Descartes reply: 'That's right. I suppose I have to admit that I can give no good reason to accept my explanation. But that doesn't really bother me any more, now that I am an "externalist". Circularity in my proofs is no objection to my theory if "externalism" is correct. I still do believe my theory, after all, and as long as that theory is in fact true—whether I can give any reason to accept it or not—scepticism will be false and I will in fact know the things that I clearly and carefully claim to know.'

I take it that that response is inadequate. The 'externalist' Descartes I have imagined would not have a satisfactory understanding of his knowledge. It is crucial to what I want to say about 'externalism' that we recognize some inadequacy in his position. It is admittedly not easy to specify exactly what the deficiency or the unsatisfactoriness of accepting that position amounts to. I think this much can be said: if the imagined Descartes responded only in that way he would be at best in the position of saying. 'If the story that I accept is true, I do know the things I think I know. But I admit that if it is false, and a certain other story is true instead, then I do not.' If 'externalism' is correct, what he would be saying here is true. His theory, if true, would explain his knowledge. The difficulty is that until he finds some reason to believe his theory rather than some other, he cannot be said to have explained how he knows the things he knows. That is not because he is assuming that a person cannot know something unless he knows that he knows it. He has explicitly abandoned that assumption. He admits that people know things whether they know the truth of his theory or not. The same of course holds for him. And he knows that implication. That is precisely what he is saying: if his theory is true he will know the things he thinks he knows. But he is, in addition, a theorist of knowledge.

He wants to understand how he knows the things he thinks he knows. And he cannot satisfy himself on that score unless he can see himself as having some reason to accept the theory that he (and all the rest of us) can recognize would explain his knowledge if it were true. That is not because knowing implies knowing that you know. It is because having an explanation of something in the sense of understanding it is a matter of having good reason to accept something that would be an explanation if it were true.

The question now is whether an 'externalist' scientific episte-mologist who rejects Descartes's explanation and offers one of his own is in any better position when he comes to apply his theory to his own knowledge than the imagined 'externalist' Descartes is in. He begins by asking about all knowledge in a specified domain. A philosophically satisfactory explanation of such knowledge must not explain some of the knowledge in the domain in question by appeal to knowledge of something else already in the domain. But the scientific student of human knowledge must know or have some reason to believe his theory of knowledge if he is going to under-stand how knowledge is possible. His theory about our belief-forming mechanisms and their reliability is a theory about the interactions between us and the world around us. It is arrived at by studying human beings, finding out how they get the beliefs they do, and investigating the sources of the reliability of those belief-forming mechanisms. Descartes claimed knowledge of God and his goodness, and of the relation between those supernatural facts and our earth-bound belief-forming mechanisms. A more naturalistic epistemologist's gaze does not reach so high. He claims knowledge of nothing more than the familiar natural world in which he thinks everything happens. But he will have an explanation of human knowledge, and so will understand how people know the things they do, only if he knows or has some reason to believe that his scientific story of the goings-on in that world is true.

If his goal was, among other things, to explain our scientific knowledge of the world around us, he will have an explanation of such knowledge only if he can see himself as possessing some knowledge in that domain. In studying other people, that presents no difficulty. It is precisely by knowing what he does about the world that he explains how others know what they do about the world. But if he had started out asking how anyone knows anything at all about the world, he would be no further along towards understanding how any of it is possible if he had not understood how he himself knows what he has to know about the world in order to have any explanation at all. He must understand himself as knowing or having reason to believe that his theory is true.

It might seem that he fulfils that requirement because his theory of knowledge is meant to identify precisely those conditions under which knowledge or good reason to believe something is present. If that theory is correct, and he himself fulfils those conditions in his own scientific investigations of human knowledge, he will in fact know that his theory of knowledge is true, or at least he will have good reason to believe it. He studies others and finds that they often satisfy the conditions his theory says are sufficient for knowing things about the world, and he believes that theory, and he believes that he too satisfies those same conditions in his investigations of those other people. He concludes that he does know how human beings know what they do, and he concludes that he therefore understands how he in particular knows the things he knows about the world. He is one of the human beings that his theory is true of. So the non-Cartesian, scientific 'externalist' claims to be in a better position than the imagined 'externalist' Descartes because he claims to know by a reliable study of the natural world that his explanation of human knowledge is correct and Descartes's is wrong. In accepting his own explanation he claims to fulfil the conditions his theory asserts to be sufficient for knowing things.

I think this theorist would still be in no better position than the position the imagined 'externalist' Descartes is in. If his theory is true, he will in fact know that his explanation is correct. In that sense he could be said to possess an explanation of how human beings know the things they know. In that same sense the imagined 'externalist' Descartes would possess an explanation of his knowledge. He accepts something which, if true, would explain his knowledge. But none of this would be any help or consolation to them as epistemologists. The position of the imagined 'externalist' Descartes is deficient for the theory of knowledge because he needs some reason to believe that the theory he has devised is true in order to be said to understand how people know the things they think they know. The scientific 'externalist' claims he does have reason to believe his explanation of knowledge and so to be in a better position than the imagined 'externalist' Descartes. But the way in which he fulfils that condition, even if he does, is only in an 'externalist' way, and therefore in the same way that the imagined Descartes fulfils the conditions of knowledge, if he does. *If* the scientific 'externalist's' theory is correct about the conditions under which knowledge or reasonable belief is present, and if he does fulfil those conditions in coming to believe his own explanation of knowledge, then he is in fact right in thinking that he has good reason to think that his explanation is correct. But that is to be in the same position with respect to whether he has good reason to think his explanation is correct as the imagined 'externalist' Descartes was in at the first level with respect to whether he knows the things he thinks he knows.

It was admitted that if that imagined Descartes's theory were true he would know the things he thinks he knows, but he could not be said to see or to understand himself as possessing such knowledge because he had no reason to think that his theory was true. The scientific 'externalist' claims to have good reason to believe that his theory is true. It must be granted that if, in arriving at his theory, he did fulfil the conditions his theory says are sufficient for knowing things about the world, then if that theory is correct, he does in fact know that it is. But still, I want to say, he himself has no reason to think that he does have good reason to think that his theory is correct. He is at best in the position of someone who has good reason to believe his theory if that theory is in fact true, but has no such reason to believe it if some other theory is true instead. He can see what he *would* have good reason to believe if the theory he believes were true, but he cannot see or understand himself as knowing or having good reason to believe what his theory says.

I am aware that describing what I see as the deficiency in this way is not really satisfactory or conclusive. It encourages the 'externalist' to re-apply his theory of knowing or having good reason to believe at the next level up, and to claim that he can indeed understand himself to have good reason to believe his theory because he has good reason to believe that he does have good reason to believe his theory. That further belief about his reasons is arrived at in turn by fulfilling what his theory says are the conditions for reasonably believing something. But then he is still in the same position two levels up that we found the imagined 'externalist' Descartes to be in at the first level. If the imagined Descartes's claim to self-understanding was inadequate there, any similar claim will be equally inadequate at any higher level of knowing that one knows or having reason to believe that one has reason to believe. That is why our reaction to the original response of the imagined 'externalist' Descartes is crucial. Recognition of its inadequacy is essential to recognizing the inadequacy of 'externalism' that I have in mind. It is difficult to say precisely what is inadequate about that kind of response, especially in terms that would be acceptable to an 'externalist'. Perhaps it is best to say that the theorist has to see himself as having good reason to believe his theory in some sense of 'having good reason' that cannot be fully captured by an 'externalist' account.

So even if it is true that you can know something without knowing that you know it, the philosophical theorist of knowledge cannot simply insist on the point and expect to find acceptance of an 'externalist' account of knowledge fully satisfactory. If he could, he would be in the position of someone who says: 'I don't know whether I understand human knowledge or not. If what I believe about it is true and my beliefs about it are produced in what my theory says is the right way, I do know how human knowledge comes to be, so in that sense I do understand. But if my beliefs are not true, or not arrived at in that way, I do not. I wonder which it is. I wonder whether I understand human knowledge or not.' That is not a satisfactory position to arrive at in one's study of human knowledge—or of anything else.

It might be said that there can be such a thing as unwitting understanding, or understanding you don't know you've got, just as there can be unwitting knowledge, or knowledge you don't know you've got. Such 'unwitting understanding', if there is such a thing, is the most that the 'externalist' philosophical theorist about human knowledge could be said to have of his own knowledge. But even if there is such a thing, it is not something it makes sense to aspire to, or something to remain content with having reached, if you happen to have reached it. We want witting, not unwitting, understanding. That requires knowing or having some reason to accept the scientific story you believe about how people know the things they know. And in the case of knowledge of the world around us, that would involve already knowing or having some reason to believe something in the domain in question. Not all the knowledge in that domain would thereby be explained.

I do not mean that there is something wrong with our

explaining how people know certain things about the world by assuming that they or we know certain other things about it. We do it all the time. It is only within the general epistemological enterprise that that otherwise familiar procedure cannot give us what we want. And when I say that 'externalism' cannot give us what we want I do not mean that it possesses some internal defect which prevents it from being true. The difficulty I am pointing to is an unsatisfactoriness involved in *accepting* an 'externalist' theory and claiming to understand human knowledge in general in that way. And even that is too broad. It is not that there is any difficulty in understanding other people's knowledge in those terms. It is only with self-understanding that the unsatisfactoriness or loss of complete generality makes itself felt. 'Externalism', if it got the conditions of knowledge right, would work fine for other people's knowledge. As a third-person, observational study of human beings and other animals, it would avoid the obstacles to human understanding apparently involved in the first-person Cartesian project. But the question is whether we can take up such an 'external' observer's position with respect to ourselves and our knowledge and still gain a satisfactorily general explanation of how we know the things we know. That is where I think the inevitable dissatisfaction comes in.

The demand for completely general understanding of knowledge in a certain domain requires that we see ourselves at the outset as not knowing anything in that domain and then coming to have such knowledge on the basis of some independent and in that sense prior knowledge or experience. And that leads us to seek a standpoint from which we can view ourselves without taking for granted any of that knowledge that we want to understand. But if we could manage to detach ourselves in that way from acceptance of any truths in the domain we are interested in, it seems that the only thing we could discover from that point of view is that we can never know anything in that domain. We could find no way to explain how that prior knowledge alone could yield any richer knowledge lying beyond it. That is the plight the traditional view captures. That is the truth in scepticism. If we think of our knowledge as arranged in completely general levels of epistemic priority in that way, we find that we cannot know what we think we know. Scepticism is the only answer.

But then that seems absurd. We realize that people do know

many things in the domains we are interested in. We can even explain how they know such things, whether they know that they do or not. That is what the third-person point of view captures. That is the truth in 'externalism'. But when we try to explain how we ourselves know those things we find we can understand it only by assuming that we have got some knowledge in the domain in question. And that is not philosophically satisfying. We have lost the prospect of explaining and therefore understanding all of our knowledge with complete generality.

For these and other reasons I think we need to go back and look more carefully into the very sources of the epistemological quest. We need to see how the almost effortlessly natural ways of thinking embodied in that traditional enterprise nevertheless distort or misrepresent our position, if they do. But we should not think that if and when we come to see how the epistemological enterprise is not fully valid, or perhaps not even fully coherent, we will then possess a satisfactory explanation of how human knowledge in general is possible. We will have seen, at best, that we cannot have any such thing. And that too, I believe, will leave us dissatisfied.

9

Epistemological Reflection on Knowledge of the External World

We can and do reflect in very general terms on human beings and their place in the world, and we do so for a number of reasons and in a variety of ways. We can notice similarities between human beings and other parts of nature, or differences between them and most other things, or even respects in which they are unique in the world as we know it. Human beings are born and grow and they decline and die. They are the only things in the universe who laugh. Human beings also act. Unlike rocks on a mountainside or branches of a tree, they do not just move, they do things. Other animals also do things, but humans differ from them in the extent to which they think about what to do, and then act as a result of that deliberation. And, not coincidentally, human beings also know things about the world around them. Knowledge is essential to deliberation and to informed action.

No one would deny or question these sweeping platitudes about human beings and the human condition. It is equally uncontroversial that humans can become curious and reflect on some of these very general features of human life and try to understand them better. This could be called 'anthropology' in the most general sense. Not simply the study of this or that group of human beings, or of this or that social or cultural arrangement among them, but anthropology as the study of human beings in general, or of apparently universal features of human beings or human life as such.

If we take an interest in human action in general we might ask what it takes for an event or a movement to count as an action performed by an agent, and how such a thing is possible. The question

This essay represents my response to Michael Williams's *Unnatural Doubts: Epistemological Realism and the Basis of Scepticism* (Oxford, 1991) as presented in a symposium devoted to that book at Northwestern University. It was first published in *Philosophy and Phenomenological Research*, 56: 2 (June, 1996). I am grateful to Michael Williams and participants in the conference for helpful critical comments.

can be found especially pressing once we acknowledge certain other general facts of the world and understand them in a certain way. Human agency must be understood as occurring in a world of events related as cause and effect which are seen as instances of general laws of nature holding universally. If that too is a very general feature of our world, any satisfactory account of human beings must accommodate itself to that fact. When we look more closely into human deliberation and action, it can then come to seem that it really is not possible at all in such a world. And that is absurd, or paradoxical. The possibility of human action thereby becomes a philosophical problem.

Similar thoughts can arise about human knowledge. What exactly is knowledge, and how do human beings know the sorts of things they have to know to live the kind of lives they lead? These are very general questions, but they are not for that reason alone illegitimate or somehow suspect, any more than other similarly general 'anthropological' questions are suspect. I think they are questions which human beings—or at least some human beings—very naturally come to ask. In fact, humans are the only beings in nature who ask such reflective questions about themselves.

Just as in the case of action, so too in the case of knowledge certain problems or obstacles seem naturally to arise once we acknowledge what seem to be certain other equally uncontroversial facts of human beings and their world. Or at least problems or obstacles *have* arisen when some of our greatest thinkers have reflected on human knowledge in this very general way. Speaking 'anthropologically', we can say that human beings gain knowledge of the world through sense-perception. And when we look more closely into how sense-perception works, and what exactly we perceive, it can become difficult to see how perceptual knowledge of the world is possible. It can be made to look as if it is not possible at all. And that is absurd, or paradoxical.

My own interest in what is usually called 'epistemology' is mainly in what goes on in the reflections which can seem so convincingly to lead to such paradoxical conclusions. I would like to know exactly how they work, and what, if anything, understanding them better would reveal. The enterprise I find most interesting really amounts to reflection on a certain kind of human reflection: the focus is not primarily on human knowledge itself, but on the kind of reflection on human knowledge in general which seems to lead to the conclusion that there isn't any. This is still reflection on human beings—on something human beings do. My question is what goes on when humans reflect on themselves in the ways we have become familiar with in Western philosophy. And how are the absurd or paradoxical conclusions of those reflections to be understood? Or, if they really do mean what they seem to mean, how are they to be avoided?

I think the most fruitful way of pursuing these questions is to raise what Michael Williams calls the 'deep and important issue'[1] to which he devotes much of his *Unnatural Doubts*: the relation between philosophical reflection on knowledge and the mundane procedures of coming to know things and assessing the knowledge we think we've got in the familiar activities of everyday life. If the philosophical reflections follow the same pattern as those everyday reflections, except perhaps in being more general, then it would seem that we must accept the paradoxical conclusions if they are fairly arrived at. If we cannot accept them, as it seems we cannot, we must find some way in which the philosophical reflection goes wrong or misleads us, and so in some sense is not exactly parallel to everyday assessments in which we rightly find that we do not know what we thought we knew. I am fully in accord with Michael Williams in his sense of the depth, and the difficulty, of this kind of enquiry. Our shared feeling does not appear to be widely held in philosophy today.

I think reflection on this kind reflection can be expected to reveal something interesting and deep about human beings, or human aspiration. It is perhaps too sweeping to speak of human beings in general. Perhaps only certain traditions or cultures in the history of humankind have engaged in these reflections as we know them. But all of us here belong to at least one such tradition or culture, so we cannot help engaging in, or trying to come to terms with, the reflections I have in mind.

We do not need to ask only about human knowledge in general. We can be interested for different reasons in our knowledge of particular sub-classes of all the things we know. We can ask in a fully general 'anthropological' spirit how humans come to know what is food for them, for example, or what is dangerous to them, or how they come to recognize their parents or their siblings. We can ask

[1] p. xii.

at an even more general level, for example, how human beings can know anything about what is going to happen in the future. How does anyone know anything about what has not yet happened at the time he acquires that knowledge? Knowledge (or at least reasonable belief) of that kind is essential to deliberation and informed action. Understanding how it is possible in general is the so-called 'problem of induction'. Or, to take another sub-class of all the things we know, how can someone know about the mental or psychological states of any person who is not himself? That is the so-called 'problem of other minds': a certain class of propositions is identified in relation to an individual who is not himself the subject of any of those propositions, and then we ask how that person can know that any of those propositions are true.

Another class of propositions of which we all know many members to be true are those which are true or false independently of the experiences or thoughts or even the existence of any human beings who might know or believe them. This includes all truths about things that are 'to be met with in space' in the sense in which G. E. Moore explained them in his well-known 'Proof of an External World'. 'Things to be met with in space', Moore said, are 'logically independent' of anyone's perception or knowledge of them in the sense that 'from the proposition, with regard to a particular time, that [such a thing] existed at that time, it *never* follows that [anyone] perceived it at that time' or that anyone 'was having any experience of any kind at the time in question'.[2] Of course, someone might be perceiving one of those things at some particular time—there is no suggestion that the things are unperceivable—but from the fact that the thing he is perceiving exists, it does not *follow* that he or anyone is perceiving it, or perceiving anything. Nor, we might add, does it follow that anyone knows anything about the thing, or even knows anything at all about anything. There are a great many truths about objects or states of affairs that are independent of us in this sense, and it seems a perfectly legitimate, if admittedly somewhat unusual, question to ask how anyone knows any such propositions to be true.

These questions about human knowledge are formulated in terms of what is known, not in terms of how it is known. A type of proposition or truth is first identified, and it is then asked how

[2] G. E. Moore , 'Proof of an External World', in his *Philosophical Papers* (London. 1959), 144.

human beings know or reasonably believe any propositions of that kind to be true. It seems that no ideas about how or even whether human beings in fact know things of that kind, or know anything else, are needed to frame the questions in the first place. But the questions are to be answered in the light of whatever other uncontroversial facts about the world and about human resources and capacities we must accept as well. This is just the point that, 'anthropologically' speaking, human knowledge must be accounted for within the world as it actually is.

Williams, as I understand him, denies that we can start off by independently identifying propositions of a certain kind in this way and then going on to ask an epistemological question about how humans know any of them. Or at any rate he denies that that is what actually happens in the epistemological reflections we are all familiar with. He thinks that in posing a completely general question of that kind we have already accepted certain epistemological doctrines—in particular, the doctrines he calls 'foundationalism' and 'epistemological realism'.[3] 'Foundationalism' is the view that knowledge of an independent world must be inferred or derived from prior knowledge of the deliverances of sense-experience alone which themselves imply nothing about such an independent world. 'Epistemological realism' is something I will come back to. For the moment it does not matter exactly what these epistemological doctrines amount to; the point is that according to Williams they are something that must be accepted from the outset by anyone who can even so much as raise a problem about our knowledge of the external world in general.

I must say that I find that implausible. It does not seem to me that elaborate theoretical constructions of the kind Williams has in mind are required in order for anyone even to take up—or be taken up by—the traditional problem. Just think how convincing, or at least exasperating, those familiar reflections about knowledge can seem even to those who come upon them for the first time and have apparently never formulated a sophisticated philosophical doctrine about anything.

Williams denies that it is all as innocent as it might seem. He wants to explain how and why the epistemological enterprise goes

---

[3] The crucial role of 'foundationalism' is first broached on pp. 56 ff. It is later argued that substantive foundationalism presupposes epistemological realism (p. 115).

wrong and leads us down a garden path to scepticism. I share that aim. In insisting as he does that it is not as 'intuitive' or 'natural' as he thinks I find it, I think he exaggerates the differences between us. I agree that there must be some ideas or thoughts or ways of thinking that are responsible for things going awry in the ways we know they do. The conclusion we reach is paradoxical. He says that he does not just want to avoid that conclusion, as I do; he seeks a 'theoretical diagnosis' of scepticism's appeal.[4] He puts it that way, I believe, because he thinks that any ideas or ways of thinking that could possibly be at work there and have such devastating effects must amount to a philosophical 'theory' of some kind. That is what I find implausible; what can have such devastating effects seems to me much more likely to be not a philosophical theory but whatever it is that gives rise to philosophical theory in the first place. But that is not the most important question. What matters to both of us is not whether you call those distorting ideas or ways of thinking a 'theory', but what they actually are, and how they work. That is what both of us want to understand.

Williams says he seeks a 'theoretical diagnosis' of the sceptical reasoning. He contrasts that with what he calls a 'refutation' of scepticism, which he does not seek.[5] He says a 'refutation' is in fact incompatible with a 'theoretical diagnosis' which amounts only to an identification of the 'theoretical commitments'[6] of the traditional epistemologist: the assumptions he must make in order for his project to be feasible and to yield such paradoxical conclusions. I find this contrast puzzling. What I don't understand is what Williams' own attitude is towards those 'theories' which he identifies as essential to the traditional epistemologist's case. He strongly suggests that simply coming to see that certain 'theories' are crucial in that way will reveal to us that they are not 'forced on us',[7] that they are ideas which we 'might do well to abandon'[8] or 'might abandon without strain'.[9] Once the case for scepticism is shown to be 'theoretically loaded', he thinks it 'will cease to be compelling'.[10]

Why should that be? It sounds as if it doesn't even matter what the 'theories' in question happen to be. If it does matter, then it will matter whether the 'theories' in question are themselves compelling. If they are not, is that because they can be seen to be wrong or to have no good reason in their favour? If that is why the

---

[4] 32 ff.   [5] 32.   [6] 32.   [7] 32.   [8] 166.   [9] 18.   [10] 42.

sceptical reasoning fails to establish its conclusion, how does pointing out that deficiency differ from refuting the sceptical reasoning? Of course, it does not prove that the conclusion is false, but if the reasoning rests on false assumptions it is unsound, and if it rests on unsupported assumptions its conclusion has not been established. The question would then be whether those assumptions can be supported or not. A 'theoretical diagnosis' as Williams describes it does not appear to answer that question. It is not a refutation of the epistemologist's reasoning. It serves only to identify the assumptions or 'theories' that the reasoning rests on. But something's being an assumption or a 'theory' is not enough simply in itself to render it less than compelling. So how will a 'theoretical diagnosis' alone enable us to avoid the paradoxical conclusion?

This is connected with a substantive issue mentioned earlier on which Williams and I really do disagree. He thinks that 'epistemological foundationalism' is present from the beginning, in the very formulation of the initiating question. He does not see it as something we can feel forced to accept by the epistemologist's reflections themselves. I don't think it is there from the very beginning. I don't find a 'foundationalist' philosophical theory present from the beginning in the philosophical 'problem of induction' or the 'problem of other minds' either. So I would ask whether Williams thinks that in simply picking out propositions about the future or about states of affairs which have not so far been observed to be true by anyone, a philosopher is thereby already committed to an epistemological doctrine which implies scepticism about induction? Or is a philosopher who focuses his attention on all those propositions about the psychological states of persons other than the person who entertains those propositions thereby smuggling into the very formulation of his question a 'foundationalist' assumption that all knowledge of other minds must be inferred from prior knowledge of non-psychological truths about the mere movements of human bodies? It seems to me that the original partitioning of the propositions or truths is all right. It is in what happens after that, when we try to say how we know those things, that the difficulties begin.

What happens in the case of the external world is that we want to understand how *any* propositions about an independent world are known to be true by *anyone*. And we must explain that knowledge in the light of other facts about human beings which we feel we cannot deny: in particular, that human beings get their knowledge of the world somehow from sense-perception—'either from the senses or through the senses', as Descartes put it.[11] No divine messages from on high, no extra-sensory access to things around us, are to be assumed to be at work. So far, that is simply a very general 'anthropological' fact about the human condition. The question is how knowledge of the world is possible in the light of that fact.

Williams regards that 'anthropological' fact as uncontroversial. It can be expressed as what he calls a 'truism': that 'without functioning sense organs, I would never form any beliefs about the external world and so would never come to know anything about it either'.[12] But he thinks it is a 'truism' about the *causes* of our beliefs and knowledge, and that no sceptical conclusion about knowledge of the world follows from it when understood in that way. As a causal thesis, it is not equivalent to, nor does it imply, epistemological 'foundationalism' according to which knowledge of the deliverances of the senses is prior to and so must form the basis of any knowledge of an independent world. That 'foundationalist' doctrine does eventually lead to scepticism about the external world, and Williams thinks the philosopher who holds that all knowledge comes from sense-experience is smuggling it into his understanding of that otherwise uncontroversial fact about the origins of human knowledge. What is true is really only a causal or genetic 'truism'.

I agree that the 'truism' about the sensory sources of human knowledge does not imply the philosophical doctrine that knowledge of the world must be inferred or derived from some prior basis restricted to the deliverances of sense-experience alone. But I also think that those philosophers who accept that 'truism' about sense-perception and are led to scepticism about knowledge of an independent world do not think that it alone is equivalent to or implies that philosophical doctrine either. I believe they are led to a sceptical conclusion by carrying out their investigation with only a causal or genetic reading of the idea that sense-perception is necessary for human knowledge in general. So I think the trouble begins, if it does, only after the philosopher has picked out the kinds of propositions he is interested in, and only after he has accepted

---

[11] *The Philosophical Writings of Descartes*, ii, tr. J. Cottingham, R. Stoothoff, D. Murdoch, (Cambridge, 1985), 'First Meditation', 12.
[12] 69.

the general 'anthropological' fact that human knowledge of those propositions requires sense-perception.

Williams is willing to concede for the sake of argument that there is something called 'experiential knowledge'[13] which is restricted to the deliverances of sense-experience alone and itself implies nothing about an independent world. There is in that sense a 'logical gap' between 'statements about appearance' and 'statements about reality'.[14] He calls that the 'neutrality of experience' *vis-à-vis* reality,[15] and he insists that it does not imply that knowledge of the one kind of statement is 'epistemically prior' to, or must serve as the 'basis' of, knowledge of the other. He even concedes that there might be an asymmetrical relation between the two kinds of knowledge: something he calls the 'autonomy of experience'.[16] That would mean that 'experiential knowledge' is possible without any knowledge of independent objects, but not vice versa; knowledge of reality always carries some 'experiential knowledge' in its train. But again he points out that that does not imply that knowledge of an independent reality must be based on or inferred from that 'experiential knowledge'. He can find no philosophical thesis or doctrine that implies the 'epistemic priority' of 'experiential knowledge' over knowledge of independent objects.

I agree that it would be invalid to move directly from any of those weaker 'logical' doctrines he considers to the thesis that 'experiential knowledge' is the epistemically prior 'basis' of any knowledge we might have of an independent world. But because he can find nothing that implies that thesis, or no deductive argument for it, Williams appears to think that the traditional epistemologist must be simply assuming it from the very beginning or smuggling it into his understanding of his very starting-point. 'How else could it get in there?' he seems to be asking. I think we should not treat that as a rhetorical question; we should try to answer it. Rather than insisting that the philosopher must be assuming some a priori thesis that would imply the doctrine, we should look closely at the way the epistemological reasoning actually goes, or has gone, in the hands of its ablest practitioners, and see where the idea of the epistemic priority of 'experiential knowledge' comes from. That reasoning, after all, is where all the 'data' for our reflections on this kind of reflection reside. That is what our diagnostic discussion should be about; not merely about the logical relations, or lack of them, among abstract philosophical theses or doctrines.

What is at stake in the problem of the external world is all of our knowledge of independent objects or states of affairs. The causal or genetic 'truism' that such knowledge comes from sense-perception implies at least that we would have no knowledge of an independent world at all unless there had been particular occasions on which we came to know something 'from the senses or through the senses'. To investigate our knowledge of the world in general we cannot investigate each particular item of knowledge of the world, or each occasion on which we came to know something from sense-perception, on its own, one by one. The philosopher considers one such occasion which can be regarded as optimal for gaining perceptual knowledge of the world. He carefully scrutinizes what goes on in that case, and lets it serve as representative of what goes on on all those occasions on which we take the senses to be operating at their best under conditions we regard as best for the acquisition of knowledge from sense-perception.

He chooses a situation in which any one of us would unproblematically say or think, for example, that we know that there is a fire in the fireplace right before us, and that we know it is there because we see that it is there. But when we ask what this seeing really amounts to, various considerations are introduced to lead us to concede that we would see exactly what we see now even if no fire was there at all, or if we didn't know there was one there. (I omit the details of this reflection: I assume they are well enough known for present purposes.) This kind of procedure, if not the terms in which it is typically conducted in philosophy, is familiar to all of us in everyday life, or in the slightly more specialized example of a cross-examining attorney who gets a witness to retreat from his original claim to have seen the accused go through the door to saying that he saw a man in a grey hat and coat go through the door, or perhaps only that he saw a figure in a grey hat and coat which, for all he saw, could even have been a woman. That we perceive *something or other* in the case of the fire is not brought into doubt by the introduction of alternative, uneliminated possibilities. But we are led to conclude that, whatever we do see to be so in that case, we do not simply see *that there is a fire there.*

Even after we have made that concession, it does not immediately follow that we do not know that there is a fire there. But we now face the problem of explaining how in that situation we nevertheless do know that there is a fire there. We do not see that it is there, since we could see exactly what we now see and there be no fire. So how, given that we do perceive what we do, do we know about the presence of a fire? This so far is still a straightforward question which simply awaits an answer. Take the question of how, given what you see on your television screen, you know that certain events are now occurring in Washington. Or how, given that you see coats and hats moving in the street below, you know that there are people inside them. I think we believe we could give good answers to those questions. We would appeal to many other things we know to explain the connection in those particular cases between what we see and what we claim to know. We know how television works and we know what kinds of things usually carry coats and hats of the kinds we see.

But in philosophy we want to understand how *any* knowledge of an independent world is gained on *any* of the occasions on which knowledge of the world is gained through sense-perception. So, unlike those everyday cases, when we understand the particular case in the way we must understand it for philosophical purposes, we cannot appeal to some piece of knowledge we think we have already got about an independent world. Because of the genetic 'truism' about the perceptual source of all knowledge, no such piece of knowledge would have been acquired unless there had been some occasion on which we gained knowledge of an independent world by sense-perception. And what goes on, or how knowledge of an independent world is acquired by sense-perception, on any such occasion is precisely what we are trying to understand.

If, in reflecting on our present situation with the fire, we reach the stage of conceding that we do not simply see that there is a fire there, we must admit that if we do know that there is a fire there it must be by seeing what we see plus something else. We must then admit that the same is true of any other, even optimal, occasion on which we come to know something by sense-perception. So any knowledge of the independent world that we might appeal to to help us in the present case would be knowledge we possess only if there have been other occasions on which we came to know something about the independent world by sense-perception. But the particular example we are considering is meant to serve as a way of examining how we ever get any knowledge of an independent world by sense-perception on any such occasion. We cannot answer the question of how we know in the present case by appeal to an exactly similar case in which the question of how we know is left unanswered.

This, I believe, is in broad outline how we come to see our knowledge of an independent world in general as problematic relative to the apparently less problematic knowledge we have of what we perceive. The priority of 'experiential knowledge' over knowledge of objects is in that sense a kind of 'discovery' or outcome which we are led to by applying familiar everyday concepts and distinctions in the course of what is admittedly a special philosophical reflection on our knowledge of the world as a whole. Of course, I have not filled in every step of that reasoning or done what it takes to make it as convincing as it can be. I am simply reminding you of the general pattern of a traditional epistemological investigation we are all familiar with. My aim is not to establish the sceptical conclusion here and now, but only to draw attention to those special features of the philosophical investigation which make it impossible to rely on the reassuring kinds of answers we find it so easy to give to what sound like similar questions in everyday life.

I think the special generality we seek in philosophy, combined with the 'truism' about the perceptual source of all human knowledge, and with the introduction of certain possibilities of error which are not normally raised in everyday life is what together makes the question impossible to answer satisfactorily. The way in which the particular example under consideration must be treated as representative of perceptual knowledge in general is the key. That is what I think we have to understand better than we do.

Williams does take up the idea that 'in the context of a distinctively philosophical investigation of our knowledge of the world, the crucial ideas about epistemic priority are *forced* on us by our ordinary understanding of knowledge and justification'.[17] That is what I think happens. If so, it would perhaps explain how we can be so impressed, or perhaps even convinced, by the completely general philosophical reasoning when we first encounter it. But Williams thinks it is not the special nature of the investigation that does it. Or if it is, it is only because that investigation takes on the

[17] 89.

character of a 'distinctively philosophical investigation' only if we already accept what he calls 'epistemological realism.'[18]

That is not the view, as the name might suggest, that we have direct or unmediated knowledge of independently existing objects or states of affairs. That would be the very opposite of scepticism. It rather is a view to the effect that beliefs (and here I take Williams to mean the 'objects' or contents of our beliefs) 'stand in natural epistemological relations' to each other, that 'a belief's intrinsic epistemic status derives from the content of the proposition believed', that 'every belief has an inalienable epistemic character which it carries with it wherever it goes and which determines where its justification must ultimately be sought'.[19]

I find this view difficult to understand. I don't know what 'epistemic relations' between propositions themselves are supposed to be, independently of the propositions' being believed or accepted by particular agents at particular places and times. Can one proposition, considered simply in itself, be a justification or a reason for some other proposition, considered in itself? Can a proposition, considered simply in itself, be justified, or unjustified? I see that one proposition can imply another, or be incompatible with another, but how can propositions themselves have reasons for or against them, or how can one proposition justify another proposition? Of course, a person can have reasons for or against believing a proposition, his acceptance of it can be justified or unjustified, but that is a different matter. There it is his believing that is reasonable or unreasonable, justified or unjustified, to some degree or other, not simply the proposition he believes. 'Epistemological realism' appears to hold that what is believed, and not the believing of it, has 'an inalienable epistemic character'. Williams himself favours an opposed view which he calls 'contextualism', according to which 'no proposition, considred in abstraction, . . . [has] an epistemic status it can call its own'.[20] That seems right to me, so to that extent I suppose I too am a 'contextualist'.

My difficulty in understanding 'epistemological realism' leaves me in no position to assess its truth or falsity. But it does enable me to say with some confidence that 'epistemological realism' is probably not something that must be accepted in order to appreciate the 'distinctively philosophical' character of the traditional investigation of our knowledge of the world, or that it is built into

[18] 130.   [19] 116.   [20] 113.

that project from the very beginning. I don't believe 'epistemolog-ical realism', but I do retain some sense of the force of the philo-sophical investigation. I have tried to sketch how it can seem to lead so inevitably to scepticism once you appreciate its special char-acter. And I don't think 'epistemological realism' plays any role in the account I have given.

The closest one needs to get in the traditional investigation to what I think Williams is trying to get at with his 'epistemological realism' is the 'truism' that knowledge of an independent world comes from particular occasions on which something is known through sense-perception. Without any occasions on which some-thing is known through sense-perception there would be no knowl-edge of an independent world. In that sense knowledge of the world can be said to depend on sense-perception. That does not mean that propositions about an independent world, when consid-ered in abstraction, stand in some invariant 'epistemic' relations to propositions about human sense-experience, considered in abstrac-tion. It means only that human beings are such that, in the world as it is, they do not get any knowledge of the world without getting some knowledge through sense-perception. If that is true, it is a truth about human beings and the world they live in, not merely about relations among the propositions they know to be true when they have such knowledge. You could reflect forever on the propo-sition that there is a fire in the fireplace, abstractly considered, and 'analyse' its meaning to your heart's content, without ever discov-ering by that means that it is a proposition which can be known to be true by human beings only if there are occasions on which they know something through sense-perception. That is not an 'intrin-sic' or 'inalienable' feature of the content of that proposition, abstractly considered. It is a truth (if it is) about human beings. The human knowing of such propositions to be true is what we are interested in, not simply the alleged relations among the proposi-tions known.

I find intriguing and very promising Williams's suggestion that there really is no such thing as 'our knowledge of the external world in general' which could serve as a single object of the philosopher's scrutiny.[21] He sees some form of what he calls 'contextualism' as a way of developing that idea further. But as Williams conceives of

---

[21] This is asserted in the first sentence of the preface (p. xii) and argued at length in chs. 3, 4, 5, and 9.

it here, I believe, what is determined by context is the type or standard of justification required for acceptance of a given proposition on a particular occasion. What is required for belief in the truth of a given proposition in one context might not be required in another, or what is up for justification or assessment in one context might be taken for granted or go without saying in another. That certainly sounds plausible as a description of what actually goes on when people are trying to find out and confirm or disconfirm the things they are interested in in science and in everyday life. But I think there is a danger for Williams in accepting such a story for general philosophical purposes, given his idea that there is no making sense of something called our knowledge of the external world in general.

If this 'contextualism' gives the general form of an account which we could appeal to to explain how we know or justify our acceptance of any or all of the propositions we think we know about an independent world, we would seem to have something very much like a positive general theory of our knowledge of the world after all. Even though the kind and degree of justification available or demanded might differ from proposition to proposition and from occasion to occasion, if the propositions in question are all about an independent world in the sense of being true or false independently of us and our experiences, and if those propositions are all justified in one way or another in some context or other, and they are true, then we might well be said to have knowledge of the truth of all of them. We could be said to have knowledge of an independent world after all. But Williams's idea is that there is no such knowledge in general for us to have a theory about.

This suggests that the kind of 'contextualism' that would be required to put an end to the philosophical theory of knowledge in the way he hopes for must find not only that one's reasons for saying something, but even *what one says* in using a given sentence to make a statement of knowledge itself can vary without even a common core from context to context. There would be in that sense no such thing as, simply, knowing that there is a fire in the fireplace. Not simply because one's reasons for assertively uttering the sentence 'I know there is a fire in the fireplace' might vary from context to context—no traditional philosopher would have reason to deny that—but rather because there is no single, fixed content to what is being said on every occasion, in every context, by the assertive use of that sentence. Or at least there would not be enough of a core to allow the philosopher to generalize from the single special case he considers to a conclusion which holds of any knowledge by anyone of any independent objects or states of affairs in the world.

This is too vague and programmatic as it stands, and I am not sure enough about it to say more now. I think J. L. Austin's celebrated opposition to epistemology might well have had some such idea behind it. It raises deep issues about meaning and truth that would lead us far afield. But as far as I can see, Williams's own reason for thinking there can be no such thing as knowledge of the external world for the philosopher to study is not really that he thinks some such version of 'contextualism' is true. His reason is simply that thinking that there *is* such a single object of epistemological study is the same as, or is a result of, thinking that 'epistemological realism' is true. That, as I have said, is what I find implausible, and not convincingly demonstrated in Williams's book. I am happy not to accept 'epistemological realism'. But I think that leaves me just where I was with respect to the problem of traditional epistemology. I agree that there must be distortion or confusion or mistake or fantasy in there somewhere. And I think we would learn a lot about human knowledge, and about the human urge to philosophize, if we could ever find what it is and where it comes from.

Williams quotes with approval Thompson Clarke's ground-floor question: 'What is the sceptic examining: our most fundamental convictions, or the product of a large piece of philosophizing about empirical knowledge done before he comes on stage?'[22] I think Williams and I (as well as Clarke) would all agree that the answer is 'The latter'. But that leaves wide open the question of how we so easily and unwittingly come to think of empirical knowledge in what turns out to be such a disastrous way: what the so-called 'philosophizing' is, and what its 'product' amounts to. It does not seem to me likely that it amounts to a substantial body of fairly elaborate philosophical doctrines or theses arrived at even before getting curious about human knowledge of the world in general. I think it is much more likely to amount to a way of thinking of ourselves, or perhaps I should say a wish to think of ourselves, in a certain

---

[22] 1, quoting from Clarke, 'The Legacy of Skepticism', *Journal of Philosophy* (1972), 754.

way—something that perhaps eventually issues in philosophical doctrines of the kind Williams has in mind.

That is why I spoke earlier of human aspiration. The philosophical problem of knowledge of the world might well be an expression of an aspiration we can all appreciate and sympathize with: a desire to understand ourselves in a certain way, to get into a certain position with respect to human knowledge and perhaps the human condition generally. It takes the form of a desire to get outside that knowledge and that condition, as it were, while somehow retaining all the resources needed to see them as they are. Who can say what illumination might be gained into human beings and human reflection by understanding better how and why such a detached position can seem so tempting while remaining forever unavailable to us?

10

Scepticism, 'Externalism', and the Goal of Epistemology

Scepticism has been different things at different times in the history of philosophy, and has been put to different uses. In the last hundred years or so it has been understood primarily as a position—or threat—within the theory of knowledge. It says that nobody knows anything, or that nobody has good reason to believe anything. That view must be of central significance in epistemology, given that the goal of the enterprise is to explain how we know the things we think we do. It would seem that any satisfyingly positive theory of knowledge should imply the falsity of scepticism.

Scepticism need not always be taken as completely general. It has more typically been restricted to this or that particular kind of alleged knowledge or reasonable belief: we have no reason to believe anything about the future, for example, even if we know a great deal about the past and the present; we know nothing about the world around us, although we know what the course of our own experience is like; or I know what the physical world and my own thoughts and experiences are like, but I know nothing about the minds of other persons. Scepticism is most illuminating when restricted to particular areas of knowledge in this way because it then rests on distinctive and problematic features of the alleged knowledge in question, not simply on some completely general conundrum in the notion of knowledge itself, or in the very idea of reasonable belief. It is meant to be a theory about human beings as they actually are, and about the knowledge we think we actually have in the circumstances in which we find ourselves.

Scepticism in the theory of knowledge involves much more than

This essay was my contribution to a Joint Session symposium on philosophical scepticism with Ernest Sosa. It was published with his 'Philosophical Scepticism and Epistemic Circularity' in *Proceedings of the Aristotelian Society: Supplementary Volume* (1994). Reprinted by courtesy of the Editor of the Aristotelian Society: © 1994.

the bare assertion that no one knows anything or has any reason to believe anything of a particular kind. If all animate life were suddenly (or even gradually) wiped off the face of the earth no one would then know anything or have any reason to believe anything about the world, but that would not make scepticism about the external world true. A philosophical theorist wants to understand human knowledge as it is, as human beings and the world they live in actually are. But again not just any denial of human knowledge in a certain domain counts as philosophical scepticism. Human beings as they are right now do not know the causes of many kinds of cancer, or of AIDS, or the fundamental structure of matter. But universal ignorance in a particular domain does not make scepticism true of that domain. Scepticism holds that people as they actually are fail to know or have good reason to believe the sorts of things we all think we already know right now. Anti-scepticism, or a positive theory of knowledge, holds the opposite. It would explain how human beings, equipped as they are and living in the world they live in, do in fact know the sorts of things they think they do.

Theories of knowledge which conflict in this way nevertheless typically share many assumptions about human beings and their cognitive and perceptual resources. It is agreed on all sides, for example, that if human beings know things about the world around them, they know them somehow on the basis of what they perceive by means of the senses. The dispute then turns on whether and how what the senses provide can give us knowledge or good reason to believe things about the world. Knowledge of matters which go beyond perception to the independent world is seen, at least temporarily, as problematic. A successful positive theory of knowledge would explain how the problem is solved so that we know the things we think we know about the world after all.

It must be admitted, I think, that what many philosophers have said about perceptual knowledge is pretty clearly open to strong sceptical objections. That is, *if* the way we know things about the world is the way many philosophers have said it is, *then* a good case can be made for the negative sceptical conclusion that we do not really know such things after all. That is why scepticism remains such a constant threat. If you don't get your description of the human condition right, if you describe human perception and cognition and reasoning in certain natural but subtly distorted ways, you will leave human beings as you describe them incapable of the very knowledge you are trying to account for. A sceptical conclusion will be derivable from the very description which serves to pose the epistemological problem. Thus did the ancient sceptics argue, conditionally, against the Stoics: 'if human knowledge is arrived at in the way you say it is, there could be no such thing as human knowledge at all.' Even if true, that does not of course show that scepticism is correct. It shows at most that human knowledge or the human condition must be understood in some other way. The threat of scepticism is what keeps the theory of knowledge going.

The point is that scepticism and its competitors among more positive theories of knowledge are all part of the same enterprise. They offer conflicting answers to what is for all of them a common question or set of questions. The task is to understand all human knowledge of a particular kind, or all reasonable belief concerning a certain kind of matter of fact. Scepticism is one possible outcome of that task. In that sense, scepticism, like its rivals, is a general theory of human knowledge. But it is not a satisfactory theory or outcome. It is paradoxical. It represents us as having none of the knowledge or good reasons we ordinarily think we've got. No other theory or answer is satisfactory either if it does not meet and dispel the threat of scepticism. I think many philosophical theories of knowledge have failed to do that, despite what their defenders have claimed for them.

In fact, I find the force and resilience of scepticism in the theory of knowledge to be so great, once the epistemological project is accepted, and I find its consequences to be so paradoxical, that I think the best thing to do now is to look much more closely and critically at the very enterprise of which scepticism or one of its rivals is the outcome: the task of the philosophical theory of knowledge itself. Its goal is not just any understanding of human knowledge; it seeks to understand knowledge in a certain way. Both scepticism and its opposites claim to understand human knowledge in that special way, or from that special philosophical point of view. I would like to enquire what that way of understanding ourselves and our knowledge is, or is supposed to be. I wonder whether there is a coherent point of view from which we could get a satisfactory understanding of ourselves of the kind we apparently aspire to. Many would dismiss scepticism as absurd on the grounds that there is no such point of view, or that we could never get ourselves into the position of seeing that it is true if it were true. But to adopt a more positive theory of knowledge instead is still to offer a description of the human condition from that same special position or point of view. If we cannot get into that position and see that scepticism is true, can we be sure that we can get into it and see that scepticism is false?

The coherence and achievability of what we aspire to in the epistemological enterprise tends to be taken for granted, or left unexplored. But that question is prior to the question whether scepticism or one or another of its positive competitors is the true theory of human knowledge. What does a true theory of knowledge do? What does a philosophical theorist of knowledge seek?

These are large and complicated questions to which we obviously cannot hope to get a definitive answer today. Distinguishing them from the question of the relative merits of scepticism and its competitors might none the less help to locate the target of Ernest Sosa's opposition to something he calls 'scepticism'. He gives that label to the view that 'there is no way to attain full philosophical understanding of our knowledge' or that 'a fully general theory of knowledge is impossible'.[1] That is obviously not what I have just called 'scepticism', which is itself a fully general theory of knowledge. Sosa considers a two-step argument for the view he has in mind which would show exhaustively that any general theory of knowledge possessing a certain feature would be what he calls 'impossible', and that any general theory lacking that feature would be 'impossible' too. So there couldn't be a fully general theory of knowledge. The conclusion certainly does follow from those two premisses, but Sosa doubts the second premiss. He thinks some theories which lack the feature in question have not been shown to be defective in the way the original argument was meant to show. The surviving theories are what he calls 'externalist'.

Theories of the first type hold that a belief acquires the status of knowledge only by 'being based on some justification, argument, or reason'.[2] That requirement is what makes them 'impossible', according to Sosa, because in order to succeed they would have to show that our acceptance of the things we think we know is justified in each case by good inferences or arguments which are not circular or infinitely regressive. That is what it would take to 'legitimate' those beliefs, and that cannot be done. Every inference has

¹ Sosa, 'Philosophical Scepticism', 263.   ² Ibid. 273.

to start from something, so without circular or regressive reasoning there must always be something whose acceptance by us is left unsupported by inference, and so cannot be accounted for as knowledge by theories of this type. But a fully general theory of knowledge must account for everything we know. Sosa concludes that there could be no fully 'general, legitimating, philosophical understanding of all one's knowledge'.[3] This is equivalent, I believe, to saying that no such theory avoids the conclusion that we know nothing. What he is saying of theories of this first type is that if, in order to know things, we had to satisfy what those theories say are conditions of knowledge, then we would not know anything, since we cannot satisfy those conditions. So theories of the first type depict us as knowing nothing. They cannot be distinguished, in their consequences, from the view that I (but not Sosa) have called 'scepticism'.

I take it to be the main point of Sosa's paper to show that certain 'externalist, reliabilist' theories escape that fate. They can be fully general and still succeed where theories of other kinds fail. He thinks there is 'a very wide and powerful current of thinking [which] would sweep away externalism root and branch',[4] and he wants to resist that 'torrent of thought'.[5] He concentrates here on the reasons he thinks William Alston and I have given for thinking that, as he puts it, 'externalism will leave us ultimately dissatisfied'.[6] He appears to equate that charge with what he calls the 'unacceptability in principle'[7] of 'externalism'.

What exactly are these objections? For my part, I do think there is a way in which 'externalism' would leave us 'ultimately dissatisfied' as an answer to the completely general philosophical question of how any knowledge of the world is possible. I tried to indicate what I have in mind in the paper that Sosa refers to and discusses.[8] But I do not suggest that 'externalism' is unsatisfying because it cannot avoid depicting us as knowing nothing about the world and so is indistinguishable from the view that I call 'scepticism'. Nor would I argue that it is inconsistent or viciously circular or internally deficient in some other way which prevents it 'in principle' from being true or acceptable. Sosa says the objections are 'grounded in what seem to be demands inherent to the traditional

---

[3] Ibid. 267.   [4] Ibid. 266.   [5] Ibid.   [6] Ibid. 266–7.   [7] Ibid. 267.
[8] 'Understanding Human Knowledge in General', Ch. 8 above.

epistemological project itself',[9] and I think his efforts to meet the objections are intended to defend not only 'externalist' theories but also by implication that very epistemological project as well. My own doubts about 'externalism' could perhaps be said to be 'grounded in' or at least connected with demands inherent to that project, but that is because they are doubts not only about 'externalism' but about the coherence or feasibility of the general epistemological project itself. That question is what I think should be our primary target, not just one or another of the answers offered to it. We need to examine more critically what we want or hope for from the traditional epistemological project of understanding human knowledge in general.

Alston's objections might well have a different source. I suspect that in opposing 'externalism' as he does he is working towards what he sees as a more adequate theory of knowledge, perhaps one which would recognize some beliefs as 'evident' or 'prima facie justified' in a way that 'externalism' cannot explain. But to support a theory that competes with pure 'externalism' as the right answer to the philosophical question is not to bring that whole philosophical project itself into question. Although I think there are many points on which we would agree, I shall therefore leave Alston to one side. That leaves me with the question: does Sosa's defence of 'externalism' show that it does not have that feature which I think means it must always leave us dissatisfied, and so by implication that the goal of epistemology must always leave us dissatisfied as well, or does he really accept the point and not regard it as a deficiency in his 'externalist' theory?

The question is complicated because Sosa sees opposition to 'externalism' as coming from some competing philosophical conception or theory of knowledge. His defence amounts to arguing that any theory from which the objections could come must be a theory of his first general type, and so can be discredited 'for simple, demonstrable logical reasons'.[10] If it is a conflict between competing theories of knowledge, 'externalism' must win, since it does not have the fatal defect those other theories have. In order to bring out my doubts about the kind of satisfaction offered by 'externalism' I can grant that point. I would like to reveal something that I think remains unsatisfying about 'externalism' even if it is the best

---

[9] Sosa, 'Philosophical Scepticism', 267.   [10] Ibid. 286.

philosophical theory of knowledge there is or could be. I do not want to put a better theory in its place; I want to ask what a philosophical theory of knowledge is supposed to be, even at its best. Revealing the unsatisfactoriness of even the best answer to the philosophical question can perhaps help draw attention to its unsatisfiable demands.

We aspire in philosophy to see ourselves as knowing all or most of the things we think we know and to understand how all that knowledge is possible. We want an explanation, not just of this or that item or piece of knowledge, but of knowledge, or knowledge of a certain kind, *in general*. Take all our knowledge of the world of physical objects around us, for example. A satisfactory 'theory' or explanation of that knowledge must have several features. To be satisfyingly positive it must depict us as knowing all or most of the things of the sort that we think we know. It must explain, given what it takes to be the facts of human perception, how we none the less know the sorts of things we think we know about that world. To say simply that we see, hear, and touch the things around us and in that way know what they are like, would leave nothing even initially problematic about that knowledge. Rather than explaining how, it would simply state that we know. There is nothing wrong with that; it is true, but it does not explain how we know even in those cases in which (as we would say) we are in fact seeing or hearing or touching an object. That is what we want in a philosophical explanation of our knowledge. How, given what perception provides us with even in such cases, do we thereby know what the objects in question are like? What needs explanation is the connection between our perceiving what we do and our knowing the things we do about the physical objects around us. How does the one lead to, or amount to, the other?

Suppose there is an 'externalist, reliabilist' theory of the kind Sosa has in mind which accounts for this. I mean suppose there are truths about the world and the human condition which link human perceptual states and cognitive mechanisms with further states of knowledge and reasonable belief, and which imply that human beings acquire their beliefs about the physical world through the operation of belief-forming mechanisms which are on the whole reliable in the sense of giving them mostly true beliefs. Let us not pause over details of the formulation of such truths, although they are of course crucial and have not to this day been put right by anybody, as far as I know. If there are truths of this kind, although no one has discovered them yet, that fact alone obviously will do us no good as theorists who want to understand human knowledge in this philosophical way. At the very least we must believe some such truths; their merely being true would not be enough to give us any illumination or satisfaction. But our merely happening to believe them would not be enough either. We seek understanding of certain aspects of the human condition, so we seek more than just a set of beliefs about it; we want to know or have good reason for thinking that what we believe about it is true. This is why I say, as Sosa quotes me: 'we need some reason to accept a theory of knowledge if we are going to rely on that theory to understand how our knowledge is possible'.[11]

Sosa does not dispute that as a condition of success for understanding human knowledge. He disputes my going on to say that 'no form of "externalism" can give a satisfactory account'[12] of our having such a reason to accept it and so understanding our knowledge of the world in purely 'externalist' terms. He thinks my only support for that second claim comes from what he calls a '*metaepistemic requirement*'[13] which does not follow from the conditions of success admitted so far. It comes, he thinks, from 'a deeply held intuition that underlies a certain way of thinking about epistemology'.[14] He thinks I have an 'anti-externalist' conception of knowledge according to which 'what is important in epistemology is justification', which in turn requires 'appeal to *other* beliefs that constitute one's reasons for holding the given belief'.[15] That is what can only lead in a circle or down an infinite regress, and so in Sosa's terms it is an 'impossible' theory of knowledge. Without that requirement, he thinks, the objection vanishes.

Now I want to say that I do not accept any of that. As far as I know, I do not hold an 'anti-externalist' theory of knowledge with which I seek to oppose 'externalism'. I do not think that everything a person knows requires justification which involves appeal to other beliefs, and so on. I think that what I am drawing attention to about 'externalism' is something that can be recognized by anyone who has a good idea of what the general epistemological

---

[11] Sosa, ibid. 272, quoting from 'Understanding Human Knowledge in General', Ch. 8 above, p. 114–15.
[12] p. 115 above.   [13] Sosa, 'Philosophical Scepticism', 272.
[14] Ibid. 273.   [15] Ibid.

project is after. Of course, it could be that I am unwittingly imposing the 'anti-externalist' requirement that Sosa's diagnosis says I
am. He thinks I must be; I don't think I am. But rather than searching my soul, which I am sure would be of limited general interest,
let me again present for public assessment the way I think 'externalism' must leave us dissatisfied. I find in any case that Sosa has
not really considered the reasons I actually gave.

We agree that an 'externalist' theorist of knowledge must know
or have good reason to believe that his explanation of our knowledge of the physical world around us is correct in order to understand in that way how that knowledge is possible. How will he know
or have good reason to believe that? Well, his theory is in part a
theory of the conditions under which people in fact know or have
good reasons to believe things about the world. If that theory is
true in particular of the theorist's own acceptance of that theory,
then the theorist has what his own theory says is knowledge of or
reasonable belief in the truth of that theory. I believe this is the
situation Sosa is describing when he says: 'We can legitimately
and with rational justification arrive at a belief that a certain set of
faculties or doxastic practices are those that we employ *and* are
reliable.'[16] He thinks there is 'no obstacle in principle'[17] to our
achieving such a state. I do not disagree with that.

That Sosa thinks the resistance to 'externalism' must be based
on some such 'obstacle in principle' is suggested by his immediately
going on to ask 'why could we not conceivably attain thereby a
general understanding of how we know whatever we do know?'[18]
It is clear that his question at that point is rhetorical. His idea is
that if we can have what an 'externalist' theory calls good reason
to believe our 'externalist' theory, it could thereby give us a satisfactory general understanding of our knowledge. For me his question is not rhetorical. I think we can see why, even with what counts
for an 'externalist' as good reason to believe his theory, there would
remain something ineliminably unsatisfactory about the position a
theorist would then be in for gaining a philosophical understanding of his knowledge of the physical world in general.

The difficulty I have in mind does not show up in understanding
the knowledge which other people, not myself, have about the
world. I understand others' knowledge by connecting their beliefs

---

[16] Ibid. 285.   [17] Ibid.   [18] Ibid.

in the right way with what I know to be true in the world they live in. I can discover that others get their beliefs through the operation of belief-forming mechanisms which I can see to be reliable in the sense of producing beliefs which are largely true. But each of us as theorists of knowledge is also a human being to whom our theory of knowledge is meant to apply, so we must understand ourselves as knowers, just as we understand others. *All* human knowledge of the world is what we want to understand.

If I ask of my own knowledge of the world around me how it is possible, I can explain it along 'externalist' lines by showing that it is a set of beliefs I have acquired through perception by means of belief-forming mechanisms which are reliable. Suppose that is what I believe about the connection between my perceptions and the beliefs I acquire about the world. As we saw, my merely happening to believe such a story would not be enough for me to be said to understand in that way how that knowledge is possible. I must know or have good reason to believe that that story is true of me. As a good 'externalist'. I do of course believe that I do. I think that I acquired my belief in my 'externalist' explanation of human knowledge by means of perception and of the operation of the same reliable belief-forming mechanisms which give me and others all our other knowledge of the world around us. So I think I do know or have good reason to believe my theory; I believe that I fulfil the conditions which that very theory says are sufficient for knowing or having good reason to believe it. Do I now have a satisfactory understanding of my knowledge of the world? Have I answered to my own satisfaction the philosophical question of how my knowledge of the world is possible? I want to say No.

It is admittedly not easy to describe the deficiency in a few words. It is not that there is some internal defect or circularity in the 'externalist' theory that I believe. Nor is there any obstacle to my believing that theory or even to my having good reasons in the 'externalist' sense to believe it. *If* the theory is true, and *if* I did acquire my belief in it in the way I think I did, *then* I do know or have good reason to believe it to be true. To appreciate what I still see as a deficiency, or as less than what one aspires to as a philosophical theorist of knowledge, let us consider the merits of a different and conflicting, but still 'externalist', account of our knowledge of the world.

I have in mind a fictional 'externalist' whom I shall call

'Descartes'. The theory of our knowledge of the world which he accepts says that there is a beneficent, omnipotent, and omniscient God who guarantees that whatever human beings carefully and clearly and distinctly perceive to be true is true. The real René Descartes held a closely similar theory, but he tried to prove demonstratively that it is true. He was accused of arguing in a circle. My 'externalist' Descartes offers no proofs. He believes that when people carefully and clearly and distinctly perceive things to be true, they are true; God makes sure of that. That is how people come to know things. He also acknowledges that what he himself needs in order to know or have good reason to believe his own theory of knowledge is to fulfil the conditions it says are sufficient for knowing or having good reason to believe something: to acquire belief in it by carefully and clearly and distinctly perceiving it to be true while God guarantees that it is true. Suppose he examines the origins of his own theory and carefully and clearly and distinctly perceives that he did acquire his belief in it in just that way. Does he now have a satisfactory understanding of his knowledge of the world? Has he got what he can see to be a satisfactory answer to the philosophical question of how his knowledge of the world is possible? I want to say No.

Your seeing and sharing my reservations about the adequacy of 'externalism' and so about the feasibility of the epistemological project depend on your finding the position of this 'externalist' Descartes unsatisfactory in a certain way as an understanding of his knowledge. The question is what is wrong with it. I think most of us will say first that what is wrong is that his theory is simply not true; there is no divine guarantor of the truth of even our most carefully arrived-at beliefs, and he is therefore wrong to think that he acquired his belief in his theory in that way. Even if that is so, is it the only deficiency in his position? I think it is not.

We cannot deny that he does believe his explanation of human knowledge, and does believe that he came to believe that theory by a procedure which his theory says is reliable, so we have to admit that *if* his theory and his account of how he came to believe it were true, *then* he would know or have good reason to believe his explanation of knowledge. But if we say that the falsity of his theory is the only deficiency in his position we would have to admit that if his theory and his belief about how he came to believe it were true, then he would have a satisfactory understanding of all of his

knowledge of the world. That implies that whether he understands
how his knowledge is possible or not depends only on whether the
theory which he holds about how he came to believe it is true or
not. If it is true, he does understand his knowledge; if it is not, he
does not. An 'externalist' theorist of this fictional kind who reflects
on his position could still always ask: 'I wonder whether I understand how my knowledge of the world is possible? I have a lot of
beliefs about it. If what I believe about it is true, I do; if it is not, I
don't. Of course, I believe all of it is true, so I believe that I do
understand my knowledge. But I wonder whether I do.' I think
anyone who can get into only that position with respect to his
alleged knowledge of the world has not achieved the kind of satisfaction which the traditional epistemological project aspires to. He
has not got into a position from which he can see all of his knowledge of the world all at once in a way that accounts for it as reliable or true.

Sosa's 'externalist, reliabilist', I believe, can get himself into no
better position for understanding himself. If what distinguishes his
position from that of my 'externalist' Descartes is only that his
theory is in fact true while that fictional character's theory is false,
then he too will be in a position to say no more about himself than
'If what I believe about my knowledge is true, I do understand it;
if it is not, I do not. I think I do, but I wonder whether I understand
my knowledge or not?' This is where the difficulty of describing the
deficiency in his position comes in. It will not be true to say simply
that although he believes his theory, he has no reason to believe it.
If we imagine that his 'externalist' theory and his account of how
he came to believe it are in fact true, as I have been conceding, then
in that sense he does have good reason to believe his explanation
of human knowledge. But still his own view of his position can look
no better to him than the fictional 'externalist' Descartes's position
looks to him.

It would be to no avail at this point for him to try to improve his
position by asking himself whether he knows or has good reason
to believe that he does know or have good reason to believe his
theory. Answering that question would be a matter of coming by
what he believes is a procedure that his theory says is reliable to
the belief that he knows or has good reason to believe his theory.
Again, if he did come to believe that in that way, and his theory is
in fact true, he will in fact know or have good reason to believe a

second-order claim about the goodness of his reasons for believing his theory. But still he could then make only the same sort of conditional assertion about his position one level up, as it were, as he made earlier. The 'externalist' Descartes could do the same. He could carefully and clearly and distinctly perceive that he came to believe his theory to be true of himself by what that very theory says is a way of coming to know or have good reason to believe. He could then come to a similarly true conditional verdict about his position. Both he and Sosa's 'externalist' could say at most: 'If the theory I hold is true, I do know or have good reason to believe that I know or have good reason to believe it, and I do understand how I know the things I do.' I think that in each case we can see a way in which the satisfaction the theorist seeks in understanding his knowledge still eludes him. Given that all of his knowledge of the world is in question, he will still find himself able to say only 'I might understand my knowledge, I might not. Whether I do or not all depends on how things in fact are in the world I think I've got knowledge of.'

Those of us who are inclined to think that Sosa's 'externalist's' theory is in fact true and the fictional Descartes's theory false will say that he does know and perhaps that he does understand his knowledge and that the fictional Descartes does not. But that does not show that that theorist's position gives him a satisfactory understanding of his own knowledge. As I said, the difficulty does not show up in one's understanding all of someone else's knowledge of the world; it is only when each of us seeks to understand our own knowledge of the world in general that we reach this unsatisfactory position.

If we do recognize a certain ineliminable dissatisfaction in any such 'externalist' attempt at self-understanding I do not think it is because of hidden attachment to an opposing 'internalist' theory which requires that everything we know must be justified by reasonable inference from something else we believe. We can be 'externalists' and still reach at best what I think is an unsatisfactory position, even if we do in fact have what 'externalism' regards as knowledge of or reasonable belief in that 'externalist' theory. I think the dissatisfaction, if we recognize it, is felt to come from the demands of the epistemological project itself, or perhaps we could say from the complete generality of the project. Whatever we seek, and what the theorists I have imagined appear to lack, is something that 'externalism' alone seems unable to explain or to account for.

Sosa grants that the epistemological goal can never be reached if the successful theory is expected to provide what he calls a 'legitimating' account. He means by that an account which 'specifies the reasons favouring one's beliefs',[19] and he thinks no theory that is 'internalist' in his sense can do that without circularity or regress. But surely the goal of understanding how we know what we do does require that the successful account be 'legitimating' at least in the sense of enabling us to understand that what we have got *is* knowledge of, or reasonable belief in, the world's being a certain way. We should be able to see that the view that I call 'scepticism' is not true of us, and we want to understand how we get the knowledge we can see that we've got. 'Externalism' implies that *if* such-and-such is true in the world, *then* human beings do know things about what the world is like. Applying that conditional proposition to ourselves, to our own knowledge of the world, to our own knowledge of how that knowledge is acquired, and so on, even when the antecedent and so the consequent are in fact both true, still leaves us always in the disappointingly second-best position I have tried to illustrate, however far up we go to higher and higher levels of reiterated knowledge or reasonable belief. We want to be in a position knowingly to detach that consequent about ourselves, and at the same time to know and so to understand how any or all of that knowledge of the world comes to be. And that would require appealing to or relying on part of our knowledge of the world in the course of explaining to ourselves how we come to have any knowledge of the world at all.

There are indications that Sosa acknowledges and accepts the situation I have tried to describe. Believing that our belief-forming mechanisms are reliable when they are in fact reliable, and coming by what are in fact those very mechanisms to believe that they are reliable, he says, is 'the very best conceivable outcome'[20] of the epistemological project. 'How could we possibly improve our epistemic situation?' he asks.[21] The thought that someone else could find his own 'epistemic situation' equally good on the basis of a competing theory of knowledge, he admits, might cause some dissatisfaction or discomfort, but he thinks that is 'discomfort we must learn to

---

[19] Sosa, 'Philosophical Scepticism', 273.   [20] Ibid. 282.   [21] Ibid.

tolerate'.[22] He concedes that in explaining, even to ourselves, how we know our 'externalist' theory of knowledge to be true, we must appeal to that very theory, and so cannot avoid, as he puts it, 'begging the question' or 'arguing circularly'[23] in our attempts to account for our knowledge. But again, he asks, 'once we understand this, what option is left to us except to go ahead and "beg" that question?'[24] I think his thought is that without doing that, we would have no chance of answering the epistemological question at all. We have to 'tolerate' the 'discomfort' of relying on a 'self-supporting argument'[25] for our theory simply because we could not arrive at a 'successful and general theory of knowledge'[26] in any other way.

Here, perhaps, we approach something that Sosa and I can agree about. What I have tried to identify as a dissatisfaction that the epistemological project will always leave us with is for him something that simply has to be accepted if we are going to have a fully general theory of knowledge at all. He appears to think, as I do, that it is endemic to the epistemological project itself. We differ in what moral we draw from that thought.

I want to conclude that we should therefore re-examine the source of, and so perhaps find ourselves able to resist, the not-fully-satisfiable demand embodied in the epistemological question. I think its source lies somewhere within the familiar and powerful line of thinking by which all of our alleged knowledge of the world gets even temporarily split off all at once from what we get in perception, so we are presented with a completely general question of how perception so understood gives us knowledge of anything at all in the physical world. If that manoeuvre cannot really be carried off successfully, we have no completely general question about our knowledge of the world to answer. We could still ask how we know one sort of thing about the physical world, given that we know certain other things about it, but there would be no philosophical problem about all of our knowledge of the world in general. What then would 'externalism' or any other fully general theory of knowledge be trying to do?

Sosa wants his 'externalism', even with its admitted 'discomfort', to serve as a bulwark against the 'relativism', 'contextualism', and 'scepticism' which he sees as rampant in our culture. I share his

---

[22] Ibid. 284.   [23] Ibid. 289.   [24] Ibid.   [25] Ibid.   [26] Ibid.

dark view of our times, but if those widely invoked 'isms' are thought of as competing answers to a fully general question about our 'epistemic situation' in the world, I think the resistance has to start further back. It is what all such theories purport to be about, and what we expect or demand that any such theory should say about the human condition, that we should be examining, not just which one of them comes in first in the traditional epistemological sweepstake. In that tough competition, it still seems to me, scepticism will always win going away.

Kantian Argument, Conceptual Capacities, and Invulnerability

Kant's transcendental philosophy was to be an exhaustive investigation of the necessary conditions of the possibility of thought and experience in general. And it was to proceed a priori, completely independently of observation and empirical theory. Reason alone was to discover its own scope and limits; the conditions of its possible employment were to be 'deduced' from thought and experience as they actually are. Any such enterprise could be expected to—and in that master's hands obviously did—yield lasting illumination of the enormous richness of interconnections among our various ways of thinking of ourselves and the world. Kant showed how and why in order to think certain kinds of thoughts, or to possess a certain kind of mental capacity, we must possess and exercise certain others, and then still others in turn. Human thought was thereby revealed as incredibly more complicated and much more of a piece than any atomistic picture of discrete impressions and ideas coming and going in the mind could possibly convey.

What is most striking and original about this radical Kantian turn in philosophy—and was meant to be its distinctive and most revolutionary feature—is that many of the conditions of thought and experience uncovered by this transcendental investigation are found to concern not merely the ways we do (or even must) think about or experience the world, but also the ways things are (or even must be) in the world that our thoughts and experiences are about.

For example, not only is it to be shown that if we think of the world as containing events which happen independently of us in a single space and time then we must also think of each of those

This essay was first published in P. Parrini (ed.), *Kant and Contemporary Epistemology* (Dordrecht, 1994 © 1994. Reprinted with kind permission from Kluwer Academic Publishers.) An earlier version was presented at a conference on that subject, I am grateful to the many members of conference whose helpful comments led to improvements, and to Anthony Brueckner for his comments on a later but still intermediate version.

events as linked to its predecessors in accordance with a general law, it is also to be 'deduced' that all events *are* linked to their predecessors in accordance with a general law. The transcendental investigation is to reveal not only that we must *think* that every event has a cause if we can think of anything's happening at all, but that every event *does* (or even must) have a cause. That is a strong conclusion to be derived from premises only about how we do or must think. It seems on the face of it to say nothing itself about how we think or experience things, and to be true or false independently of all such broadly psychological facts. But it too is to be revealed as a necessary condition of our experiencing things in certain ways.

The same is true of the conclusion that everything that exists is either a substance or an attribute of a substance, and of the other 'principles' of nature which Kant 'deduces' from the possibility of thought and experience. They too are, at least overtly, what I will call non-psychological; they appear to state or imply nothing about anyone's thinking or experiencing things in certain ways. And yet their independent truth is to be shown by transcendental investigation to be implicated in, and so required for, our thinking and experiencing things as we do. This is what sets transcendental philosophy apart from all metaphysics that had gone before, and it represents a new conception—or perhaps the first truly distinctive conception—of what philosophy itself is or should be.

Of course we are familiar with the unremarkable fact that certain non-psychological things must be so in order for us to think and experience things as we do. We know that our brains and sense-organs must function appropriately, and that the things around us must have certain characteristics and must affect us in certain ways, if we are going to enjoy anything like human thought and experience as it is. But in those thoughts the "must" is a causal "must", and it is known to hold, if it does, by empirical investigation. What is striking about the Kantian enterprise is that discoveries of apparently non-psychological conditions of thought are to be made purely a priori, independently of all experience. The necessity involved is not causal. That things are a certain way is said to be a necessary condition of our thinking and experiencing things as we do, in a stronger or different or at any rate non-causal sense of "necessary".

If there were things that were necessary conditions of thought in

that sense we would see that they *must* or simply *have to* be true
in pretty much the same way in which we recognize, for example,
that someone who says that he is speaking *must* be saying something true. It is not possible for me to speak truly while saying that
I am not speaking. Not because it is not possible for what I am then
saying to be true. What I am saying is that I am not speaking, and
it is possible for that to be true; I am often not speaking. But it is
not possible for it to be true when I am speaking, and so not even
when I am saying that I am not speaking. Similarly with such self-
guaranteeing thoughts as 'I am thinking' or even 'There is thought'.
It is not possible for those statements to be false if someone is
thinking them, although it is possible for them to be false; there
could have been no thought. But then if there are necessary conditions of thought in general—certain things that must be true if
there is any thought at all, or any thoughts or experiences of certain
specific kinds—then it will not be possible for any of those things
to be false if anyone thinks anything, or thinks or experiences in
those particular ways, either. The fulfilment of all the conditions of
thought is required or guaranteed by any thinking that occurs
which presupposes them. That holds for thinking anything at all,
even thinking (mistakenly) that those conditions are not or even
might not be fulfilled. We would therefore *have to* find those conditions to be fulfilled, in a pretty reassuring sense of "have to". We
could never correctly find them not to be so. Anyone who was
inclined to doubt that they are so, or to wonder whether they are
so, or even to look around for evidence that they are so, could be
relieved of his doubts and absolved from his quest once and for all
by a demonstration that they are indeed necessary conditions of
thought and experience in general, or conditions of the particular
kinds of thought and experience which the doubter engages in.
Those necessary conditions, if there are any, would belong to a
privileged class of propositions or 'principles' which in that sense
would enjoy a certain kind of invulnerability. They could not be
false if we think or experience anything.

I think this is part of what Kant himself saw as the distinctive
and most important pay-off of his transcendental philosophy. It is
what alone would put metaphysics on the secure path of a science.
It would put an end to the conflicts of dogmatic metaphysics, in
which one side confidently asserts a speculative verdict about the
fundamental nature of things and the other side just as confidently

asserts its opposite. And it would put an end to the perhaps more enlightened but still unsatisfactory kind of scepticism represented by Hume. He could find nothing more than custom and habit behind our acceptance of the synthetic proposition that every event has a cause. But Kant thought that if Hume had concerned himself more directly with the necessary conditions of thought and experience in general his good sense would have saved him from such a disastrous conclusion in that case. He would have seen that 'Every event has a cause', although synthetic, must be true if we can think of an independent world at all. It is therefore discoverable a priori; there is no need to seek support for it through a course of experience which it itself in part makes possible.

Here we can distinguish two aspects of the revolutionary Kantian strategy which Kant himself did not pause to distinguish. There is first the idea of the invulnerability of certain fundamental ingredients in our conception of the world. There could be no serious doubt or any threat of general scepticism about those broad features of our conception of the world which are themselves necessary conditions of our thinking about or experiencing anything at all. And there is secondly the question of how that invulnerability is to be established. For Kant it is to be shown by proving that certain apparently non-psychological truths about the world are indeed necessary conditions of the possibility of thought and experience. Those truths would thereby be shown to enjoy a special privileged security which could never be achieved by any conclusion of merely dogmatic metaphysics however convincing it might seem. The truth of transcendentally achieved results would be presupposed in any intelligible attempt to doubt or deny them.

It is with this second aspect—the attempt to provide positive proofs of metaphysical conclusions about the world from premises about features of human thought and experience—that the Kantian enterprise reveals its truly distinctive character. It must explain how we can proceed deductively, or in some sense necessarily, from facts about how we think and experience things to conclusions which appear to say how things are independently of all human thought and experience. Even if we allow that we can come to see how our thinking in certain ways necessarily requires that we also think in certain other ways, and so perhaps in certain further ways as well, and we can appreciate how rich and complicated the relations among those ways of thinking must be, how can truths about the world which appear to say or imply nothing about human thought or experience be shown to be genuinely necessary conditions of such psychological facts as that we think and experience things in certain ways, from which the proofs begin? It would seem that we must find, and cross, a bridge of necessity from the one to the other. That would be a truly remarkable feat, and some convincing explanation would surely be needed of how the whole thing is possible.

Kant's answer was transcendental idealism. The world of which, for example, 'Every event has a cause' or 'Everything is either a substance or an attribute of a substance' is true is not really a world which is in every sense fully independent of all thought and experience. It is a world which, transcendentally speaking, depends on or is 'constituted' by the possibility of our thinking and experiencing things as we do. The principle 'Every event has a cause', when taken transcendentally, as a necessary condition of the possibility of thought and experience, is not true independently of the possibility of all thought and experience. The world of which it is true is only the 'phenomenal' world which is somehow 'constituted' by the possibility of our thought and experience of it. Idealism, or the world's dependence on the mind, at least when that is thought of transcendentally, is therefore the price one has to pay for establishing the invulnerability of fundamental features of our thought. Metaphysics can reach secure positive results in Kant's a priori way only because the world of which those transcendental results hold is an idealist world, or a world understood idealistically. 'Reason has insight only into that which it produces after a plan of its own.'[1]

There are those who do not see idealism as a price one has to pay. Or if they do, many are apparently all too happy to pay it. But whoever accepts idealism, for whatever reason, is under some obligation to say what it is: what it means, for example, to say that the sun and the planets, and the mountains and continents which have been on this particular planet so much longer than we have, are nevertheless in some sense dependent on the possibility of human (or any other) thought and experience. And there is the challenge of saying in what ways idealism is superior to, or even different from, the sceptical doctrines it was meant to avoid. How

[1] I. Kant, *Critique of Pure Reason*, tr. N. Kemp Smith (London, 1953), Bxiii.

it differs, for example, from Hume's view that we simply cannot avoid believing that every event has a cause, and cannot help acting for all the world as if it were true, but that it is not really true of the world as it is independently of us.

In our own day Professor Peter Strawson has pursued a somewhat scaled-down form of the revolutionary Kantian strategy, keeping at least at arm's length what he has variously referred to as the 'complications', the 'incoherences', 'the phantasmagoric quality', even the 'doctrinal fantasies of transcendental idealism'.[2] Those putative doctrines are, as he says, 'the chief obstacles to a sympathetic understanding of the *Critique*'.[3] But he finds—or hopes—that they are not essential to the basically Kantian programme of 'determining the fundamental general structure of any conception of experience such as we can make intelligible to ourselves'.[4] That is what he carries out with such depth and brilliance in *The Bounds of Sense* and, more or less independently of Kant, in his earlier *Individuals: An Essay in Descriptive Metaphysics*.[5] Together those books have done more to bring Kant into contemporary philosophy, at least but not exclusively in the English-speaking world, than any comparable works of our time.

For Strawson, as for Kant, there were to be impressive metaphysical pay-offs from an examination of the framework of those fundamental ideas and principles which can be found to be necessary to any coherent conception of a world which we can form or find intelligible. There will be ways of thinking and experiencing which will be unavoidable for any being who can conceive of and experience an independent world of enduring spatio-temporal objects, for example. And it is a task of considerable intricacy and delicacy to tease out their connections with further cognitive capacities and to show that they too are required for the kind of thinking which makes possible our conception of an independent world. But for Strawson, as for Kant, the project originally appeared to promise conclusions which seemed to go beyond the way we do, or even must, think about and experience the world, and to reach as far as requiring something of the world itself. Not only must we think of, and so believe in, enduring particular objects in a single spatio-temporal system if we are to think of a world independent

---

[2] P. F. Strawson, *The Bounds of Sense* (London, 1966), 170 ff., 39, 235, 51.
[3] Ibid. 22.   [4] Ibid. 44.
[5] P. F. Strawson, *Individuals: An Essay in Descriptive Metaphysics* (London, 1959).

of ourselves at all, but it also seemed to be required that there actually *be* such objects.[6] The necessary conditions of our thinking in
the ways we do appeared to include highly general facts or states
of affairs which are non-psychological in the sense of apparently
containing nothing about how we think. They were essentially
richer than the merely psychological starting-points from which
they were to be derived, and the gap was to be bridged by some
form of Kantian or transcendental argument.

The question which in Kant led to the horrors of transcendental
idealism therefore arises for this apparently more austere version
of the Kantian strategy as well. How can we proceed 'deductively',
or by necessity, from premisses only about our thinking in certain
ways to conclusions about the independent world which we thereby
think about? Having abandoned, or not even flirted with, transcendental idealism, Strawson was inclined, some of the time, to
deny that any general explanation was really needed here. The particular derivations were to speak for themselves, and to be seen to
succeed, or to fail, independently of any 'high doctrine' that might
be hauled on stage to help support them.[7] That strategy is perhaps
best, if indeed it does enable us to see in particular cases that the
transcendental arguments in fact succeed.

But most of the time, no doubt feeling the pressure to provide
some account of the otherwise questionable linkage between
thought and the world, Strawson appealed to what he called a
general 'principle of significance' to the effect that there can be no
meaningful or legitimate employment of concepts which does not
relate them to empirically ascertainable conditions of their application.[8] That principle, which he found essential to Kant's programme in any case, would be enough in itself to secure at least the
empirical knowability of whatever non-psychological propositions
about the world could be shown must be intelligible to us if we are
to have any meaningful thoughts or experiences of an independent
world at all.

That would be a way of establishing something Kant sought: the
transcendental invulnerability of those truths and hence those ways
of thinking from any completely general sceptical attack. And it
would apparently do so without transcendental, or any other kind
of, idealism. But the 'principle of significance' which would achieve

---

[6] See ibid., e.g. 38–40, 53–4.   [7] Strawson, *The Bounds of Sense*, 44.
[8] Ibid. 16–18 and elsewhere.

that happy result does not stand on its own in Kant. It appears to
get its support, such as it is, from the dreaded doctrines of transcendental idealism. Strawson tries to free it from that support,
both in Kant and for his own use. But then it stands out as a so-far
unsupported and controversial thesis about meaning in general.
And even if some such 'principle of significance' turned out to be
acceptable, a blanket appeal to it would leave us with no special
core of fundamental truths which are uniquely invulnerable
because of their central position in our thought. A completely
general thesis linking meaning and empirical ascertainability would
mean the end of all forms of epistemic scepticism. Everything we
could intelligibly think would be knowable as true, or as false; if it
were not, it would mean nothing. There would be no need then to
explore the presuppositions of thinking in certain ways, or to trace
interconnections among various aspects of our thought, in order to
identify a special core of privileged and so invulnerable truths. All
propositions would be equally immune from sceptical attack, and
for the same simple reason.

But if we do not help ourselves to a general 'principle of significance' from the outset, an attempt to pursue something like the
general Kantian project would still seem to require a truly remarkable bridge of necessity leading from premises about our ways of
thinking to conclusions about the way things are. If we let the particular arguments speak for themselves at this point, and judge
them on their merits as they stand, a certain general (dare I say
'sceptical'?) pattern of response immediately suggests itself.

Without questioning the demonstrated connections *within* our
thought, we might agree that thought of an independent world, for
example, ultimately requires that we possess an elaborate conception of particular objects which endure and are reidentifiable in a
single spatio-temporal system. That is still only about how we do,
or must think. But why, we will ask, does our possession of such a
conception, our *thinking* of and *believing* in such objects, also
require that there actually *be* such objects, or even that we can
know or have good reason to think that there are? We know why
Kant thought there had to be. But if we do not go in for transcendental idealism, why would the existence or even the knowability
of such objects be derivable from our thinking in certain ways?
Would not the most that we can see to be necessarily connected

with our thinking in a certain way be only our having to *think* or *believe* that certain other things are true, and not the actual truth of those other things as well?[9]

That is a question and not, as it stands, an argument, and certainly nothing like a proof of impossibility. But to overcome this surely plausible (even if ultimately misguided) response, and to establish positive conclusions about the world without the use of a general 'principle of significance', something more would have to be added to the proffered derivations themselves. Whatever that extra something might be, it seems essential now to the positive task of making a place for a 'scientific', or decidable, or non-dogmatic metaphysical investigation that would reach beyond our thought and deliver conclusions about the non-psychological world.

On further reflection in recent years Strawson has drawn back from the hope of extracting positive metaphysical conclusions from the more austere form of Kantian or transcendental argument.[10] That is in part because he is now inclined to view the issue of scepticism as completely 'idle'[11]—not just practically but philosophically. The beliefs or attitudes it would question he sees as in fact inescapable for us; 'we simply cannot help accepting them';[12] they are an expression of a 'naturally implanted disposition'[13] which we are powerless to resist. Any fully general or philosophical sceptical doubt directed against them is therefore 'idle, unreal, a pretense', and resorting to argument or philosophical theory to render our fundamental beliefs invulnerable to such a sceptical attack would be equally 'idle'.[14] He now finds this form of what he calls 'naturalism' sufficient in itself as an antidote to the threat of philosophical scepticism. He is accordingly willing to concede that perhaps his earlier transcendental arguments did fall somewhat short of securing the full invulnerability of our beliefs which they had seemed to promise. But even if that is so, he thinks it doesn't matter; there was no real need for them to promise any such thing in the first place.[15]

Strawson's giving up on the project of wholesale validation or defence of fundamental beliefs in this way does not mean that he

---

[9] This was the challenge of my 'Transcendental Arguments', (ch. 2 above).

[10] See P. F. Strawson, *Skepticism and Naturalism: Some Varieties* (London, 1985), ch. 1.

[11] Ibid. 19.   [12] Ibid. 20.   [13] Ibid. 13.   [14] Ibid. 19.   [15] Ibid. 22.

has abandoned the broadly Kantian project of discovering what makes possible our thought and experience as it actually is. He finds that there is still good reason to investigate the major structural elements of our thought and experience of the world and to trace out the connections among its various parts and features. Typically, this will involve claims to the effect that one type of thought or conceptual capacity is a necessary condition of another, so that the second would not be possible without the first. Of course, that is not to say that such connections are easy to establish, or that one can always be certain that the connection is truly necessary. But the point now is that those connections, even if correctly and success-fully drawn, are drawn only *within* our thought. The investigation is to show only how one way of thinking is connected with another, and how our having one set of thoughts or beliefs about the world requires that we also have certain other thoughts and beliefs. It is to establish, in Strawson's words, 'a certain sort of interdependence of conceptual capacities and beliefs: e.g., . . . that in order for self-conscious thought and experience to be possible, we must take it, or *believe*, that we have knowledge of external physical objects or other minds'.[16] It is not necessarily to establish that there are such objects or minds. The conditions of thinking in certain ways are not to be proved to extend to what I am calling the non-psychological world beyond our thought. So it is no longer to be established by transcendental argument that there actually is a world of external physical objects or a world of embodied, thinking persons, or that we know that there is. The descriptive metaphysician can be content to follow the advice of E. M. Forster's motto: 'only connect'.[17] And the connections now are only *within* our thought.

It is because Strawson now finds no need to take seriously the general question of validation or justification of our beliefs that he is happy to concede that effective 'transcendental' argument might not reach beyond connections within our thought to try to estab-lish metaphysical conclusions about the world beyond it. He thinks that any sceptical 'challenge' would be 'idle' and so can safely be ignored; it does not need to be 'refuted'. This withdrawal from the positive metaphysical project, like Kant's own endorsement of it, seems still to be based on an assumption which Strawson shares with Kant. Both appear to assume that scepticism will be disarmed

[16] See P. F. Strawson, *Skepticism and Naturalism: Some Varieties* (London, 1985), 21. [17] Ibid. 22.

by argument alone only if it can be refuted, and the propositions which it would challenge are positively proved by transcendental means, and so put out of harm's way. Here again we can distinguish the same two questions. There is first the question of the security or invulnerability of certain fundamental ingredients of our thought against sceptical attack. And there is the further question of whether that security is to be established by arriving at positive metaphysical results—by proving the truth of the propositions our acceptance of which the sceptic would question. I said that Kant did not separate the two questions, and they appear to remain tied together in this response by Strawson. It is precisely because he now thinks scepticism and the issue of invulnerability is 'idle' that he is no longer concerned to prove positive metaphysical conclusions about the world.

I would like to suggest that by keeping the two questions separate we can agree with Strawson that Kantian transcendental argument alone, without unpalatable philosophical excesses, cannot take us as far as positive non-psychological conclusions as to how things are, but we can remain somewhat more optimistic than he seems to be on the admittedly elusive issue of security or invulnerability. Strawson finds the question 'idle' because he thinks that nothing could ever lead us to change our minds on such fundamental matters; there is simply no point in considering it. But there might be more of interest in the threat of a sceptical 'challenge' to our thought than simply whether it could ever get us to change our minds. As Kant himself suggested, scepticism might still be a benefactor of human reason or of human understanding in some other way, even if we know from the outset that it will never affect our actual beliefs directly. That, at any rate, is a possibility still worth exploring, even restricting ourselves now to our 'conceptual capacities and beliefs'[18] alone, and the (perhaps necessary) connections among them.

I would like to sketch in the barest outlines one way in which I think that might be possible.

What calls into question the validity of the last step of would-be transcendental arguments from the way we think to the way things are is the apparently simple logical observation that something's being so does not follow from its being thought or believed to be

---

[18] Ibid. 21.

so. Something's being so does not follow from everyone in the world's believing it to be so, from everyone's fully reasonably believing it, even from every reasonable person's being completely unable to avoid believing it. It might of course be overwhelmingly unlikely, perhaps even in some sense unthinkable, that we are all wrong about some simple and universally acknowledged matter of fact, but it cannot be said that our being right about it can be derived, of necessity, from nothing more than the fact that we all believe it. Our being wrong, given that we believe something, is not in that sense an impossibility. That we all think things are a certain way is one thing; that things are that way is another.

This thought alone does not amount to anything we could call scepticism about our knowledge of the way things are, or even in itself to any threat to that knowledge. But it is a thought from which scepticism, or a certain kind of challenge to knowledge, typically begins. The human possibility of error seems to be a constant challenge, or to be somehow generated into a constant challenge, to human knowledge. The most ambitious form of transcendental argument would wipe out the alleged challenge right at the beginning, by demonstrating of some of the things we believe that their truth is a necessary condition of our thinking and believing them. That would imply that the thought from which the putative challenge appears to begin is actually a contradiction; what it thinks is possible is not really a possibility after all. We simply could not have all those beliefs if they were in fact all false.

That seems to me too strong, or too quick. I think we must grant that there *is* such a possibility, at least in the sense that the truth of our beliefs does not follow simply from our having them. Given only that we believe them, it is still possible for them to be false. But even if the goal of transcendentally proving positive metaphysical truths from facts of thought and belief alone is therefore unreachable, as Strawson is now willing to concede, it seems to me that the more modest project that he calls 'connective analysis'[19] might still reveal a way in which no such potentially threatening challenge can even get going. If we carefully restrict ourselves to necessary links among our ways of thinking themselves, without venturing beyond 'a certain sort of interdependence of conceptual capacities and beliefs',[20] there might still be a way to uncover some-

---

[19] See P. F. Strawson, *Skepticism and Naturalism: Some Varieties* (London, 1985), 25.   [20] Ibid. 21.

thing we can recognize as a kind of invulnerability in our fundamental beliefs about the world—something that amounts to more
than the natural fact (if it is a fact) that nothing will ever lead us
to give them up. That is the suggestion I think is worth exploring.
I can describe it here only in the most general terms.

Any scrutiny of human knowledge will contain the thought that
human beings think or believe or experience certain things; the task
is then to gain a correct general understanding of how or whether
those thoughts and experiences are appropriately related to the
world they are about. That involves thinking of human beings as
having certain determinate beliefs and experiences. Suppose we
ask, in a Kantian spirit, how it is possible for us to think of ourselves in that way. That is a question that has not always been taken
seriously in philosophy, despite Kant's detailed demonstration of
how complicated it really is. Certainly before Kant, and even to a
surprising extent after his day, there has been a tendency to assume
that there really is no difficulty about this: that each of us somehow
simply recognizes in ourselves what thoughts or experiences we are
undergoing at any particular time, and that when we think of the
mental life of others we think of them as having the same sorts of
things as we know we have. That whole way of conceiving of mental
or psychological phenomena has of course come under attack from
several different directions in philosophy since Kant, but it seems
to me that it has still not disappeared completely. I do not have
time here to enter into its difficulties. I will take it for granted that
it does not work. When we abandon it, we are left with the task of
understanding something which must now be seen as a truly formidable achievement—our ability to think of a world as containing certain mental or psychological phenomena, and to ascribe
psychological attitudes and experiences of particular determinate
kinds to some of the things that populate the world.

That is a complex human achievement, and our being able to
think of human beings in those psychological ways can be expected
to have complex conditions of its own. In particular, there might be
expected to be many other ways in which we must think, or other
beliefs which we must have, in order to be able to think of human
beings as having the thoughts and beliefs about the world which
we understand them to have. Our thoughts about human beings are
after all only part (however interesting and important a part) of
everything we think and believe about the world. And the question
is whether, and in what ways, the several different parts of our

thought about the world are, or even must be, connected. Are there ways in which we must think about the world, ways in which we must believe things to be non-psychologically, or independently of us, in order for us to have the ability to attribute psychological states such as thoughts or beliefs or experiences with determinate contents to the people we believe to be in the world? That is a Kantian question. And it is a question which can be expected to have implications for epistemology, or the philosophical understanding of human knowledge. But as I have expressed it, it is a question only about how we think. Trying to answer it would not have to take us beyond what Strawson calls our 'conceptual capacities and beliefs'. To search for beliefs or ways of thinking which anyone must possess or engage in in order to think of human beings as the bearers of psychological states in the ways we do is to search for nothing more than interconnections or interdependences within our ways of thinking themselves.

The basic thought is still the Kantian thought that there are conditions of the attribution to human persons of thoughts, beliefs, and experiences with determinate contents. The particular suggestion I am making is that it is likely to require an understanding of the relations in which those people and those thoughts and experiences stand to the world the thoughts and experiences are about. And that in turn would require some knowledge, or at least some beliefs, on our part as to what that non-psychological world is like. We make sense of people as believing or experiencing certain things only to the extent to which what we think they believe or experience is something intelligible to us. And we must also see the people we understand as part of the wider world which we believe in; their psychology makes sense to us only in relation to that. So to understand people as believing things or as experiencing things we must be able to connect the psychological states we attribute to them with facts or happenings in the surrounding world that we take the beliefs and experiences to be about. If we ourselves had no beliefs about what is so in the world, and about what people are most likely to be interested in or paying attention to, we would be in no position to attribute any beliefs or experiences to anyone. We interpreters and ascribers of beliefs and other psychological states understand the world to contain persons with beliefs and experiences which have determinate contents only because we ourselves are engaged in and have beliefs about the same non-psychological world that we take their beliefs and experiences to be directed towards.

This seems to place limits on the amount and kind of error or falsehood we can understand our fellow-believers in the world to be involved in, or at least constraints on our way of understanding whatever false beliefs we think they have got. We need some reason, in what people say and do, for thinking that they have got certain beliefs and not others, and if we regard their beliefs in particular cases as false it must be because we have some explanation of how, given the way things are, they have come to get things wrong. That too of course requires beliefs on our part as to how things are. And it could be that disagreement in some cases or at one level reveals agreement on more general matters or at a higher level of abstraction.[21]

For example, suppose Strawson were right in his fundamental claim that anyone who thinks of a world independent of himself at all must think of it as containing enduring particular objects in a single spatio-temporal system. And suppose further that for any of us to think of people as having such beliefs about the world around them, we must ourselves also have beliefs to that effect. That highly general condition would still leave great latitude in our ascription of particular beliefs to people at particular times. We might find them wrong about where particular objects are on particular occasions, or even about whether there are certain kinds of things anywhere at all. We might find large groups of people wildly wrong about whole classes of objects which we know do not exist at all and never have. But that would not be to find them wrong in the more general, or more abstractly described, belief that there are enduring objects existing independently of us in a single spatio-temporal system.

If our thinking of the world as containing people with beliefs about that world were connected with our own thinking of the non-psychological world in those same ways, what could we then make

---

[21] The limits on the error or falsity which we can find in the beliefs of others are central to Donald Davidson's conception of the project of 'radical interpretation' and its consequences. See his 'Radical Interpretation' and 'On the Very Idea of a Conceptual Scheme' in his *Inquiries into Truth and Interpretation* (Oxford, 1984). The anti-sceptical consequences of the project are drawn out more explicitly in his 'A Coherence Theory of Truth and Knowledge' in E. Lepore (ed.), *Truth and Interpretation* (Oxford, 1986), and 'Three Varieties of Knowledge', in A. Phillips Griffiths (ed.), *A. J. Ayer: Memorial Essays*, (Cambridge, 1991).

of the alleged possibility that the world as it is independently of us simply might not even in general be the way we think it is? Could we find threatening the apparently sceptical possibility that, although we *believe* in a world of particular objects enduring in space and time, the world as it is independently of us might not be that way at all?

The thought in question would be the thought that, although we believe many things about a world independent of us and our experiences, perhaps none of those beliefs is true. I want to concede that there is a sense in which that is a possibility: the truth of our beliefs about an independent world does not follow from our having them. But the apparently threatening possibility is a possibility with two parts. It includes people believing that there is an independent world, and it includes the falsity of those beliefs— there being no such independent world. If we can make sense of there being people with beliefs in an independent world only because we also believe that there is an independent world, then our coming to think that the first half of the alleged possibility is realized would guarantee that we could not then think that the second half of it is realized. We could never consistently come to find that both halves of the apparently threatening possibility are actual.

In that respect the situation is structurally similar to what is expressed by the apparently paradoxical sentence 'I believe that it is raining, and it is not raining.' This is not something anyone is ever likely to say. One could not consistently put it forward as something one holds to be true. But that is not because what it says is something that simply could not possibly be true. It *is* possible for me to believe that it is raining when it is not raining; the falsity of the second conjunct does not follow from the truth of the first. The two conjuncts are perfectly consistent with each other.

I am suggesting that the apparently threatening sceptical possibility is analogous: it does not follow from our having a set of beliefs about the world that those beliefs are true; their falsity is consistent with our having them, just as the truth of what we believe is compatible with their not being believed. There is such a two-part possibility. But although the possibility of my believing that it is raining, and its not then raining, is also a possibility with two parts, it is not something that I could ever consistently discover to be so. If I discovered and so believed that the second conjunct was true (it is not raining), I could not then consistently believe that it is raining, so the first conjunct would then be false. And if I did believe that it is raining, and so the first conjunct were true, I could not then consistently believe that the second conjunct is true. There is a difference between something's being inconsistent or impossible (which my believing that it is raining, and its not raining, is not) and something's being impossible for me consistently to believe. It is impossible for me consistently to believe both that I believe that it is raining and that it is not raining.

In the case of our making sense of the apparently threatening sceptical possibility, the basic idea is that our fundamental 'conceptual capacities and beliefs' are linked; we cannot even see people as believers in an independent world of enduring objects without ourselves also believing in such an independent world. If that were so, then to think that the beliefs which we take people to have about the world are false even at that high level of generality we would have to think that there is no such independent world after all. To think that, or to try to think it, would be to abandon the belief in an independent world of enduring objects. And our having that very belief is (by hypothesis) a condition of our thinking that people believe that there is an independent world in the first place. The idea is that we could not attribute that general belief to them unless we believed it was true. It is only because we think that the second half of the apparently threatening possibility is not realized that we can think that the first half is. We could not find both halves to be true together.

If that were the position we were in with respect to our belief in an independent world, it would not be because there is simply no logical possibility of anyone's having beliefs about an independent world without those beliefs being true, but rather because our thinking that people have such beliefs requires that we ourselves believe in an independent world of enduring objects. A condition of our thinking of people's beliefs and other psychological phenomena in the ways we do is that our view of the non-psychological world they interact with is of a world characterized by the contents of those very beliefs, at least those of a high level of generality. So to abandon our belief that the world is that way would mean that we could no longer attribute a belief in an independent world to anyone. Now there is, perhaps, no necessity or inevitability in our attributing that belief to human beings. It is not that human beings simply must have such a belief, or set of beliefs. But if we were to abandon the thought that human beings do believe in an independent world of enduring objects, we could no longer have the apparently threatening possibility to contend with. We have to think that people believe *something* in order even to find intelligible the thought that perhaps those beliefs are not really true, let alone to be challenged or threatened by that possibility. Someone who does not think that human beings have any beliefs about the world at all is in no position to undertake a general scrutiny of human knowledge and belief about the world. So if we understand and accept the terms of the question about our beliefs in an independent world, we could never consistently discover that those beliefs, at the highest levels of generality, are not true.

This anti-sceptical strategy which I am sketching in such schematic form obviously raises many questions. I single out only two by way of conclusion. How close is it to Kant? And how reassuring would it be, even if 'connective analysis' worked as well as anyone could hope?

It is close to Kant in the kind of security it would reveal in some of our fundamental beliefs about the world. If there were things that we had to believe to be true in order to acknowledge that humans have those very beliefs and experiences which we attribute to them, then we could not discover that although we all believe the world to be those ways, it really is not as we believe it to be. A necessary connection between our thinking of ourselves as having those beliefs and our believing their contents to be true would mean that we could never find such a putative possibility to be realized. And that would certainly provide a certain kind of reassuring invulnerability with respect to those beliefs. Their status would be recognizably secure, but not because, as with Kant, it is necessarily true that the world is that way—that the world could not possibly have failed to contain particular enduring objects in space and time, for example. The security would also not derive from its being necessarily true that if we believe that the world is a certain way, in general, then the world is that way. The only necessity involved here would be the necessity with which one 'conceptual capacity' or way of thinking is connected with another. But if there are such connections between our believing in certain psychological phenomena such as beliefs and our thinking of the non-psychological world in certain ways, then the two could not be pulled apart completely in our thoughts and beliefs. We could not discover that those beliefs about the world which enjoy such a special status in our thought about the psychological states of beings in the world are not true.

Kant called his special metaphysical conclusions 'synthetic', not analytic: it is not a contradiction to say that not every event has a cause. But he described such propositions as 'necessary'. That is partly because he thought they were discoverable a priori, and he appears to have thought not only that necessity is a 'sure criterion'[22] of the a priori, but also that whatever is knowable a priori must be necessary. Otherwise, there would be no explanation of its being known a priori. What his 'deductions' of various principles certainly showed, if they were valid, is that we could not think that there is an independent world, or perhaps could not even think at all, unless we believed, for example, that every event has a cause. Having discovered that, one might naturally express the discovery by saying 'Every event *must* have a cause.' And agreeing with Hume that the causal principle is not analytic, one might then think one had discovered a way that the world simply had to be—it had to be such that the causal principle is true of it, in the sense that things could not have been otherwise.

That is the thought which seems to lead so easily to transcendental idealism. If it is necessarily true, and so knowable a priori, that the world is that way, the only explanation of that a priori knowledge of such a world would seem to be that the world of which it is true is the 'phenomenal' world—the world only as it is possible for us to experience it and know it. Its being as it is is 'constituted' by the possibility of our thinking of it and experiencing it in the ways we do. Of such a world it could be said that it is necessarily true that if we believe it to be a certain way, in general, then it is that way. There would be no other explanation of its having those necessary features which can be discovered a priori.

The development I am suggesting of Strawson's more austere Kantianism does not go that far. Without approaching transcendental idealism, I think we can still recognize what we might even call a certain transcendental invulnerability in any beliefs which we could see to be required for our thinking of people as having those very beliefs and experiences which we think they have. If we find

---

[22] *Critique of Pure Reason*, B4.

that our belief that there are enduring particular objects in space and time is one of those beliefs, for example, then we might say 'There *must* be such objects.' But the most we will have discovered is that we cannot hold that we have the beliefs and experiences we have without also holding that there are enduring objects in space and time. We will have found that the world cannot be thought to be one way without its also being thought to be another: it cannot be thought to contain beliefs about an independent world of enduring objects without also being thought to contain enduring objects. And there is, or ought to be, no invitation to transcendental or any other kind of idealism in that.

But that raises the second question: how reassuring would that alleged invulnerability be? There is no firm general answer; it is best approached piecemeal, with particular arguments before us to consider. But schematically, and in the abstract, we can see that in a fairly robust sense we could no longer take seriously the possibility that although we have all those beliefs and experiences, the world is not in fact the way we believe it to be. If entertaining that possibility is a first but necessary step on the way to producing a general challenge to our putative knowledge that the world is that way, then we could never find ourselves confronted with such a challenge because we could never find that possibility to be realized. Our regarding the beliefs as in general true is a condition of our finding that people have those beliefs. And perhaps that would be reassuring, at least with respect to the philosophical question.

But our being in a position to dismiss or ignore that possibility would not mean that by discovering some of the conditions of our thinking of ourselves as having certain determinate beliefs we had proved positively that we *do* know what we think we know about the world. We would not have demonstrated that the threat could not succeed because the world really is the way we take it to be, and that we know that it is. No such conclusion follows from the austere 'connective analysis' I am contemplating. And it will perhaps be found to be less than fully satisfying to have to admit that we still have not proved that we do know what we think we know. The most we would legitimately have established is that we cannot seriously entertain a certain thought from which a completely general scrutiny and hence a possibly threatening challenge to human knowledge might be thought to arise. There would so far be nothing on that horizon that even looks like a threat. But still, we might feel the need to ask, *do* we know the things we believe to be true about the world or not? Even if I could never consistently continue to believe both that I believe that it is raining, and that it is not raining, I still might want to answer the question 'Do I know that it is raining right now, or not?'

Now taken one way, the question whether we know something which we believe or think we know is a perfectly intelligible question. It is a question about the truth or reliability of our current beliefs, and the way to answer it is to examine or re-examine the facts or the credentials of those beliefs as best we can. For much of what we believe, the unexciting answer will turn out on further investigation to be 'Yes, we do know them, as far as we can tell so far.' We look out, or go out, into the rain, and then we know, and perhaps also know that we knew. Or if we find no rain, or no reason to believe that there is any, we realize we do not know, and we give up the belief that it is raining. But when the question is asked philosophically, with a completely general scrutiny of human knowledge in mind, it will admittedly remain unanswered by an exploration of connections among 'conceptual capacities' alone. If the most that it can establish is that we cannot suppose certain of our beliefs to be false while still holding to the idea that we have those very beliefs, it might be found tempting at that point to extend the challenge or the doubt to those psychological phenomena themselves. We might be brought to wonder whether we are even right in thinking that we have those very beliefs after all. Perhaps that thought is incoherent, but again it must be conceded that nothing about the interdependences among our conceptual capacities and beliefs can alone establish that we have those beliefs. And that can seem to open up an even more radical form of scepticism; maybe we do not even believe what we think we believe!

But as before, if that putative possibility is going to threaten us, we must be able to take it seriously in turn, and to do so we would have to see ourselves as not really having those beliefs. What would then become of the problem about human knowledge and belief? If we no longer think of ourselves or anyone else as having the beliefs and ways of thinking which we wanted to submit to philosophical scrutiny, what exactly would the alleged sceptical challenge be a challenge to? We would seem eventually to be left with nothing to talk about, and nothing to say. Perhaps we would then have reached a point in philosophy at which, as Wittgenstein put it, 'one would like just to emit an inarticulate sound'.[23]

---

[23] L. Wittgenstein, *Philosophical Investigations*, tr. G. E. M. Anscombe (Oxford, 1953), §261.

12

Radical Interpretation and Philosophical Scepticism

I

There is a very general philosophical question which asks how, on the basis of what human beings get through the senses, they can ever have good reason to accept the beliefs, hypotheses, and theories they hold about the world. What is in question are the credentials or the degree of well-foundedness of what is taken to be a fully formed conception of the world and our place in it, as embodied in everything we believe. To show how (or which of) those beliefs amount to knowledge, or to beliefs we have good reason to hold, would be to explain, philosophically, how knowledge of the world is possible. If there are no such reasons, or our best reasons are inadequate, scepticism is the right answer; we do not know what we think we know.

Donald Davidson regards this philosophical question as misguided. He thinks that if we understood better how we could even be in a position to ask it, we would see that it can present no threat of general scepticism. In this respect, his approach is akin to that of Kant. Kant thought an understanding of the possibility of thought and experience in general was essential to, perhaps sufficient for, an understanding of the possibility of knowledge. This idea too is present in Davidson.

Kant found that what had been seen as potential obstacles to our knowledge of the world were demonstrably illusory and so posed no real threat. They rested on the assumption that each person can know what experiences, thoughts, and beliefs he has while leaving open the question of whether he has reason to believe

Reprinted by permission from *The Philosophy of Donald Davidson*, ed. Lewis E. Hahn (LaSalle, Ill., 1999: Open Court Publishing Company), copyright © 1999 by the Library of Living Philosophers.

anything about the world around him. But experience and knowledge of things in the independent world was for Kant a condition of making sense of oneself as having any experiences, thoughts, and beliefs at all. Davidson too argues against the alleged priority of knowledge of one's experiences or the contents of one's own mind over knowledge of the 'external' world. By reflection on what we must know in order even to understand the question from which traditional 'empiricist' epistemology appears to begin, he concludes that there can be no genuine barriers to knowledge of the world.

This seems to me by far the most fruitful and most promising general strategy for getting to the bottom of the appeal and frustration of philosophical scepticism. The distinctive Kantian concern with the sources of the very idea of an objective world promised real progress. But Kant's own treatment of objectivity ended up with something that looks like a typically philosophical theory of knowledge after all. Not content with securing the invulnerability of our knowledge against sceptical attack, he argued positively that our having a conception of a world and of ourselves as potential knowers of it is enough in itself to guarantee that the world must be in general just as we believe it to be. This too is a line of argument Davidson appears to pursue. Kant thought it was something he could prove, and the proofs were to proceed a priori, independently of all experience. He then felt the understandable need to explain how such a priori knowledge of the world is possible. It turned out that the only explanation was 'transcendental idealism'; we can have a priori knowledge of the world only because the world we know in that way is in some sense 'constituted' by the possibility of our knowing it. 'Idealism' had to be true if there was to be a satisfactory explanation of how human knowledge of the world is possible.

Davidson's exposure of the ineffectiveness of philosophical scepticism is in a very broad sense Kantian. The outcome, if correctly reached, would be philosophically reassuring. I want to ask how far he goes, or how far must he go, in a Kantian direction for his anti-sceptical strategy to succeed. What exactly can be established along Davidson's lines about the invulnerability of our knowledge of the world? And is there an idealist price to be paid for whatever invulnerability can be secured in that way?

II

I am primarily concerned with the status of Davidson's conclusion, and with its implications, so I will accept more or less without question the reasons he gives for it. His starting-point, like Kant's, is distinctive in bringing to the centre of philosophical attention the conditions of our having the very beliefs that constitute the subject-matter of the traditional epistemological assessment. Anyone who asks or wonders whether he has any reason to think that his beliefs are true must have some idea of what beliefs are. To have the concept of belief is to possess a certain capacity, including the capacity to ascribe beliefs to people under the appropriate conditions—to know when to assert things which in English can be rendered in sentences of the form '*a* believes that *p*'. That involves ascribing a belief with some determinate content; to believe is to believe *that* something or other is so. A sentence in the declarative or indicative mood which is intelligible to the ascriber must appear in the place of '*p*' in his sentences of the form '*a* believes that *p*'.

Davidson explores what is involved in ascribing beliefs with determinate contents, and what a person has to do, think, or know in order to have the concept of belief. From the conditions he identifies he derives the conclusion that 'belief is in its nature veridical'.[1] That is what is meant to block any threat of general scepticism and to erase any potentially troubling epistemological challenge. Whether that conclusion sustains those reassuring results depends on exactly what 'belief is in its nature veridical' means and how it is supported. 'Belief can be seen to be veridical', Davidson holds, 'by considering what determines the existence and contents of a belief.'[2] And that in turn can be seen by understanding the conditions of correct attribution of beliefs and other propositional attitudes. It is a matter of the successful 'interpretation' of one person by another.

Interpretation requires that the person to be interpreted do or produce something that can be treated as an utterance—something to be interpreted. The interpreter must recognize that the speaker takes a certain attitude to what he produces; he holds something

---

[1] 'A Coherence Theory of Truth and Knowledge', in D. Henrich (ed.), *Kant Oder Hege?* (Stuttgart, 1983), 432.　　[2] Ibid.

to be true, for instance, or he prefers something to be true rather than something else. If some such attitude is discoverable, the interpreter's easiest road into the thoughts of others is to start from those things which a speaker assents to, or holds true, or prefers true, on particular types of occasion but not always. Because what is so can be seen to change from occasion to occasion, and assent and dissent can be seen to change with it, the interpreter can ascertain the conditions under which sentences of that kind are assented to or held true, and the conditions under which they are not. He can then hazard hypotheses as to what causes the speaker to assent to or to dissent from the sentence in those circumstances. And that provides him with the meaning of that sentence.

Identifying the cause of a speaker's utterance or assent for the purposes of interpretation involves more than simply finding some cause or other. There will be many different causes in each case, all of which initiate causal chains leading up to the utterance. Some of those chains begin at different points inside the speaker's body; other longer chains start earlier and so contain those shorter chains as parts. Some even longer chains begin in prehistoric times; others begin later but still many years before the utterance. The interpreter must pick out one cause, and he does so by responding himself to something in the environment and so converging on a common cause both of his own response and of the utterance or assent of the speaker. By correlating the two he gives content to the speaker's utterance. He makes sense of what he recognizes as instances of the same kind of utterance on the part of the speaker by connecting them with what he recognizes as instances of the same kind of object or event in the world which he and the speaker are both interacting with. And his recognition of that recurrent aspect of the world is marked by an actual or potential utterance of his own. Davidson sums up the situation this way:

Without this sharing of reactions to common stimuli, thought and speech would have no particular content—that is, no content at all. It takes two points of view to give a location to the cause of a thought, and thus to define its content. We may think of it as a form of triangulation: each of two people is reacting differentially to sensory stimuli streaming in from a certain direction. If we project the incoming lines outward, their intersection is the common cause. If the two people now note each other's reactions ... each can correlate these observed reactions with his or her stimuli from the world. The common cause can now determine the contents of an utterance and a thought. The triangle which gives content to thought and speech is complete. But it takes two to triangulate. Two, or, of course, more.[3]

With the sentences directly correlated with certain kinds of stimuli handled in this way, those sentences that a speaker will continue to assent to through obvious changes in local circumstances can be understood through their connections with these basic 'occasion' sentences. One sentence is connected with others through their shared parts and their grammatical and logical relations. Beliefs and meanings of utterances with internal structure are ascribed to speakers only holistically, as part of a large body of beliefs or meanings.

III

One immediate consequence of these conditions of interpretation is that an interpreter cannot find speakers to have beliefs without himself having an opinion as to their general truth or falsity. In order to interpret, he must be able to notice that speakers hold certain sentences true, and, at least with respect to sentences directly correlated with current stimuli, he must be able to notice the occasions on which speakers do and those on which they do not have that attitude to those sentences. For that he himself needs beliefs about what is so on those occasions. He needs both beliefs about the world and beliefs about the beliefs of others. His having views about what beliefs speakers hold therefore could not leave open for him any serious question as to the truth-values of most of the beliefs he thinks they hold. Their holding the beliefs they do could not be in that sense 'epistemically prior' for him to the truth or falsity of those beliefs. But no one could have thoughts or beliefs of his own unless he were subject to interpretation by others with whom he is or could be in communication.[4] So even to have beliefs is to be capable of attributing beliefs to others, and so to have beliefs about what others believe as well as about what is so. The three kinds of belief are interdependent. Without any one of them,

---

[3] 'Three Varieties of Knowledge', in A. Phillips Griffiths (ed.), *A. J. Ayer: Memorial Essays* (London, 1991), 159–60.

[4] See e.g. 'Thought and Talk', in *Inquiries into Truth and Interpretation* (Oxford, 1984) 157; 'Three Varieties of Knowledge', 160.

one could not match others' beliefs with conditions in the world and so with beliefs of one's own, so one could not attribute to anyone beliefs with determinate content.

The 'triangulation' that Davidson sees as essential to thought therefore stands in the way of any line of thinking that would accord 'epistemic priority' to one's own thoughts or beliefs over truths about the world, or to truths about the observable world over truths about the contents of the minds of others. There can be 'no "barriers", logical or epistemic, between the three varieties of knowledge'.[5] But with no barriers or relations of priority between sets of beliefs of those different kinds no serious argument for epistemological scepticism in its traditional forms could get off the ground. That is why Davidson holds that 'if I am right that each of the three varieties of empirical knowledge is indispensable, scepticism of the senses and scepticism about other minds must be dismissed'.[6]

That negative result, if secured, would seem enough in itself to remove the threat of epistemological scepticism. But Davidson finds behind the persistent idea of levels of epistemic priority an unquestioned assumption which remains a standing invitation to the traditional epistemological question and so to its inevitably sceptical outcome. It is the assumption that 'the truth concerning what a person believes about the world is logically independent of the truth of those beliefs'.[7] If that were so, it would always seem to make sense to ask, of a given set of beliefs, whether any of them are true, and to entertain the possibility that all of them are false even though they are all held to be true. Davidson wants to show that the assumption is not correct; its acceptance is the source of the fatal epistemological step. He thinks that, given what beliefs are and how their contents are determined, the truth of everything we believe is not in general 'logically independent' of our having those very beliefs. It is in that sense that 'belief is in its nature veridical'. Of course, any particular belief may be false even though it is held to be true. But it does not follow that *all* our beliefs might be false. Not only does Davidson reject that inference as fallacious, he holds in addition that its conclusion is not true. 'Nor could it happen', he says, 'that all our beliefs about the world might be false.'[8]

The idea of the essential 'veridicality' of belief, or of the 'logical' dependence of beliefs upon their truth, is expressed at different times in different ways. They are probably not all equivalent. Nor

---

[5] 'Three Varieties of Knowledge', 161.   [6] Ibid. 156.   [7] Ibid. 154.
[8] 'Epistemology Externalized', *Dialectica* (1991), 193.

are they all fully satisfactory as they stand. To say that *most* of interpreted speakers' beliefs must be true would seem to require some
way of counting beliefs, which is not an encouraging prospect. To
say that falsity is attributable only 'against a background' or 'in a
setting' of largely shared or true belief[9] remains largely metaphor,
if it is not explained in terms of numbers of beliefs. To say that successful interpretation shows that there is 'a general presumption of
truth for the body of belief as a whole',[10] or that 'there is a legitimate presumption that any one of [a person's beliefs], if it coheres
with most of the rest, is true',[11] seems in a way too weak. It could
be said that anything that is believed has some presumption in its
favour, simply by being believed by someone. But presumptions
can be overturned, and to say that in interpretation *not all* of them
could be overturned, or that even after revision *most* of them must
be left standing, seems once again to revert to counting.

The differences among these formulations of the point do not
matter much for my purposes here. Nor does the precise scope of
possible falsity. We can still concentrate on the central idea that the
way the contents of beliefs are determined puts certain limits on
the extent of falsity that can be found in a coherent set of beliefs.
Even with the limits left vague we can still ask about the status
of this conclusion, and about the extent of its anti-sceptical
consequences.

IV

The first step towards determining what those consequences are is
to see that what is deduced from the conditions of interpretation
so far is a conclusion about what a successful interpreter will or
must find.

What should be clear is that if the account I have given of how belief and
meaning are related and understood by an interpreter [is correct], then
most of the sentences a speaker holds to be true . . . are true, at least in the
opinion of the interpreter.[12]

Nor, from the interpreter's point of view, is there any way he can discover
the speaker to be largely wrong about the world.[13]

---

[9] See e.g. 'The Method of Truth in Metaphysics', in *Inquiries into Truth and Interpretation*, 200.
[10] 'A Coherence Theory of Truth and Knowledge', 437.   [11] Ibid. 431.
[12] Ibid. 434.   [13] Ibid.

It is an artifact of the interpreter's correct interpretation of a person's speech and attitudes that there is a large degree of truth and consistency in the thought and speech of an agent. But this is truth and consistency by the interpreter's standards.[14]

From the interpreter's point of view, methodology enforces a general presumption of truth for the body of beliefs as a whole.[15]

To speak of 'the interpreter's point of view' or 'standards' or 'opinion' is presumably to speak of what the interpreter finds or believes. The method of interpretation 'enforces' on any successful interpreter the conclusion that his speakers' beliefs are largely true.

The point is worth stressing because Davidson sometimes seems to endorse what looks like a stronger conclusion. He holds that 'a correct understanding of the . . . propositional attitudes of a person leads to the conclusion that most of a person's beliefs must be true'. That is perhaps ambiguous as between a weaker and a stronger reading. But he also says that it simply could not happen 'that all our beliefs about the world might be false';[16] any view of the world shared by communicating speakers and interpreters 'must, in its large features, be true';[17] and 'it is impossible for all our beliefs to be false together'.[18] This appears to say more than something about what successful interpreters will or must find, or what those who recognize others as having beliefs about the world must inevitably believe. It seems to imply not only that those who understand one another must be in agreement as to what the world is like, but that the world must be in general the way any agreeing believers believe it to be. 'Belief is in its nature veridical' would then mean that *any* coherent and comprehensive set of beliefs must be largely true; their being largely true is implied by their being the beliefs that people hold. What is so could not possibly diverge in general from what is widely believed to be so.

That reading of 'belief is in its nature veridical' is most strongly suggested by what Davidson says when he applies his theory of interpretation directly to the threat of scepticism. It is perhaps most explicit in the conclusion he draws from the 'triangulation' that gives content to thought and speech.

---

[14] 'A Coherence Theory of Truth and Knowledge', 435.
[15] Ibid. 437.   [16] 'Epistemology Externalized', 193.
[17] 'The Method of Truth in Metaphysics', 199.
[18] 'A Coherence Theory of Truth and Knowledge', 438.

It should now be clear what ensures that our view of the world is, in its plainest features, largely correct. The reason is that the stimuli that cause our most basic verbal responses also determine what those verbal responses mean, and the content of the beliefs that accompany them. The nature of correct interpretation guarantees both that a large number of our simplest beliefs are true, and that the nature of those beliefs is known to others. Of course many beliefs are given content by their relations to further beliefs, or are caused by misleading sensations; any particular belief or set of beliefs about the world around us may be false. What cannot be the case is that our general picture of the world and our place in it is mistaken, for it is this picture which informs the rest of our beliefs, whether they be true or false, and makes them intelligible.[19]

There is a way of taking what Davidson says here in which it does not really endorse what I am calling the stronger reading. The important fact about belief to which he draws attention is something that 'we can be led to recognize by taking up ... the interpreter's point of view'.[20] And it could well be that in drawing the conclusion he does he is simply announcing what he finds (and anyone would find) on taking up an interpreter's point of view with respect to his fellow human beings. If he is right about the conditions of interpretation, no interpreter will be in a position to find all or most of the beliefs he ascribes to people false. So Donald Davidson in particular will find himself in that position as an interpreter, and can announce his results accordingly. That could be what he is doing when he says 'our view' or 'our general picture of the world' cannot be false. After carrying out or imagining an interpretation of a group of speakers it would be perfectly understandable to report one's discovery by saying 'most of their beliefs are true', or even 'most of their beliefs must be true' or 'it is impossible for most of their beliefs to be false'. Given that one has ascribed a set of beliefs to those speakers, that would be a way of expressing the fact that one's finding most or all of those attributed beliefs to be false is inconsistent with one's having found the people in question to have those very beliefs.

That inconsistency is a consequence of the conditions of interpretation as described so far. It implies that 'belief is in its nature veridical' in the sense that belief-attribution is in its nature (largely) truth-ascribing: an interpreter must find the beliefs he ascribes to

---

[19] 'Three Varieties of Knowledge', 160.
[20] 'A Coherence Theory of Truth and Knowledge', 435.

be largely true. But that is not what I am calling the stronger reading of that thesis. The admitted necessity of finding largely true beliefs among the beliefs one attributes does not imply that the beliefs one attributes are in fact largely true. What a successful interpreter concludes ('Most of their beliefs are true') is a conclusion anyone must draw about his fellow human beings after having taken up the interpreter's point of view towards them. But it does not follow that 'Most of their beliefs are true' states a necessary condition of successful interpretation or of human beings' having any beliefs at all.

When he seems to be asserting the stronger claim Davidson does not always appear to be drawing a conclusion from his having interpreted his fellow human beings as they actually are. He says that the truth of a large number of our beliefs is 'guaranteed' by 'the nature of correct interpretation'.[21] That is true if 'correct interpretation' is interpretation carried out by interpreters whose beliefs about the world are all or mostly true. The truth of the beliefs they attribute is 'guaranteed' by the conjunction of the weaker thesis that belief-attribution is in its nature (largely) truth-ascribing and the assumption that the beliefs of the interpreters are largely true. *If* an interpretation is 'correct' in that sense, the attributed beliefs must be largely true. But the stronger reading is the consequent of that conditional proposition, taken on its own. It says that any large and comprehensive set of beliefs must be largely true—that every interpretation of such a set of beliefs must be a 'correct' interpretation in the sense specified. That stronger thesis does not follow from the conditions of interpretation accepted so far. It would be true if being a 'correct' interpretation in the sense specified were itself a condition of being an interpretation. That is in effect what the stronger reading says. But that is not supported by what has been said so far about the nature or conditions of interpretation.

What we have so far seen to be 'guaranteed' or 'methodologically enforced' by the nature or conditions of interpretation is that if a successful interpreter believes that speakers believe that p, that speakers believe that q, that speakers believe that r, and so on, then in general or in large part that interpreter will also believe that it is true that p, true that q, true that r, and so on. He and the speakers he interprets will be largely in agreement. But that what he and

---

[21] 'Three Varieties of Knowledge', 160.

those speakers all agree about *is* in fact in general true is a further step beyond the fulfilment of that admitted condition. Of course, the interpreter will *regard* everything they all agree about as true, just as the other speakers will. But that is not something that the nature of interpretation is needed to guarantee. Any believer regards as true whatever he fully believes. But from that it does not follow that what many believers agree about is all or mostly true.

The truth of most or all of what believers believe does of course follow from *what* a successful interpreter of those believers believes. In interpreting them, he comes to believe that they believe that p, that they believe that q, that they believe that r, and so on, and (in the case of complete agreement) he himself also believes that p, that q, that r, and so on. So from everything he believes it follows that those speakers' beliefs are true. But again the nature of interpretation is not needed to secure that conclusion. It is guaranteed by the fact that any statement of what a person believes, together with the statement that he believes it, implies that the person's belief is true. An interpreter believes:

1. They believe that p, they believe that q, they believe that r.
2. p and q and r.

It follows from (1) and (2) that those speakers have true beliefs. But that implication neither supports nor relies on the idea that 'belief is in its nature veridical' in the stronger sense. It holds whether or not the beliefs in question are in fact true.

V

Perhaps the clearest indication that Davidson endorses the stronger reading is that he explicitly takes up the issue of why it could not happen that speaker and interpreter understand one another on the basis of 'shared but erroneous beliefs'. He argues that that 'cannot be the rule';[22] 'massive error about the world is simply unintelligible';[23] the beliefs in question must be largely true beliefs. The argument invokes the idea of an interpreter who is 'omniscient about the world, and about what does and would cause a speaker to assent to any sentence in his (potentially unlimited)

---

[22] 'A Coherence Theory of Truth and Knowledge', 435.
[23] 'The Method of Truth in Metaphysics', 201.

repertoire'.[24] It is clear that such an interpreter, like any interpreter, would find the speakers he interprets to be largely correct. Since by hypothesis what that interpreter believes about the world is true, those speakers would in fact be correct in most of their beliefs. If the 'omnisicient' interpreter turned his attention to an ordinary, fallible interpreter at work among those speakers, he would find that interpreter also to be largely correct about the world. And by hypothesis he would be correct. But then that 'fallible' interpreter could not possibly be sharing with those he interprets a body of erroneous beliefs. His beliefs would not be largely erroneous; and those are the very beliefs he must share with those he interprets.

I do not see that this thought-experiment as described adds anything to what has already been accepted as a condition of interpretation: that belief-attribution is in its nature (largely) truth-ascribing. It is true that an interpreter who was right in everything he believed about the world would attribute to the speakers he interprets beliefs that are in fact true. But in imagining such an interpreter we are simply adding to the already accepted requirement that the interpreter himself must have beliefs about the world the further thought that in this case those beliefs are all true. And that is how each of us regards all our own beliefs, even without thinking of ourselves as omniscient. We each say of ourselves, as we can say of the imagined interpreter, that *if* our beliefs are all true, as we think they are, then anyone we interpret and understand will also have largely true beliefs.

If the 'omniscience' of the imagined interpreter meant that he simply *could not* get things wrong about the world, then of course we would be thinking of him in a way we do not think of ourselves. But omniscience in that sense seems to play no role in Davidson's story. He draws only on the fact that the 'omniscient' interpreter's beliefs about the world are all true. Of course, Davidson does not claim that there actually is such an interpreter; he holds only that if there were, all those he interpreted would also be right about the world. But that same conditional thought is a thought we have about ourselves, or about anyone, with no mention of omniscience. *If* a person's beliefs about the world are true, then given that belief-

[24] 'A Coherence Theory of Truth and Knowledge', 435.

attribution is largely truth-ascribing, anyone he interpreted would also have true beliefs about the world. Imagining an 'omniscient' interpreter adds nothing to that point.

Davidson once even seemed to suggest that the mere fact that 'there is nothing absurd in the idea of an omniscient interpreter' was enough to show that 'massive error about the world is simply unintelligible':

> for to suppose it intelligible is to suppose there could be an interpreter (the omnisicient one) who correctly interpreted someone else as being massively mistaken, and this we have shown to be impossible.[25]

I do not think the invocation of an omniscient interpreter establishes the conclusion here either. It is admittedly impossible for an interpreter to interpret speakers as massively mistaken. But to suppose it intelligible or possible for speakers to be massively mistaken is to suppose only that it is intelligible or possible in general for there to be speakers who have beliefs about the world around them that are all or largely false. To suppose that that is possible is not necessarily to suppose that one has carried out an interpretation on some speakers and found their beliefs to be largely false. If Davidson is right about the conditions of interpretation, that cannot be done. So in acknowledging the mere possibility of massive falsity of some speakers' beliefs one need not be in a position to say what any of those speakers' beliefs are. But that alone does not rule out the abstract possibility. Nor is granting that there *could* be an interpreter who is omniscient about the world incompatible with there being speakers with largely false beliefs. What is ruled out is an omniscient interpreter's having interpreted those speakers and identified their beliefs as all or mostly false. But that is ruled out by the supposition that one has interpreted those speakers oneself, or that anyone has. No one could have done so while finding those identified beliefs to be mostly false, if Davidson is right. But that does not show that the thought of there being a set of beliefs that are all or mostly false is itself an impossibility or a contradiction.

One conclusion Davidson draws from his speculation about an 'omniscient' interpreter does seem to me warranted, taken strictly as he expresses it.

[25] 'The Method of Truth in Metaphysics', 201.

Once we agree to the general method of interpretation I have sketched, it becomes impossible correctly to hold that anyone could be mostly wrong about how things are.[26]

If belief-attribution is in its nature (largely) truth-ascribing, then no one who carries out an interpretation could correctly hold both that the speakers he has interpreted have such-and-such beliefs, and that those beliefs are all or mostly wrong. The conditions of interpretation, if Davidson is right about them, rule that out. That is to say, the verdict 'Those speakers believe that p, believe that q, believe that r, and so on, and all or most of those beliefs are false' is not something that a successful interpreter could consistently believe about a set of attributed beliefs. Ascribing beliefs to people is not consistent with ascribing falsehood to all or most of them. But that is not to say that that impossible-to-reach verdict states something which could not possibly be true. That is what is implied by 'belief is in its nature veridical' on the stronger reading: no body of beliefs could be all or mostly false. I do not think that stronger conclusion is implied by anything Davidson says about an omniscient interpreter. And the weaker conclusion about belief-attribution is validly drawn from the conditions of ordinary or 'fallible' interpretation, with no reliance on omniscience at all.

VI

If the stronger thesis is to be guaranteed by 'the nature of correct interpretation' alone, then, it must be drawn from some conditions of interpretation beyond those described so far. We have seen so far that an interpreter must have beliefs about the world, and that those beliefs will in large part agree with the beliefs he attributes to those he interprets. That is because of the importance of causality. Davidson says we cannot:

in general fix what someone means independently of what he believes and independently of what caused the belief. . . . we can't in general first identify beliefs and meanings and then ask what caused them. The causality plays an indispensable role in determining the content of what we say and believe.[27]

----

[26] 'A Coherence Theory of Truth and Knowledge', 435.   [27] Ibid.

He sometimes describes that role by saying that, at least for simple occasion sentences, 'the stimuli that cause our most basic verbal responses also determine what those responses mean, and the contents of the beliefs that accompany them'.[28] This in turn is meant to carry the implication that whatever any group of speakers' beliefs happen to be, they simply have to be largely true:

as long as we adhere to the basic intuition that in the simplest cases words and thoughts refer to what causes them, it is clear that it cannot happen that most of our plainest beliefs about what exists in the world are false.[29]

The beliefs in question cannot be false because, if they were, they would not have been held; what in fact caused those beliefs would not have been so. And if it had not been so, it could not have caused them.

If anything is systematically causing certain experiences (or verbal responses), that is what the thoughts and utterances are about. This rules out systematic error.[30]

This description of the role of causality seems to say that it is not the responses of an interpreter that determine the meaning of a speaker's utterance and so the content of his belief, but that, at least for a sentence directly correlated with current stimuli, it means whatever in fact causes it. This must be understood in the light of Davidson's insistence that communication and mutual understanding among speakers are necessary for meaning and thought. What an utterance means cannot be identified simply as *the* cause of the utterance. For one thing, there are too many available causes, all along an indefinitely extended causal chain. Since there must be convergence on a common cause between two or more speakers, an utterance's meaning what it does involves both speaker's and interpreter's responses. For the indispensability of causality directly to support the stronger reading of the impossibility of massive falsity, then, there would have to be no possible difference between what in fact cause verbal responses and what an interpreter takes their causes to be. This is perhaps what Davidson is getting at in the sentence I have italicized here:

What stands in the way of global scepticism of the senses is, in my view, the fact that we must, in the plainest and methodologically most basic cases,

---

[28] 'Three Varieties of Knowledge', 160.
[29] 'Epistemology Externalized', 195.   [30] Ibid. 199.

take the objects of a belief to be the causes of that belief. *And what we, as interpreters, must take them to be is what they in fact are.* Communication begins where causes converge: your utterance means what mine does if belief in its truth is systematically caused by the same events and objects.[31]

It is not easy to find good reasons for holding that what an interpreter takes the cause and so the meaning of an utterance to be *must* be what is in fact the cause of that utterance. Davidson at one point appeals to the conditions of interpretation. If utterances mean what causes them, he says:

> it is clear that it cannot happen that most of our plainest beliefs about what exists in the world are false. The reason is that we do not first form concepts and then discover what they apply to; rather, in the basic cases the application determines the content of the concept. An interpreter who starts from scratch—who does not already understand the language of a speaker—cannot independently discover what an agent's beliefs are about, and then ask whether they are true. This is because the situations which normally cause a belief determine the conditions under which it is true.[32]

This appears to be an explanation of why utterances mean what causes them and so why 'it cannot happen that most of our plainest beliefs . . . are false'. It appeals to the fact that an interpreter cannot discover what an agent's beliefs are without also believing that they are largely true. But that admitted impossibility does not itself imply that most or any of the attributed beliefs are true. Nor is the truth of most of an agent's beliefs needed to explain why interpreters 'cannot independently discover what an agent's beliefs are about, and then ask whether they are true'. That is explained by the fact that interpreters attribute beliefs only by correlating the utterances they interpret with conditions which they believe to hold in the world they share with their speakers; they cannot discover what those speakers' beliefs are without also believing certain things to be the causes of those utterances. That interpreters must take the utterances to mean whatever in fact causes them, or that 'the situations which normally cause a belief determine the conditions under which it is true', does not follow from, nor is it needed to account for, that condition of interpretation.

This is not to deny the importance of causality in interpretation. Interpretation always takes place in some setting or other, and

---

[31] 'A Coherence Theory of Truth and Knowledge', 436.
[32] 'Epistemology Externalized', 195.

there must be utterances or something similar to be interpreted. Those utterances, like everything else that happens, will all be caused to happen, and they can be interpreted only by an interpreter's connecting them with the world they are responses to—with what causes them. But on Davidson's view it takes more than an utterance's simply being caused for it to mean something, and more than that for it to mean what caused it. Everything that happens is caused, but not everything that happens means something, or means what caused it. Meaning and thought for Davidson require communication, and the 'triangulation' he sees as essential to communication shows that the identification of meanings and thoughts 'rests . . . on a social basis'.[33]

This means that there is meaning and the expression of belief only where there is communication, not simply wherever there is causation of utterance. And there is communication only where there is expression of thought and belief, not mere utterance. If A hears B utter the sound 'Gavagai' in all and only those situations in which A would be caused to utter 'Rabbit', that alone does not give A an interpretation of B's 'Gavagai'. Even if what causes B's utterance is that there is a rabbit in the vicinity, and that too is what causes A to utter 'Rabbit', that still does not give A an interpretation of B's utterance. As described so far, it could just be parallel behaviour, like two people caused to sneeze by all and only the same things. To reach an interpretation, A must believe on the appropriate occasions that there is a rabbit in the vicinity, and he must know that he himself is or would be expressing that belief in intentionally uttering 'Rabbit'. Noticing what is so when B intentionally utters 'Gavagai', he could then see that B makes that utterance because there is a rabbit in the vicinity, and so he could conclude that that is what B means by it. That is what it takes for B to be expressing the belief that there is a rabbit in the vicinity in making that utterance on that occasion.

What then does it take for A to have that belief, or to be expressing that belief in uttering his 'Rabbit', on that occasion? That is the same kind of question about A that A had about B. The answer is the same. A's simply being caused by the presence of a rabbit to utter 'Rabbit' does not imply that he means by it that there is a rabbit in the vicinity, or that he or it means anything at all. The question cannot be settled by considering only the single speaker A. 'It takes two points of view to give location to the cause of a thought, and thus to define its content.'[34] But 'points of view' in the sense required here are not to be understood merely as spatial and causal positions in the world. Two sneezers occupy different 'points of view' on the common cause of their sneezing in that sense. 'Points of view' relevant to meaning involve having perceptions and thoughts and beliefs. On Davidson's view thoughts with propositional content are present only if there is communication or reciprocal interpretation. At work in all such interpretation are beliefs on the part of an interpreter about the utterances of others, beliefs about their causes, and beliefs about his own beliefs. And since an interpreter has beliefs at all only because he communicates with others and is interpreted by them in turn, those others must have beliefs as well. It is what they all take to be the causes of their utterances that determines the interpretations they put upon those utterances and so what they mean. Causality is indispensable, but the notion of cause plays its role in interpretation within the scope of the psychological verbs expressing the propositional attitudes of interpreters and speakers. A interprets B by having beliefs about what causes B's utterances, and B does the same for A.

If A believes that an utterance by B is caused by the presence of a rabbit, and B believes that an utterance by A is caused by the presence of a rabbit, they could each attribute meaning to the other's utterance, and so ascribe to each other the belief that there is a rabbit in the vicinity. They could communicate with each other on that basis. That their utterances are in fact caused by the presence of a rabbit is not required in order for that communication to take place. That is to say, it does not follow from 'A believes that B's utterance is caused by the presence of a rabbit' and 'B believes that A's utterance is caused by the presence of a rabbit' that their utterances are caused by the presence of a rabbit. It does not follow from those two sentences that there is a common cause of A's and B's utterances at all, or even that each of their utterances singly is caused by something. Of course, we know that their utterances were in fact caused by something, given that everything that happens is caused by something. And in the example as described, we know that they had a common cause, the presence of a rabbit.

---

[34] 'Three Varieties of Knowledge', 159.

But that alone is not sufficient to determine that their utterances mean that there is a rabbit in the vicinity. Another common cause of their utterances is the birth of that rabbit and its subsequent meanderings through space until it appeared before them. But that is not what their utterances mean. Their *taking* the common cause to be the presence of a rabbit is required for their each meaning that there is a rabbit. And it is possible for them to take that to be so without its being so. The presence of a rabbit does not follow from their both believing that the presence of a rabbit is the common cause of their utterances. That is what I mean by saying that it is at least possible for what interpreter and speaker take to be the cause of an utterance not to be the actual cause of that utterance. I do not mean to suggest that that often or even ever happens, especially where a large number of utterances and beliefs are concerned. The point is only that the conditions of interpretation as Davidson describes them do not alone guarantee that what interpreters take the causes of utterances to be is what they in fact are.

If that were required for interpretation, it looks as if the stronger reading of 'belief is in its nature veridical' would then be a consequence of the nature of interpretation; beliefs attributed on the basis of interpreted utterances would have to be largely true. But if it is not a necessary condition of interpretation that the actual causes of utterances are what interpreters and speakers take their causes to be, as I think it is not, the guaranteed truth of attributed belief is not supported by the conditions of radical interpretation as described so far.

VII

Rather than explore further conditions or further possible support for what I am calling the stronger reading of 'belief is in its nature veridical', I want to conclude by explaining why I think Davidson need not, and I hope does not, accept that reading. I have said why I cannot see that it follows from his account of radical interpretation; nor is it needed to explain why the conditions of interpretation are what he says they are. What is more, I do not think it is needed to block the threat of philosophical scepticism in the highly promising way he has in mind; the weaker reading alone, and the conditions of interpretation as described so far, suffice. The stronger reading appears to involve the adoption of a standpoint on our knowledge of the world which many philosophers, including Kant, have certainly aspired to. One of the greatest merits of Davidson's position as I understand it is to show why there is no such standpoint.

Even the stronger reading according to which any reasonably comprehensive set of beliefs must be largely true would not refute philosophical scepticism in the sense of implying that what it says is false. Scepticism says that no one knows or has good reason to believe anything about the world, and 'belief is in its nature veridical' does not imply the negation of that. It does not imply that those who hold largely true beliefs thereby *know* those beliefs to be true or have good reason to hold them. Not all true beliefs constitute knowledge. Davidson himself makes this point.[35] The strategy he envisages would therefore 'serve to rescue us from a standard form of scepticism', but not by establishing its falsity.

A sceptical threat is generated in epistemology by a line of thinking which begins, innocently enough, with the uncontroversial thought that something's being so does not follow from its being believed to be so. The truth of something does not follow from everyone in the world's believing it, even fully reasonably believing it, or their being completely unable to avoid believing it. When all our knowledge, or all knowledge of a certain general kind, is then brought under scrutiny, there is a move to the more general thought that everything we believe, or everything of the kind in question, could be false consistently with our believing it.[36] This thought alone does not amount to scepticism. It is at most the logical point that there is a failure of implication from beliefs to truth, and so in that sense a possibility that the beliefs we hold are all or mostly false. The epistemological challenge that is eventually raised is to explain how we know that that possibility is not actual: how we know that our beliefs are in fact true. Various sceptical considerations are introduced at that point to show, in one way or another depending on the case, why the question cannot be given a satisfactory answer.

[35] 'A Coherence Theory of Truth and Knowledge', 438.
[36] There are exceptions to this when what is believed is itself something about believings or believers. For example, since 'There are beliefs' or 'Somebody believes something' must be true if anybody believes anything, they could not be believed (or disbelieved) without being true. Similarly for everything that follows from such propositions.

The stronger reading of 'belief is in its nature veridical' would block this line of thinking right at the beginning. On that reading it is *not* possible for all or most of a reasonably comprehensive set of beliefs to be false. So the thought from which the epistemological question is meant to arise would be a contradiction; what it says is possible would not really be a possibility at all. That would leave nothing intelligible that we could be pressed to show is not actual; we could never get as far as having to answer a question that sceptical considerations might show cannot be given a satisfactory answer. That really would eliminate any threat of philosophical scepticism from that quarter, but not by giving a reassuringly positive answer to the epistemological question. No such question would have been intelligibly raised.

I think this way with scepticism is too quick, and if it rests on the strong thesis that a set of all or mostly false beliefs is impossible, I think it is unsound. I think we must grant the abstract possibility of a set of beliefs' being all or mostly false in the minimal sense that the truth of all or most or even any of them does not follow simply from their being held.[37] To insist otherwise seems to me to threaten the objectivity of what we believe to be so. It would be to deny that, considered all together, the truth or falsity of the things we believe is independent of their being believed to be so. I think there are other good reasons for not accepting that stronger reading. But at the very least, if that thesis does not follow from Davidson's conditions of interpretation, as I have argued it does not, then this quick and decisive elimination of scepticism cannot be derived from the theory of interpretation alone.

What can be derived from the conditions of interpretation, if Davidson is right about them, is that belief-attribution is in its nature largely truth-ascribing. Anyone who believes people to have a specific set of determinate beliefs will take those beliefs to be largely true. An interpreter's verdict 'Those people believe that p, believe that q, believe that r, . . . and all or most of those beliefs are false' is not something that anyone could consistently believe about a specified set of attributed beliefs. That is weaker than saying that no comprehensive set of beliefs could possibly be all or mostly false, but I think it can still serve to block the potentially sceptical line of thinking right at the beginning.

---

[37] I exclude exceptions of the kind mentioned in n. 36.

An epistemological investigation of human knowledge is meant to examine the beliefs that human beings have actually got. The possibility from which the potentially threatening line of thinking begins is the possibility of our having all the beliefs we now have while they are all false. I think we must grant, as against the stronger reading, that there is a sense in which that is a possibility: the (for the most part) truth of our beliefs does not follow from our having them. But the possibility we grant has two parts. If we believe the first part—that we do have all the beliefs we now take ourselves to have—then we cannot consistently find the second part to be true—that those beliefs are all or mostly false. The conditions of belief-attribution require that the beliefs we find people to have are beliefs which we hold to be mostly true. If we found them all to be false, and so found the second half of the possibility to be true, we could not then consistently find the first part of that possibility to be true. We could no longer ascribe all those beliefs that we had originally ascribed. The possibility from which the sceptical line of thinking begins is therefore not one which anyone could consistently find to be actual. It involves the presence of certain specific beliefs, but attribution of those beliefs requires our finding them to be largely true. Believing a certain set of propositions to be all or mostly false precludes our assigning them as contents of the beliefs of any people we find to have beliefs.

An enquirer's relation to the apparently innocent possibility from which a sceptical threat is thought eventually to arise is therefore parallel to a speaker's relation to the possibility expressed in the paradoxical sentence 'I believe that it is raining, and it is not raining'. That is not something one could consistently believe or assert. But not because it is something that could not possibly be true. It is possible for a person to believe that it is raining when it is not raining. The first conjunct does not imply that the second is false; what the whole sentence says is in that sense a genuine possibility. But no one could consistently believe that that possibility is actual, that both conjuncts are true. If she believed the second conjunct—that it is not raining—she could not consistently believe that it is raining. If that first conjunct were true, and she did believe that it is raining, she could not then consistently believe that the second conjunct is true. There is a difference between something's being simply inconsistent or impossible (which someone's believing that it's raining, and its not raining, is not) and something's being impossible for anyone consistently to believe or discover.

If the apparently innocent possibility from which the epistemo-logical reasoning would begin is not a possibility anyone could consistently believe to be actual, it can be eliminated from serious consideration right at the beginning. There would be no need to insist on the stronger view that it is simply impossible for human beings to have a comprehensive set of beliefs that are all or mostly false. Even if the falsity of most or all of a set of beliefs is in general consistent with their being believed, the conditions of belief-attribution as Davidson describes them imply that there can be no potentially unanswerable epistemological challenge. For any specific set of beliefs we take ourselves to possess, the question 'Given that the truth of those things we believe does not follow simply from our believing them, how do we know that they are not all or for the most part false?' presents no serious general threat. Not because we could not possibly fail to be right in whatever set of beliefs we happened to have. And not because we could determine, in some way other than by acquiring beliefs, that our beliefs are for the most part true. There can be no general threat because our considering the specific attributed beliefs we are asking about guarantees that we find those beliefs to be for the most part true. Our having them and their being all or mostly false is not a possibility we could consistently believe to be actual, so it is not a possibility we could be pressed to explain how we know is not actual.

That is not to say that we therefore *know* that all or most of the things we believe are true. That would be the negation of scepticism, and it does not follow from this anti-sceptical strategy. The goal is only to block a familiar route to scepticism, not to show that scepticism is false. A certain possibility is to be removed from consideration as the source of a potentially unanswerable threat. That would leave us just where we were, or just where we are now, with respect to knowing the things we think we know about the world.

Scepticism is a negative verdict on a body of putative knowledge made in that sense from a position outside it; none of the very beliefs in question can be appealed to in making the assessment. The denial or negation of scepticism would accordingly be a positive verdict on that body of knowledge made from that same position outside it. It would share with the scepticism it opposes a common question and so a common standpoint from which the question is asked; they would differ only in the answers they give to that shared philosophical question. But that philosophical question does not seem to be what we answer when we straightforwardly conclude after careful consideration that most of the things we now believe are true, or even that we know that they are. That mundane answer is given from within whatever knowledge we take ourselves to have at the time.

The great importance of concentrating as Davidson does on the conditions of thought and so of belief-attribution is that it promises to reveal how and why we could never intelligibly get ourselves into the kind of disengaged position from which the general epistemological question can be raised with its special significance and force. If that is so, we could never get as far as facing the philosophical challenge, let alone trying to construct a non-sceptical answer to it. We can face a general challenge to our beliefs only if we take ourselves to have many beliefs. But we understand ourselves to have the beliefs we do only by for the most part endorsing them and so finding ourselves in a world in which they are largely true.

Kant's way of showing that no general epistemological challenge could arise resembled the stronger reading of 'belief is in its nature veridical' in claiming that any world we could even so much as think of must possess certain very general structural features. He thought he could identify those features; in those fundamental respects, the world must be just as we believe it to be. That is why no coherent line of thinking could possibly bring those central parts of our conception of the world into question. The success of that strategy depended on there being necessary connections between the world's being thought of in those ways and the world's being those ways; the truth or falsity of those general structural beliefs could not be 'logically independent' of their being held. And that was to be proved, as for Kant all necessities could be proved, only a priori.

One danger of all such proofs is their proving what turns out to be too much. It has turned out that some of the general features Kant thought he had proved to be present in any world that anyone can conceive of are not even present in this world. An opposite danger is not being able to reach the conclusions that the proofs purport to establish. From our thinking in certain ways it was to be deduced, by necessary steps, that things are that way. At the very least, some explanation is then needed of how such audacious conclusions could be reached. Kant had his explanation: a priori knowledge of the world is possible only because the world's being in general the way it is is dependent on the forms of human sensibility and thought. We can know a priori only that which is in some sense dependent on or 'in us'. That is a form of idealism, but since it is meant only to explain how any a priori knowledge is possible, it is 'transcendental' idealism. It is a thesis assertable only from a position in which we comprehend the world as a whole, and all of human thought and belief about it, and see why the two must in general correspond. Kant's way of showing that we can never achieve a disengaged position from which a sceptical verdict on our knowledge of the world might be reached was to show that human knowledge of the world is possible only because we can achieve a disengaged position from which we can see that idealism is true.

If 'belief is in its nature veridical' were true in its stronger reading, some comparable explanation would surely be needed of how and why such a remarkable thing must be true. If it followed from the conditions of belief-attribution alone, no further explanation would perhaps be needed, but I have argued that it does not follow. Any richer explanation would seem then to be answering a question which we could never get ourselves into a position to ask, if the conditions of belief-attribution are as Davidson describes them. That is why I think his strategy against philosophical scepticism precludes acceptance of the stronger thesis linking every comprehensive set of beliefs with the world's being in general as those beliefs say it is.

Davidson appears to repudiate the disengaged question to which the stronger thesis would be an answer when he writes:

Communication, and the knowledge of other minds that it presupposes, is the basis of our concept of objectivity, our recognition of a distinction between false and true belief. There is no going outside this standard to check whether we have things right, any more than we can check whether the platinum-iridium standard kept at the International Bureau of Weights and Standards in Sevres, France, weighs a kilogram. We can, of course, turn to a third party and a fourth to broaden and secure the interpersonal standard of the real, but this leads not to something intrinsically different, just to more of the same, though the augmentation may be welcome.[38]

If 'there is no going outside this standard to check whether we have things right', there is presumably no 'going outside' it even to assert that we have got things right, that our beliefs are for the most part true. We can of course assert the things we believe, and say

---

[38] 'Three Varieties of Knowledge', 164.

something to the effect that all or most of our beliefs are true. And if we have to we can even check to see whether they are. But what we say at the end of all that is a straightforward verdict on how our beliefs have measured up to what we now find to be the way things are. It involves or leads to nothing intrinsically different from what we had before, but just to more of, and perhaps to a welcome improvement of, what we already believed.

For Davidson the key to understanding ourselves as having thoughts and beliefs is to understand ourselves as part of a community of persons with thoughts and beliefs.

A community of minds is the basis of knowledge; it provides the measure of all things. It makes no sense to question the adequacy of this measure, or to seek a more ultimate standard.[39]

This seems to reject the possibility of what I have called a disengaged question about the truth or adequacy of our beliefs as a whole. If his account of the conditions of belief-attribution shows that it 'makes no sense' to question the general 'adequacy' of the 'measure' provided by our necessarily largely shared conception of what it so, it should equally 'make no sense' even to *assert* the 'adequacy' of that 'measure'. That is what the stronger reading of 'belief is in its nature veridical' would seem to do. It would be an attempt to assure us, quite independently of what our actual beliefs happen to be and how well they stand up to scrutiny, that we *must* be getting things for the most part right about the world. I think the conditions of radical interpretation support only the weaker but still powerful anti-sceptical conclusion that the question of whether our beliefs are all or for the most part true cannot be consistently asked with the possibility of reaching a negative answer. In that way it 'makes no sense' to ask the question. But we should not conclude that the answer to the question is therefore 'Yes'. The stronger reading sounds like a positive answer to that question. But it is a question that I think Davidson's theory of interpretation has the great promise of showing we could never be faced with.

[39] 'Three Varieties of Knowledge', 164.

13

The Goal of Transcendental Arguments

The earliest use of the phrase "transcendental argument" that I am familiar with is by J. L. Austin in a 1939 Joint Session symposium on 'Are There *A Priori* Concepts?'[1] As far as I know, Kant never used the corresponding German expression, although he spoke of many different things as 'transcendental', including 'transcendental philosophy'. I have not seen the expression "transcendental argument" used anywhere in the nineteenth century, or in the twentieth before Austin. I cannot say I have searched. Strawson used the phrase to describe what he was doing in the first half of his *Individuals* in 1959.[2] Other arguments apparently similar to his in form or purpose, but not explicitly called 'transcendental', were widely appealed to elsewhere at that time and since. As some philosophers began to ask how arguments of that kind work, and what exactly they can achieve, the term "transcendental argument" eventually became the name of what by now seems to be almost a distinct subject. Some academic job-seekers in America now list 'Transcendental Arguments' as one of their areas of 'specialization' or 'competence' in philosophy.

Austin was examining arguments meant to show that there are certain things called 'universals'. Not that he himself was trying to prove that there are such things, but others were. An argument was needed, since they are not the sorts of things we simply stumble across. In fact, Austin says, they are 'calculated into existence by a transcendental argument'.[3] It is assumed that we 'sense' things that are many and different on different occasions. It is assumed further that we call many of these different 'sensa' by the same

---

This essay was first published in Robert Stern (ed.), *Transcendental Arguments: Problems and Prospects* (Oxford, 2000).

[1] J. L. Austin, 'Are There *A Priori* Concepts?', in his *Philosophical Papers* (Oxford, 1961), 1–22. What I say here was true at the true of the conference at which this paper was first presented. My ignorance was quickly exposed by Christopher Hookway (about the nineteenth century) and David Bell (about Kant).

[2] P. F. Strawson, *Individuals: An Essay in Descriptive Metaphysics* (London, 1959).

[3] Austin, 'Are There *A Priori* Concepts?', 2.

single name, for example, 'This is grey', 'That is grey', and so on. And it is assumed finally that this practice is in some sense "justifiable" or indispensable. We then ask how such a practice is possible. The answer given is that since we use the same single name in each case, there must be some single identical thing there in each case of which the name is the name. Call that thing a 'universal'. Since what we 'sense on each occasion is different from what we 'sense' on any other occasion, that single and identical 'universal' is not something 'sensed'. So there are 'unsensed' 'universals'.

Austin says this is a 'transcendental argument', and 'in Kant's sense':[4] 'if there were not in existence something other than sensa, we should not be able to do what we *are* able to do (viz., name things).'[5] He does not say what he thinks being transcendental means, and he says he is not going to consider 'whether, in general, such a form of argument is permissible or fruitful'.[6] He says the argument is also transcendental in another (presumably non-Kantian) sense: in proving the existence of a class of entities different in kind from 'sensa'. The entities 'proved' to exist transcend anything available in sense experience, but we know they must be there because they are required for a practice we 'justifiably' or indispensably engage in.

It is not altogether clear exactly which argument Austin is referring to in calling it 'transcendental' in Kant's sense. The statement 'if there were not in existence something other than sensa, we should not be able to do what we *are* able to do (viz., name things)' can perhaps be seen as offering a truncated argument. It contains the conditional premiss that if there were not things other than sensa we would not be able to name things, and adds to it the factual premiss that we do or are able to name things, perhaps even that we 'justifiably' do. From those two premisses it follows that there are things other than sensa.

Now this two-premiss argument[7] is simply an instance of *modus tollens*: if *p* then *q*; not-*q*; therefore not-*p*. There is nothing special, and nothing problematic, about that form of argument. There is no interesting question whether, in general, such a form of argument is permissible or fruitful. The premisses imply the conclusion truth-functionally. I don't think this is what Austin has in mind in calling an argument 'transcendental' in Kant's sense.

---

[4] Austin, 'Are There *A Priori* Concepts?', 3 n.   [5] Ibid. 3.
[6] Ibid.   [7] If, to avoid complications, it is put into the indicative.

A better candidate is the argument used to establish the conditional premiss: whatever is supposed to show that if there were not
things other than sensa we would not be able to name things. The
argument Austin considers for that conclusion is pretty bad, as he
easily shows. In fact, he says, 'it is so artless that it is difficult to state
it plausibly'.[8] For one thing, just because the same word is used on
each occasion, why should it be assumed that the word denotes one
and the same thing each time? Why can't the same word denote
many different things? Maybe it cannot, if it is a name. But then
why think it is a name? So is it even true that in applying the
word "grey" to our different sensa we are naming something? It
becomes doubtful that we engage in the very practice that the existence of 'universals' is said to be required for. It looks as if a single
unsensed thing is not required for us to do what we in fact do.

Now to say that an argument is of a certain type or form, and it
is a very bad argument, is not necessarily to say that that is a very
bad type or form of argument. That will be so, perhaps, if an argument's being of a certain type is a matter simply of the logical form
of its constituent propositions and the relations among them. An
argument of the 'affirming the consequent' type, for instance, is a
bad argument because that is a bad (i.e. invalid) form or type of
argument. Premisses of the form 'If p then q' and 'q' do not imply
'p'. But an argument might be identified as being of a particular
type or form in some other way. Arguments for the existence of
God, for example, are identified as such in terms of their conclusions: what they are trying to prove. Arguments with only contingent premisses are identified as such in terms of the modal status
of what they start from. These are two different types of argument,
but one and the same particular argument might belong to both
types. It might be a bad argument for the existence of God, but it
would be silly to conclude that therefore there is something questionable or impermissible or unfruitful about arguments with only
contingent premisses.

The argument for 'universals' that Austin considers is a bad argument, and he calls it 'transcendental' in Kant's sense, but I think
what makes it transcendental is not its logical form or its subject-
matter, but its aim or goal. We might speak rather of a transcendental strategy or project, or a transcendental enterprise. This

---

[8] Austin, 'Are There *A Priori* Concepts?', 7.

brings it closer to Kant's 'transcendental philosophy'. Particular arguments put forward to achieve that goal, or advance or promote that project, might be good or bad, sound or unsound, or even of different logical forms, without losing the label "transcendental". What they are meant to do is what counts.

It is not distinctive of transcendental arguments as Austin understands them that what they are meant to do is to prove the existence of universals. That could not be their special feature as he sees it, since he argues that there is no such independently specifiable goal. He mentions another transcendental argument that is also supposed to establish something called 'universals' as things different from 'sensa'.[9] Again, the particular argument is found questionable, but it is said to be transcendental in attempting to prove something by showing that it is required as a solution to a problem: in this case, how is it possible for science to make true statements about reality, given that they are not statements about 'sensa'? That this is a different problem means that strictly speaking the two different arguments for something called 'universals' cannot even be known to prove the existence of the same kinds of thing. Austin shows that they are not in fact the same. As he points out, the word ' "universal" *means*, in each case, simply "the entity which this argument proves to exist" '.[10] Our only conception of such things, and our only access to them, is by means of the arguments by which they are 'calculated' into existence. So we do not have a prior conception of something which we then seek a special kind of argument to prove.

The arguments Austin considers try to prove that one thing is a necessary condition of another. But that alone cannot be what makes an argument transcendental, since every argument in which one thing is deduced from another proves that one thing is a necessary condition of another. That would make all valid deductions transcendental. More specifically, the arguments he considers try to prove that something is a necessary condition of our doing something we do, or justifiably or indispensably do. That gets closer to the transcendental, but it is still too general. We eat bananas and drive automobiles, for example, so there must be such things as bananas and automobiles. Is this a transcendental argument for the existence of such things? If so, we could transcendentally prove the

⁹ Austin, 'Are There *A Priori* Concepts?', 4–5.   ¹⁰ Ibid. 5.

existence of all those things that are required for all the practices we engage in.

Kant was concerned with the necessary conditions, not simply of our doing all the things we do, but in particular of our thinking or experiencing things—of there being 'objects' of our thoughts and perceptions, in the sense of our thinking something or perceiving something. The arguments for 'universals' that Austin considers appear to fall within this range; naming things, or classifying them, or making true statements about reality, are all ways of thinking or experiencing something. To show that something is required for thought or experience would be to show that it has a very special status. We could call it transcendental status. Bananas and automobiles, for all their desirable features, do not have it. If the arguments for universals worked, universals would have it, if thinking of different things as being of the same type, or making statements about reality, are essential to thought or experience.

Understanding what transcendental arguments are, or are meant to do, means understanding this special transcendental status, and seeing the point of trying to establish that certain things have it. For Kant the point was metaphysics. That traditional enterprise, which seeks answers to the questions that matter most to us, had so far been 'a merely random groping'[11] after knowledge beyond the limits of experience, and had produced only apparently endless and irresolvable disputes. Transcendental philosophy would put it once and for all on the secure path of a science, because of the special standing of any result that could be proved to be necessary for the possibility of thought or experience. The proofs of such results could accordingly be called 'transcendental' proofs or arguments, even though Kant does not actually call them that.

Any metaphysical conclusions proved to have that special status would have to be true if there were any thought or experience. Since we obviously do think and experience things, we can say they *must* be true, those conditions *must* hold. They could not fail to hold if we think at all, so they could not fail to hold if we think they do. They could not be false if they are thought to be true, and they could not be found to be false in experience. This puts those 'principles' in a very special position in our thought. Kant sometimes speaks of them as 'necessary', but strictly speaking they would not

[11] Kant, *Critique of Pure Reason*, tr. N. Kemp Smith (London, 1953), pp. 17, 21 (Bvii, xv).

have been proved to be necessarily true by having been proved to enjoy this special standing. It would not have been shown that those principles simply could not possibly be false. But any conditions under which they would be false would also be conditions under which thought or experience would be impossible. So they must be true if thought, or if anything is thought.

This is not to say that a statement expressing a necessary condition of the possibility of thought or experience could not even be thought to be false. Of course it could, if we did not know that it enjoyed that special standing. It is also possible for us to ask, or wonder, whether a certain thing is true, even though its truth is (unknown to us) a necessary condition of thought, and hence of our asking, or thinking, anything. This is a somewhat delicate point for Kant, since he thinks that in some sense we all know all these things a priori, even that we couldn't fail to. But that apparently does not put an end to all dispute and uncertainty about them. The promise of transcendental philosophy is that such doubts or questions can be resolved by discovering by reflection that the thing in question *is* a necessary condition of thought or experience. That would settle the metaphysical question. And that discovery could be made a priori, independently of experience.

It would not be just a matter of reflecting on the contents of the concepts involved in the judgement in question. That could yield knowledge of the truth only of analytic judgements. What is needed for synthetic judgements is a proof that the truth of the judgement is something without which thought or experience, or thought or experience of certain kinds, is not possible. If that could be achieved, and achieved a priori, then substantive, synthetic principles could be known a priori. That is what transcendental philosophy promises: an explanation of our knowledge of things in so far as that knowledge is possible independently of experience. That for Kant would be to explain how synthetic a priori knowledge is possible, and so how metaphysics as a science is possible, and how speculative and dogmatic metaphysics, which lands us only in scepticism, can be left behind for ever.

How much of this elaborate Kantian story must we accept or sympathize with in order to find something special and perhaps even especially promising in transcendental arguments? To insist on the full Kantian package as involved in any transcendental project would reduce the question of transcendental arguments to

the question of whether the Kantian philosophy as a whole is permissible or fruitful. Do we need to believe in the synthetic a priori,
for example, in order to think transcendental arguments are worth
pursuing? That would mean believing in a defensible notion of analytic judgements as well, since synthetic judgements are identifiable
as such only as non-analytic judgments, or vice versa. That is a lot
to ask. Do we have to be concerned to defend or preserve metaphysics, or perhaps even want to put it on the secure path of a
science? Do we even have to believe in a priori knowledge at all?
Maybe it is possible to describe goals or targets that certain arguments might serve, or a special status they might show certain
things to have, that would be transcendental in a recognizably
Kantian sense without their having to vindicate the whole *Critique
of Pure Reason*.

One thing that *has* seemed essential to the transcendental strategy is the deduction of substantive truths about the way the world
is from nothing more than the conditions of the possibility of
thought and experience of a world. I have questioned whether that
project can succeed, or at least whether the conditions required for
its success, if otherwise acceptable, would leave us with any distinctively transcendental enterprise at all. In raising those questions
in my 'Transcendental Arguments' paper of 1968,[12] I did not have
Kant specifically in mind—contrary to what many readers appear
to have supposed. Kant had transcendental idealism to explain how
a priori knowledge of general principles of the world around us is
possible. The world was in some sense to depend on the possibility
of thought and experience of it. Of course, transcendental idealism
has problems of its own—what it is, for a start—but I thought I
could see how transcendental arguments without it would be much
more problematic than transcendental arguments that presuppose
it or would be shown to be possible if it were true. What I would
question are the efforts of those who retain what looks like the
generally Kantian transcendental strategy while dropping the transcendental idealism that was supposed to explain how the whole
enterprise was possible and could yield positive results.

Put in the most schematic terms, what is problematic is that
the conclusions of the most ambitious transcendental arguments
without transcendental idealism are apparently meant to state how

---

[12] Ch. 2 above.

things are—that there are enduring objects, for example, or that events are related causally, or that there are persons with thoughts and feelings, and so on—and in a way that in itself says nothing about anyone's thinking or believing that things are those ways. But such conclusions about the world are to be reached transcendentally by a priori reflection on the conditions of our thinking and experiencing the things we do. That appears to mean that transcendental reflection starts from statements like 'We think or experience in such-and-such ways' or 'We believe that things are so-and-so', and proceeds by necessary steps to conclusions like 'Things are so-and-so'. We start with what we can call psychological premises—statements whose main verb is a psychological verb like "think" or "believe"—and somehow reach non-psychological conclusions which say simply how things are, not that people think things are a certain way.

That is what Kant sought: metaphysical conclusions about the independent world that we can know must be true if thought and experience are possible. If we could reach such conclusions, and they really were necessary for the possibility of thought and experience, or thought and experience of the kinds we engage in, then they would have the specially inviolable status I have mentioned. There would be no room for further metaphysical dispute. But the big question about transcendental arguments understood in this way is whether or how results of that kind can legitimately be reached from those starting-points.

There *are* psychological statements from the truth of which we can unproblematically deduce non-psychological things about the world. From the fact that we know certain things, for instance. From the fact that Mary knows that it is raining in Cleveland it follows that it is raining in Cleveland. "Knows" is a psychological verb, and there is nothing psychological about its raining in Cleveland. But if would-be transcendental reflection is allowed to start from the fact that we know certain things, there would be no need for further enquiry, and certainly no need for any special argument, to determine what the world is like. We could safely say that the world is the way we know it to be.

So the premises from which transcendental reflection begins must be psychological statements about our thoughts or beliefs, but they must be—or at least appear to be—weaker than statements that directly and obviously imply that things are a certain way in the world. But the conclusions of that reflection do have to be strong enough to assert or imply that things are a certain way, non-psychologically speaking. And those conclusions must be reachable from those weaker premises by necessity. Each step of the argument is supposed to express a necessary condition of the previous steps, and so a necessary condition of the truth of the premises. The conclusion will then be a veiled or hidden necessary condition of the truth of the premises after all—something brought to light by transcendental argument.

This is one way in which scepticism can be brought into the picture to help reveal the special character of transcendental arguments. A philosophical scepticism that denies that we know, or ever can know, certain things we think we know about the world, would agree that we do think of the world in certain ways, perhaps even that we cannot help thinking or believing it to be those ways. Without that, there would be nothing for scepticism to question. But it would question or deny, and would give reasons for denying, that we can ever know whether any of those beliefs are true. Transcendental arguments as we are now understanding them, if they worked, would completely overcome any such sceptical threat, and in a special way. To say that scepticism can be used to draw attention to the special character of transcendental arguments is not to say that the only point of going in for transcendental arguments is to refute scepticism, or to suggest that that is mainly what Kant was trying to do. But explaining exactly how philosophical scepticism would be refuted, or rendered in a sense impossible, by a transcendental argument, is one way of showing something distinctive about the transcendental project. The propositions that scepticism claims we can never know are to be shown to be necessary conditions of our having the very thoughts and beliefs we need in asking the epistemological question of whether we can know such things. A positive, reassuring answer to the question is shown to be built into our asking it, and so to be guaranteed.

This would be effective against various forms of scepticism because it would draw the truth of the things that have been put into doubt directly out of our having the thoughts we need to ask the potentially sceptical question whether we have any reason to believe them. Given that we have the beliefs in question, we could discover that they are true by reflection on the conditions of our having them. So we could show that they are known after all, or perhaps, as Kant would have it, that we have known them a priori all along. In any case, the sceptical charge that our ordinary empirical support for them is inadequate in some way, and the further challenge to show what additional empirical support we could possibly have for them, would be sidestepped. We would not need any more support for them than we have already.

So if transcendental arguments as we are now thinking of them were successful, various forms of scepticism would be completely disarmed. The intelligibility of the doubts they raise would guarantee that they can be reassuringly answered. It would be only because the things the sceptic purports to question our knowledge of are true that he can ask his questions with the meaning he gives to them. Strawson said of sceptical epistemological problems that 'their statement involves the pretended acceptance of a conceptual scheme and at the same time the silent repudiation of one of the conditions of its existence'.[13] It looks as if the repudiation is not always so silent. But it would be at best an attempted repudiation. The philosopher who claims to reject, or to question our knowledge of, what are in fact necessary conditions of our thinking in the ways he is trying to challenge, would not succeed in raising a challenge we need to, or even could, take seriously.

All this would be so on the assumption that transcendental arguments deduce the truth of certain conclusions about the world from our thinking or experiencing things in certain ways. That strong condition of success is what I continue to see as the stumbling-block for such ambitious transcendental arguments. Can we ever really reach such conclusions from such beginnings? One familiar danger is that of 'proving' what turns out to be too much. Some of the things Kant thought could be shown must be true of any world anyone could make sense of have turned out not even to be true of this world. So in one way, conclusions might be too easily or too quickly reached by means of transcendental reflection. But the opposite danger is surely more troubling: that of not being able to reach substantive, non-psychological truths from premises only about our thinking or experiencing things in certain ways.

I will not rehearse the reasons for pessimism about this. I think they are familiar by now. I want instead to explore the idea of weakening the requirements of something like transcendental argu-

---

[13] Strawson, *Individuals*, 106.

ments in various ways, or bringing the goal of arguments along those lines closer to something that might be achievable, and asking where that would leave us. Giving up the idea of establishing truths about the world by transcendental reflection on the conditions of thought and experience probably means giving up the highest Kantian hopes for metaphysics as a secure science beyond all controversy. But perhaps some forms of a broadly transcendental strategy can still be deployed with profit. There might turn out to be other valuable pay-offs of reflection on the conditions of thinking or experiencing things in certain ways. Some things might still be shown to have a certain special position in our thought about the world, or certain forms of philosophical scepticism might still be exposed or rendered ineffective in illuminating ways.

I can only sketch the outlines of one way in which this might be so. What I have in mind starts from the fact that our thinking of and experiencing the world in all the ways we do is obviously a rich and complex achievement. Reflecting on that achievement involves first of all acknowledging that we do think and experience things in those ways. Those are the 'premisses' from which transcendental reflection on the necessary conditions of our thinking in those ways begins. Accepting such premisses means ascribing those thoughts and experiences to human beings. We can then reflect in a broadly Kantian spirit on the conditions of our making such ascriptions—on what must be so, how we must be able to think, and what we must be able to do, in order to think of anyone as possessing such thoughts and experiences. That is the kind of reflection that I think promises to reveal a special role or position for certain thoughts or beliefs in our conception of the world, or a certain kind of philosophical invulnerabilty for some of them, even if it falls short of the full Kantian story, or even of the conclusions of the more ambitious post-Kantian transcendental arguments.[14]

To acknowledge that people think and experience the world in certain ways, the thoughts and experiences that we think of them

[14] This is what I suggest in 'Kantian Argument, Conceptual Capacities, and Invulnerability' (Ch. 11 above), partly in response to Strawson's apparent abandonment of the most ambitious form of transcendental argument. (See his *Skepticism and Naturalism: Some Varieties* (London, 1985). He now is inclined to concede that in reflection we can get no further than drawing connections *within* our thought, noting 'a certain sort of interdependence of conceptual capacities and beliefs' (21), without being able to reach as far as truths about the way things are.

as having must be intelligible to us. We ascribe to ourselves and others thoughts and beliefs we understand. In ascribing such thoughts, we must make sense not only of the contents of the thoughts and beliefs in question, but also of people's having them. We can do that, I believe, only because we connect the thinking of the thoughts or the holding of the beliefs with the world we take them to be about. The connection is not always direct, or one–one, and we must allow for the possibility of false belief, but it seems clear that we must have some basis in what is so for ascribing the kinds of thoughts and experiences that we do. For that we need beliefs about the world, as well as beliefs about what thoughts and beliefs people have. What we believe about the connection between them is what enables us to ascribe them to people. We understand ourselves and others only by placing them in a world we believe in and to some extent understand. Our beliefs in psychological facts therefore go hand in hand with our beliefs in non-psychological facts of the world around us. I think this is very important, and not always acknowledged.

Suppose, then, that there were certain general ways in which we must think of the world in order to have any thoughts or any conception of a world at all. Suppose, for example, that it had been proved or made plausible, as Strawson argued, that to think of a world independent of us at all we must think of it as containing enduring particular objects in a single space and time. I don't mean the strong conclusion that such particulars must exist in order for us to think of the world in that way; I mean only that we must believe they exist if we have any conception of a world at all. If even that were true, it would put the belief that there are enduring particulars in a special position in our thought. It would give it a certain distinctive status.

It would mean that any conception we could have of a world independent of us must be a conception of a world in which there are enduring particulars. We do conceive of the world we live in as being independent of us, so if we knew of that necessary connection, we could say that there *must* be enduring particulars in the world. That would not be to say that it is a necessary truth that there are such things. We would have to admit that there might not have been. There might have been nothing. Nor would it even be to say that there must be such things if we have a conception of an independent world. That is the stronger view that sees the *truth* of

'There are enduring particulars' as a necessary condition of our having a conception of an independent world—that, necessarily, if we think of an independent world, there are enduring particulars. It would take the more ambitious form of transcendental argument to establish something like that. This weaker version says only that, necessarily, if we think of an independent world, we think of it as containing enduring particulars. That is a connection solely within our thought: if we think in certain ways, we must think in certain other ways.

If we could not think of a world at all without thinking of it as containing enduring particulars, then we could not think of there being anything in the world without thinking that there are enduring particulars in it. So we could not think of there being people in the world without thinking that there are enduring particulars in the world. To think of those people as believing things, and in particular as believing that there are enduring particulars, we would therefore have to believe that there are enduring particulars. So we could not ascribe that belief to people without also thinking of that belief as true. It would be a belief we could not find to be false, consistent with finding that people hold it. So we could not consistently find that people are wrong in believing that there are enduring particulars. We could see that that is a belief in which they must be getting things right. Of course, it is a very general belief, and it is only at that very general level that we could see they must be right. There would be lots of room for error about particular objects on particular occasions, but if we could make sense of people as in general holding beliefs about objects continuing to exist in space and time, we would have to find those beliefs, in general, to be true. In fact, we could not consistently find them to be wrong about that if we thought they had any beliefs about or any conception of an independent world at all.

Of course I have said nothing about how easy or difficult it might be to prove such a thing, or even how a plausible argument for it might go. But however difficult it might be, it would not require what the more ambitious form of transcendental argument requires—that a non-psychological truth about the world be deduced as a necessary condition of our thinking of the world in a certain way. But even a weaker transcendental-like argument that established only a connection between different ways of thinking, and no direct connection between our thinking and the world, would still show the thoughts or beliefs in question to have a special status or position in our thought.

The beliefs in that case would have been shown to be indispensable, and that would carry with it what I will call a certain kind of invulnerabilty. They would be indispensable because no belief that must be present in any conception or any set of beliefs about an independent world could be abandoned consistently with our having a conception of the world at all. We would have to think of any world we could think about at all as being the way that indispensable belief says it is. That would mean that any such belief would also be invulnerable in the special sense that it could not be found to be false consistently with its being found to be held by people. No one could consistently reach the conclusion that although we all believe that things are as that belief says they are, the belief is false. Even the suggestion that that is at least a possibility could be dismissed as unthreatening. If our holding the belief to be true is a condition of our even finding that belief to be held by people, the possibility of its being held and being false is one we cannot take seriously as a threat to our current beliefs.

The indispensability of a certain thought or belief implies what I am calling invulnerability. A belief's being required in order to have any thoughts or beliefs about a world at all implies the impossibility of our finding that belief to be false if held. That is because the indispensability of a belief implies the impossibility of finding that belief to be false if any thoughts or beliefs are ascribed at all. But there appears to be no implication in the other direction, from invulnerability to indispensability. Even if there are no specific beliefs that are indispensable to thought of a world, our beliefs as a whole might still enjoy the kind of invulnerability I have in mind.

This is illustrated in one way by the closely related position of Donald Davidson who, from the conditions of belief-ascription, or what he calls 'radical interpretation', concludes that most of our beliefs must be true.[15] Any conception of the world we can recognize as being held by those whose thoughts and beliefs we can find intelligible is one we will largely agree with. Otherwise we could make no sense of what those people do. The idea of belief alone is

---

[15] See e.g. his 'The Method of Truth in Metaphysics' in his *Inquiries into Truth and Interpretation* (Oxford, 1984), 199; 'A Coherence Theory of Truth and Knowledge', in D. Henrich (ed.), *Kant Oder Hegel?* (Stuttgart, 1983), 438; 'Epistemology Externalized', *Dialectica* (1991), 193.

what is said to guarantee this reassuring result, without appeal to any specific core of indispensable beliefs. Davidson appears to hold the strong view that the *truth* of most of people's beliefs is guaranteed by the necessity of everyone's finding themselves largely sharing them with anyone they can interpret. That is a stronger version of invulnerability. It is something I think it would take the more ambitious form of transcendental argument to prove. But even on that stronger conception, invulnerability does not imply the indispensability of any specific beliefs. It does not imply that there are certain beliefs that must be present, and therefore must be true, if people have any conception of a world at all. It says only that any reasonably comprehensive conception of a world, whatever it might be, will be composed of beliefs that are largely or for the most part true.

The weaker and apparently more easily reachable version of invulnerability says only that we could not find most of people's beliefs to be false consistently with our finding them to have those beliefs. And that does not imply the indispensability of any particular beliefs either. Of course, it might seem implausible that there is *nothing* specific that anyone who believes in an independent world must believe in. But even if that implausible supposition were true, people's beliefs as a whole, whatever they might be, might still enjoy this special kind of invulnerability. It could still be true that whoever finds people to have any beliefs at all could not consistently find that the beliefs they have are largely or entirely false.

This kind of invulnerability, if there is such a thing, should not be expected to apply to particular beliefs held by individual persons on particular occasions, or even to fairly large sets of beliefs held by many people. It applies at best only to very large classes of beliefs, and to people whom we find intelligible only by finding ourselves in large-scale agreement with them. But those are just the kinds of beliefs that philosophical scepticism questions. It is not concerned to show only that Mary Smith does not know right now that it is raining in Cleveland although she believes that it is, or even that all those who believe that their fate is fixed by the stars at birth have no good reason for believing what they do. Philosophical scepticism is more general. It holds that, for all we know, all our beliefs about enduring objects in space and time might be false, for example, or that we all could be massively mistaken about virtually everything. If the set of beliefs we attribute to ourselves and others enjoys as a whole the kind of invulnerability I have identified, these allegedly sceptical possibilities can represent no threat to our beliefs. We could not find ourselves massively mistaken in the beliefs we can recognize ourselves as holding. Error of such cosmic scope is not something we could discover to be so consistently with continuing to ascribe and to think of ourselves as possessing the beliefs in question.

If there is a certain invulnerability against philosophical scepticism here, it does not amount to anything as strong as a denial of what scepticism says. Philosophical scepticism says that we do not know certain things that we think we know. To show that that is false would be to show that we do know those things. The kind of invulnerability I have in mind does not imply that we do know them. Showing that the things that scepticism questions our knowledge of must be true, because their truth is a necessary condition of our thinking in the ways we do, would be a way of showing that we know them, but invulnerability as I am thinking of it does not imply that either. Establishing that strong conclusion would require the more ambitious form of transcendental argument. But invulnerability is available without having to reach such ambitious conclusions.

It does not imply that we know the things in question, and it does not imply that they are true. It does not imply that the beliefs in question are indispensable to any conception of an independent world. It does not even say that the beliefs in question are invulnerable in the sense that we could never, or never reasonably, give them up. What it implies about invulnerable beliefs is that we could never see ourselves as holding the beliefs in question and being mistaken. We could not consistently find that human beings are simply under the misapprehension or the illusion that those things are true—that they think they are true, but that really they are not.

This might not seem like much reassurance in the face of a general scepticism. That remains to be seen. But it is none the less a special or distinctive feature that some of our beliefs might be shown to have. And it could be shown without having to resort to the more ambitious and so dubiously available form of transcendental argument. It also might be shown in some cases without having to show that the beliefs in question are indispensable for thought, or for thought of an independent world. Just how much, and what kind of, reassurance it could then offer against philo-sophical scepticism would depend on the particular form of scep-ticism at issue, on what kinds of beliefs it questions, and on exactly how it tries to bring them into doubt.

Between the two extremes mentioned so far—a fixed and deter-minate set of indispensable and therefore invulnerable beliefs on the one hand, and a completely holistic invulnerability of all beliefs in general, on the other—there is much middle ground. Within it lies the terrain on which transcendental arguments or transcen-dental strategies are now perhaps most actively explored in philo-sophy, although not always under that name. I mean in so-called 'externalist' theories of mental content. These are views to the effect that what kinds of thoughts or beliefs a person can have—what the contents or 'objects' of a person's propositional attitudes can be—is determined in part by what is so in the world the person interacts with and that his thoughts and beliefs are about. What the stuff that a person interacts with and refers to with the word "water" is actually like is what is said to determine what belief he is expressing when he says 'Water is wet' or 'Water is good to drink', for example.

Some philosophers conclude from such views that if someone believes that water is wet or is good to drink, then there must be such a thing as water in the world. The person could not have had just that belief unless that were so. Others have even tried to deploy this kind of theory more directly against philosophical scepticism by arguing on the same grounds that our not being brains in vats, for example, is a condition of our having the thoughts and beliefs about the world that we actually have, so we are not in fact brains in vats. These are both versions of the more ambitious form of tran-scendental argument. They purport to deduce the truth of some-thing non-psychological about the world from premises only about our having certain thoughts or beliefs. If they worked, they would secure the invulnerability of the beliefs in question by establishing their truth, and thereby our knowledge of them. Like Davidson's 'externalist' theory of belief in general, they would secure that invulnerability without proving that the specific beliefs in question are indispensable to any thought or any conception of a world at all. Water is not something that anyone who believed in any inde-pendent world at all would have to believe in, although of course we believe that there is a lot of it in our world. And although we are not brains in vats, perhaps not all those who could think of a world at all would have to believe that they are not brains in vats. Maybe brains that did exist in vats could have a conception of the stark, slimy, electrode-filled independent world they exist in, including true beliefs about themselves (although I doubt it).

One obvious difficulty with ambitious arguments from the contents of thoughts to conclusions about the world, even given a broadly 'externalist' theory, is that our thoughts about a particular substance like water might be composed of thoughts of other kinds of things, and based on a complex set of beliefs. They might then be perfectly intelligible thoughts about water even though many of those beliefs are false and there is in fact no such stuff as the water we believe in. That was true of phlogiston, and witches, and many other things that human beings have believed in. This worry drove philosophers in the past to search for some absolutely simple thoughts whose contents could not be made up from the contents of other thoughts, so if they had any intelligible content at all there must be some absolutely simple parts or aspects of the world which those who think those thoughts have sometimes been in direct contact with. Recent 'externalist' theorists of content, to their credit, do not on the whole seek that will-o'-the-wisp known as absolute simplicity. But their views continue to face the difficulty it was hoped could be avoided in that way. Even if our thoughts have content at all only because we are ultimately connected in some ways with something that is actually so in the world, how is it to be established that water in particular must exist if we have thoughts and beliefs about water?

Less ambitious arguments that draw connections only within our thought could still be said to represent a form of 'externalism' of content. They do not aspire to conclusions about what is so. They do not ask about the conditions of anyone's possessing certain thoughts and beliefs, but only about the conditions of our ascribing certain thoughts and beliefs to people as we do. The question is how we must think of the world, and whether we must think of the non-psychological world in certain ways, in order even to think of there being persons in the world with thoughts and beliefs with the determinate contents we think of them as having. We can ascribe to our fellow human beings intelligible thoughts and beliefs about phlogiston and witches, or ghosts and goblins, without having to suppose that there are any such things. We might do the same with thoughts of water if we had a way to explain how people form thoughts about water without anyone's having actually been in contact with any of the stuff they believe in. But if there are some thoughts, or some classes of beliefs, for which that does not seem possible, for which we must believe in things of the kind in question even to attribute thoughts and beliefs about things of that kind to people, then such beliefs might be shown to enjoy the kind of invulnerability I have in mind. And they would not have to be indispensable to any conception of an independent world at all in order to enjoy that status.

There is time to sketch only one possible instance. Take all our beliefs about the colours of objects in the world. Suppose that the contents of those beliefs—what we believe when we believe that an object is coloured—cannot be reduced to or equivalently expressed in exclusively non-colour terms. That seems plausible to me. Green, for example, might be understood as a mixture of blue and yellow, and other particular colours might be understood as combinations of other particular colours, but it is difficult to think that there are things or properties that are not colours at all that could be thought of as put together in a way that would give us the idea of colour in general. If that is so, colour is not definable or explainable in non-colour terms.

That suggests in turn that we must catch on to thought of colour, we must be able to think intelligibly about the colours of things, in order to think of others as thinking or believing things about the colours of objects. We could not find them to have beliefs about the colours of things in general—we could not ascribe to them beliefs with those contents—by explaining how they form those thoughts from other thoughts they have of things that are not colours, as we might do in the case of phlogiston or goblins. The irreducibility of beliefs of that type to beliefs of a completely different type would suggest that without some beliefs of our own of that type, we could make no sense of others having beliefs of that same type.

Again, I say nothing here about how one might go about establishing such a thing. It obviously would take a lot of argument. But the argument it would take, if any could be produced, would bear a distant but still perhaps sufficiently close relation to arguments called 'transcendental' to be worthy of the name. It would show that our beliefs about the colours of things in general enjoy the special kind of invulnerability I have mentioned. Anyone who could make sense of people as having any such beliefs would have some beliefs of his own about the colours of things. No one could consistently find people to have beliefs of that kind that are all false.

Of course, one might find widespread, even persistent, disagreement about the particular colours of certain objects. One might even conclude that there are no green things at all, for instance, even though almost everyone believes that there are. But if the argument succeeded, one could not consistently conclude that there are no coloured things at all, even though almost everyone believes that there are. One could not find that human beings are under a systematic and completely general illusion in supposing, as they do, that things are coloured. That outcome, if it could be reached, could provide a measure of reassurance against the otherwise apparently disturbing philosophical view that we all are in fact under such a cosmic illusion. Many philosophers appear to endorse some such view of the human condition. Perhaps "scepticism" is not exactly the right label for what they propound, but whatever you call it, the special invulnerability of our beliefs about the colours of things would imply that no one could consistently arrive at that view. It would not follow that objects in the world *are* coloured, or that we know that they are, but the possibility of our making sense of ourselves as being under such an illusion would have been eliminated.

If beliefs about the colours of things could be shown to be invulnerable in this way, it would not be because they are indispensable to any conception of an independent world that anyone could form. If all human beings had been blind from birth, but otherwise just like us in a world like ours, they might well have developed a rich conception of the world they live in, but without having any conception of the colours of things, or even any inkling that there is such a thing as colour. They might still have located themselves in the world, and moved about in it, and known a great deal about it. So if colour beliefs are invulnerable in this way, it is not because they are indispensable, but because they form a system of beliefs that as far as we can tell is *sui generis*, or irreducible, and so cannot be acquired by construction from materials that lie outside the system. Only for large classes of beliefs with these distinctive features does the prospect of less ambitious transcendental arguments for their special invulnerabilty seem promising. How many such large classes of belief there are, and how to establish the mildly reassuring result even for one of them, are questions for further research.

One other possible example is worth mentioning—evaluative beliefs or attitudes. If it is plausible that the evaluative contents of our moral and other normative beliefs cannot in general be reduced to and so explained in terms of purely non-evaluative states of affairs, then perhaps morality, or evaluation generally, could be shown to be invulnerable in this special way. It would not mean that we all agree about the values of things, or that we must be right in the evaluations we do largely agree about. But it would mean that we could not consistently find the whole idea of the evaluative in general to be illusory. We could not find ourselves to be completely wrong about the idea that some things do have value, or that some things are better than others, while we continue to think as we do. Even that outcome could provide some reassurance in the face of radical philosophical attack on value. The large and persistent disagreements that continue among us would still be disagreements about what value, if any, particular things or courses of action actually have. We would not be disagreeing about whether anything whatever could have any value at all, even though we all think it does. That is what many philosophers have said is true of the human condition. But if the invulnerability of evaluative beliefs in general could be shown, we could not take that particular philosophical view seriously.

This brings us back to the relation between invulnerability and indispensability. If evaluative beliefs do enjoy the kind of invulnerability I have mentioned, it might ultimately be because, as I imagined in the case of enduring particulars, they are indispensable to any conception that anyone could form of an independent world. That seems to me plausible if it is true both that no one could form a conception of a world unless he could see himself as acting in it, and that making sense of people as acting in a world they understand requires attributing to them beliefs about the relative values of the different courses of action they see as available.

But this is too big a question to pursue. It is perhaps enough to have drawn attention to a possible goal of such reflection. Whether it any longer counts as 'transcendental' is perhaps of secondary interest.

14

The Synthetic A Priori in Strawson's Kantianism

Kant's 'general problem of pure reason'[1] was to be solved by following 'a special science' called 'the Critique of Pure Reason'.[2] It would examine the 'sources and limits'[3] of reason's power, and 'lay down the . . . plan' of what he called a 'transcendental philosophy'.[4] Ideally, such a philosophy would account for all of human knowledge in so far as it is possible a priori, including even our knowledge of what is already contained in our concepts. But Kant's *Critique of Pure Reason*—the book by that name—would not investigate such merely 'analytic' knowledge. It would go only as far as is needed for the examination of 'knowledge which is *a priori* and synthetic'.[5] So the whole project, and the whole question to which Kant's masterpiece is devoted, is 'How are *a priori* synthetic judgements possible?'[6]

Peter Strawson says that 'Kant really has no clear and general conception of the synthetic *a priori* at all.'[7] If that is true, what becomes of the general problem of pure reason? What then of transcendental philosophy? Does this mean that Strawson thinks Kant has no clear and general conception of the task of his *Critique of Pure Reason*, or of the problem he is trying to solve there? Not necessarily, of course. It might mean only that Strawson thinks the real problems Kant deals with so masterfully are not best expressed, or perhaps even fully intelligible, in that form.

Readers of *The Bounds of Sense* are familiar with this general idea. We are urged again and again to look through the surface features of Kant's often confused and sometimes grandiose presenta-

This paper was presented at a conference on Strawson and Kant in Reading, England, in 1999.

[1] I. Kant, *Critique of Pure Reason*, tr. N. Kenp Smith (London, 1953), B19.
[2] Ibid. A11 = B24.   [3] Ibid. A12 = B25.   [4] Ibid. A13 = B27.
[5] Ibid. A14 = B28.   [6] Ibid. B19.
[7] P. F. Strawson, *The Bounds of Sense* (London, 1966), 43.

tion of the issues to what is really at stake behind them. It is like being taken round a baroque cathedral by a wise cicerone whose practised eye and seasoned intelligence see right through all those impressive twisted columns and grimacing giants to discern what is really carrying the weight and keeping the whole improbable thing upright.

What then is the austere, unembellished truth about what is going on in the *Critique of Pure Reason*? Strawson sees its programme as that of 'determining the fundamental general structure of any conception of experience such as we can make intelligible to ourselves'.[8] That too was the project of the first half of his own earlier *Individuals*, before he turned his attention more explicitly to the work of Kant. Objective particulars in space and time, and human persons with both physical and psychological characteristics, were found to play a central role in our conception of the world, just as they do in Strawson's account of Kant's achievement.

But the task of the special Strawsonian or Kantian enterprise is not captured simply by observing that we think of the world in terms of relatively permanent spatio-temporal particulars and embodied persons as subjects of experience. That is true, but it is just a very general remark about us—about how we think of the world. Nor does it get any closer to say that there *are* relatively permanent particulars and embodied persons. That too is true, but it is just a very general remark about the way the world is. This special investigation of our conception of the world achieves its goal not simply by reaching such results, but only by our coming to see that those propositions have a certain special and 'distinctive character or status'[9] in our thought. Kant uses the term 'synthetic a priori' to capture what he thinks is that distinctive character.

But if the point of the enterprise is to discover the distinctive character or status of certain components of our experience of the world, and Kant calls that distinctive status 'synthetic a priori', what is the point of his asking how synthetic a priori judgements—or propositions that have that distinctive character—are possible? If such propositions must be present in any thought we can form, that amounts to asking how thought and experience are possible. But for Kant that distinctive character involves those propositions' being known, or knowable, in a certain way. So his question is also

[8] Ibid. 44.   [9] Ibid.

in part a question of how it is possible for an investigation into our conception of the world to yield conclusions which can be known to have such a distinctive character or status. It is not enough for something to have that distinctive status; it must be knowable or discoverable that certain things have it.

Kant thought that if there are discoverable results with the distinctive status he had in mind, then metaphysics—the attempt to discover general truths about the world—would no longer be 'a merely random groping'.[10] It could be set on 'the secure path of a science'.[11] It would be secure because there would be an explanation of how undeniable metaphysical results can be reached.

Kant's explanation of the possibility of that knowledge—what he thought was the only possible explanation—was the truth of transcendental idealism. We know that was his explanation, even if we don't know what transcendental idealism actually is, or says. To the extent to which we can understand it, it seems to leave us with the sinking feeling that the knowledge it credits us with is not really knowledge of the kind of world we thought we knew before we took up the critical enterprise. But to put it most gently—more gently than Strawson sometimes does—transcendental idealism can add nothing positive to our understanding of whatever position we are in. It is partly for these reasons that Strawson thinks there is 'nothing to demand, or permit, an explanation such as Kant's'[12] in any results that might be reached in an investigation of the fundamental general structure of our conception of the world of experience.

There are two questions here: whether the possibility of discovering the distinctive character or status of certain components of our conception of the world demands or permits an explanation such as Kant's, and whether it demands or permits an explanation at all. What the explantion might be depends on what the distinctive character or status of those special propositions is. Strawson does not deny that they have some special or distinctive character. That is crucial to his own understanding of the project.[13] So the question is what austere, unembellished description he

---

[10] Kant, *Critique of Pure Reason*, Bxv.   [11] Ibid. Bxix.

[12] *The Bounds of Sense*, 44.

[13] 'If there is such a structure [of any conception of experience which we could make truly intelligible to ourselves], if there is a set of ideas which enter indispensably into such a structure, then the members of this set will surely have a distinctive status' (ibid. 49–50).

would give of propositions of the kind that Kant called 'synthetic a priori', and whether the possibility of propositions with that character demands, or permits, explantion.

Strawson at times appears to doubt or deny that any explanation at all is needed. He thinks that in exploring the fundamental general structure of our conception of the world of experience, 'it is no matter for wonder' if we come up against certain 'necessary limits' to any such conception we can make intelligible to ourselves.[14] But:

> In order to set limits to coherent thinking, it is not necessary, as Kant, in spite of his disclaimers, attempted to do, to think both sides of those limits. It is enough to think up to them.[15]

Is that really enough? It is of course not possible to think beyond the limits of coherent thinking. Even when we think right up to those limits, or think something that expresses a necessary condition of thinking anything, we are still within those limits. To think up to what is in fact a limit of thought is, in a way, easy to do, in fact, impossible to fail at. But for the Kantian or Strawsonian philosophical enterprise we must think up to those limits while recognizing them as limits. But the point of the Kantian or Strawsonian philosophical enterprise is not simply to think up those limits, but to come to *recognize* those limits, or to *identify* some of the necessary conditions of the possibility of thought and experience. We must come to see, of some of the things we think, that they are necessary conditions of the possibility of our having any thoughts or experiences at all. And how such discoveries are possible, if they are, is something that might call for explanation even if we are never tempted by the 'doctrinal fantasies'[16] of transcendental idealism.

Kant does not simply start off with his transcendental explanation. A number of steps lead up to the felt need for it. First, he seeks some necessary conditions of the possibility of thought and experience in general. Next, he thinks he finds something which holds necessarily, and which he sees to hold necessarily. Third, he infers that his knowledge of such necessities is a priori. By "a priori" here he can be taken to mean nothing more than "non-empirical". As he says in the introduction: 'we shall understand by *a priori* knowledge, not knowledge independent of this or that experience,

---

[14] Ibid. 44.   [15] Ibid.   [16] Ibid. 51.

but knowledge absolutely independent of all experience.'[17]
And "independent" means the knowledge does not 'arise out of'
experience, not that it does not 'begin with' experience.[18]

Fourth, Kant makes an inference to the a priori on the basis of
the general principle that necessity is what he calls a 'sure criterion'
of the a priori. 'Experience teaches us that a thing is so and so, but
not that it cannot be otherwise', he says. So 'if we have a proposition which in being thought is thought as necessary, it is an *a priori*
judgment.'[19] So any discoveries we make of the necessary conditions of the possibility of thought and experience in general must
be made and so known a priori, independently of all experience,
according to Kant. So far there appears to be no appeal to, or even
mention of, transcendental idealism.

Even the next, and admittedly more problematic, step seems free
of transcendental idealism. Kant holds that the necessities he discovers, or the way he discovers them—at least those that are central
to the *Critique of Pure Reason*—cannot be accounted for as merely
'analytic'. They do not serve simply to express what is somehow
covertly contained within the very concepts they make use of. They
are in that sense 'ampliative' or 'synthetic'. This is course obscure.
"Synthetic" just means "non-analytic", so our understanding of the
idea of the synthetic a priori can be no better than our understanding of the notion of analyticity. And our understanding of the
notion of analyticity is not good. It seems to rest on the notion of
one concept or meaning somehow 'containing' or not 'containing'
another. Kant's suggestion that an 'analytic' judgement is one in
which one concept is 'extracted' from another 'in accordance with
the principle of contradiction'[20] would help if we had some independent grasp of the notion of a contradiction. But it tells us at
least that the distinctive, non-analytic propositions that he is concerned with are not such that their negations are contradictory. For
now it is enough to observe that the admitted obscurities surrounding all these notions appear to have nothing to do with transcendental idealism.

That doctrine begins to make its appearance only at the final
step, when Kant asks how it is possible for anyone to know a priori
that such non-analytic necessities hold—how synthetic a priori
judgements are possible. This is where the secret operations of 'our
faculties', and what is 'in us' and not in the world, and all the other

---

[17] Kant, *Critique of Pure Reason*, B2.   [18] Ibid. B1.
[19] Ibid. B3.   [20] Ibid. B12.

incoherences of what Strawson calls 'transcendental subjectivism' are appealed to. A priori knowledge of the fundamental structure of the world of experience is possible only because that world must conform to the constitution of our minds. If that were not so, we could at most have a posteriori knowledge of what its structure is, and not what Kant thought we do have—a priori knowledge of what its structure must be. But that kind of knowledge, he thought, is possible at all only if it is somehow knowledge of *us*, or of what 'we' bring to the 'raw material' of 'sensible impressions' to make up 'that knowledge of objects which is entitled experience'.[21] A priori knowledge is knowledge that arises out of something called 'reason', and 'reason has insight only into that which it produces after a plan of its own'.[22]

These 'fantasies' and excrescences of transcendental idealism are put forward by Kant as the only possible explanation of something he thinks he has independently identified. When Strawson says, as I quoted him at the beginning as saying, that 'Kant really has no clear and general conception of the synthetic *a priori* at all', he is making an observation about what he takes to be the incoherence and explanatory emptiness of transcendental idealism. It is *because* transcendental idealism can explain nothing that he finds Kant's question about the synthetic a priori unrewardingly unclear, and so to be set aside. But how closely are the two connected? Kant's transcendental answer to the question might be unclear or incoherent even though there remains something real, and puzzling, in the Kantian project that calls for explanation. What of the earlier steps leading up to the Kantian explanation?

First, it is clear that Strawson seeks and thinks he finds, in Kant and in his own investigations, 'statable necessary conditions of the possibility of experience in general',[23] or 'what is necessarily involved'[24] in any conception of experience which we can make intelligible to ourselves. Without asking by what specific arguments

---

[21] Ibid. B1. The connection between synthetic a priori knowledge and the subjective source of that knowledge is well expressed by Kant in a single rich sentence, also appropriately quoted by Strawson (*The Bounds of Sense*, 115 n): 'For this unity of nature has to be a necessary one, that is, has to be an *a priori* certain unity of the connection of appearances; and such synthetic unity could not be established *a priori* if there were not subjective grounds of such unity contained *a priori* in the original cognitive powers of our mind, and if these subjective conditions, inasmuch as they are the grounds of the possibility of knowing any object whatsover in experience, were not at the same time objectively valid' (*CPR* A125–6).

[22] Ibid. Bxiii.   [23] *The Bounds of Sense*, 120.   [24] Ibid. 121.

conclusions like this are supported, we can ask whether for Strawson, as for Kant, our knowledge of such necessities is a priori, or independent of all experience. The question is difficult to answer, since Strawson gives a very austere interpretation of the expression "a priori". In fact, in his revulsion from any transcendental idealist understanding of it as standing for knowledge that has a subjective source in the nature of our cognitive constitution, he seems to go so far as to understand it as not really an epistemic term for a kind of knowledge at all.

An element of our conception of the world can be called "a priori" for Strawson if it is 'an essential structural element in any conception of experience which we could make intelligible to ourselves'.[25] It can be contrasted with those less general, and so dispensable, features of our experience which at least in principle could be, or could have been, abandoned 'without imperilling the entire structure of the conception'.[26] Those features could be called, in a correspondingly austere sense, merely 'empirical'. With the so-called 'a priori' features, 'we can form no coherent' conception of how experience might have been without them.[27] This virtually identifies the 'a priori' features of our conception of the world with the necessary or absolutely indispensable features of it. It is not as if the necessity of what is known serves as a 'criterion' of its being known in a certain way, as in Kant. Something's being indispensable to any conception of experience implies nothing about how it is known, or knowable, or how it is known to have that status. It leaves untouched Kant's question of how a 'scientific', or generally reliable, metaphysics is possible.

There might be felt to be no problem—or no need for what Strawson calls 'any high doctrine'[28]—here at all, beyond the completely general question of how we know the things we think we know. Since necessary truths, or necessary connections between things, are among the things we know, no doubt our knowledege of them must be accounted for in some way. But the notion of 'independence from all experience', which is essential to an epistemic reading of "a priori", is too difficult to apply with any confidence, or too laden with dubious epistemological assumptions, to be of much help. But if we abandon an epistemic notion of the a priori altogether, and with it any general distinction between 'a priori' and

---

²⁵ *The Bounds of Sense*, 68.   ²⁶ Ibid. 50.
²⁷ Ibid. 115.   ²⁸ Ibid. 44.

'empirical' ways of knowing things, the features of the Strawsonian or Kantian conclusions which might seem to call for explanation would only concern what Kant called their 'synthetic', rather than their 'a priori' character.

In a familiar but surprising passage, Kant says that of all earlier philosophers, it was Hume who came closest to seeing the problem of how synthetic a priori judgements are possible. Closest, but no cigar, even for Hume. He did not see the generality of the problem. Or, to put Kant's point in another way, if we generalized to all propositions what Hume said in particular about the 'synthetic' proposition that every event has a cause, 'then all that we call metaphysics [would be] a mere delusion whereby we fancy ourselves to have rational insight into what, in actual fact, is borrowed solely from experience, and under the influence of custom has taken the illusory semblance of necessity'.[29] Metaphysical results of the kind Kant thought could be reached would then be unavailable, since the propositions in question would not really be necessary after all. That is why he thinks that if Hume had seen the universality of the problem 'his good sense' would have saved him from the conclusion he reached in the case of causality.

Kant's reasons for this generous assessment of Hume show that what he thinks is really important is the synthetic character of the necessary propositions he seeks. Of course, for Kant the necessity carries with it the implication that the propositions are known a priori, but it is not on the question of the a priori that he differs at this point from Hume. He is confident that Hume would have seen that he could not say the same thing about the necessary propositions of pure mathematics as he said about the proposition that every event has a cause. That would make pure mathematics impossible. I take Kant to mean by this that its propositions would not really be necessary after all, but would have only 'the illusory semblance of necessity', borrowed from experience under the influence of custom.

That is more or less the view from which John Stuart Mill was not saved by whatever good sense he had. But it is not a view by which Hume was even tempted.[30] He thought the propositions of pure mathematics are necessarily true because they express no

[29] Kant *Critique of Pure Reason*, B20.
[30] Or not quite. There is one passage in which he shows that a similar thought has occurred to him. 'Thus as the necessity, which makes two times two equal to four,

more than 'relations of ideas', so their negations are contradictory. He thought that was enough to explain how we know them too, but it cannot be said that he ever gave such an explanation. So he would not disagree with Kant about their being necessary, but about their being what Kant called 'synthetic'. Neither Hume nor Kant doubts that the proposition 'Every event has a cause' is synthetic. But Hume held that the propositions of pure mathematics are not. So the challenge represented by Hume is to explain how it is to be known that something really does hold with necessity, and not just with 'the illusory semblance of necessity', when neither its truth nor its necessity is discoverable 'analytically', by inspection of the contents of concepts alone.

This is Kant's question of how non-'analytic' and therefore synthetic necessities can be known. Is there a similar challenge facing a more austere interpretation that repudiates transcendental idealism completely and even abandons a distinction between a priori and a posteriori knowledge? Strawson recognizes and discusses a certain kind of challenge along these lines. He sees that it is important to distinguish the Kantian project as he understands it from a certain 'historical'—what he sometimes calls a 'merely historical'[31]—conception of an investigation of the fundamental framework of ideas in terms of which we make sense of our experience. On that historical view of metaphysics, the general structure we can uncover by philosophical reflection might be fundamental and unquestioned in a particular scientific epoch or culture, but it could change or be gradually and silently abandoned when scientific or social thinking enters a new historical phase. There could be great illumination in revealing the basic categories and presuppositions of what with a fairly determinate reference could be called *our* thought and experience of the world, but even the most secure results would not necessarily hold for everyone, or for all thought and experience whatever.

Strawson thinks this conception is 'very far from Kant's intentions', and if true would make the *Critique of Pure Reason* 'a less

---

or three angles of a triangle equal to two right ones, lies only in the act of the understanding, by which we consider and compare these ideas; in like manner the necessity or power, which unites causes and effects, lies in the determination of the mind to pass from the one to the other' (D. Hume, *A Treatise of Human Nature*, ed. L. A. Selby-Bigge (Oxford, 1958), 166.

[31] *The Bounds of Sense*, 121.

interesting work than we had hoped'.[32] He wants to preserve a project which he thinks 'corresponds more closely to Kant's own'.[33]

The 'historical' view of the metaphysical enterprise would restrict us to the fundamental ideas and presuppositions of a particular time and culture. But it would not have to deny that the results achieved by metaphysical reflection have a certain kind of necessity. It could find that anyone who thinks of the world in certain ways must also think of it, or at least acknowledge it as being, this and that other way as well. Within the very concepts in which a society grasps the world, there might be certain other concepts necessarily connected with them. In short, the 'historical' conception of metaphysics could endorse what Kant would call the 'analytic' character of the necessities it discovers. This would be metaphysics as the study of what Hume called 'relations of ideas'. That does not mean that it would be as easy as Hume sometimes suggests knowledge of the 'relations of ideas' can be: merely holding up an idea for inspection and gazing 'inside' it to see whether a certain other idea is included in it or not. It might require a deep enquiry of great complexity to lay bare some of the most fundamental and far-reaching ways of thinking involved in our experience and thought of the world. But any outcome reached in that way could be seen as an 'analysis' or a bringing to light of the contents of those experiences and thoughts.

The more Kantian conception of the project which Strawson favours involves the discovery of some necessities that are different from that. On the 'historical' view there is no necessity in anyone's having any particular conception of the world, even a conception with a certain fundamental structure. For all that view says, we could, or someone could, have had radically different kinds of experience, and so a radically different conception of the world. The necessities discoverable on that view would be in that sense conditional, concerned with what is necessarily involved in a certain way of thinking and experiencing things, but without implying that those are the only ways in which thought and experience of a world are possible. Other ways of thinking would contain different necessities of their own.

This is not the conception of their project shared by Strawson and Kant. They seek stronger conclusions, and so different

---

[32] Ibid.   [33] Ibid.

necessities. That Strawson aspires to something more can be seen in another way when he is struck with a possible way of taking Kant's claim to have discovered what is 'necessarily involved in any coherent conception experience'[34] that would rob it of most of its interest for him. Experience, for Kant, is possible only if it is experience of objects in a fairly weighty sense, involving the application to items in experience of certain identifiable general concepts or 'categories' which carry certain implications of objectivity. But if this were simply a matter of the definition of the word 'experience', or if the claim were simply laid down as a premiss from which the rest of Kant's investigation proceeds, Strawson thinks our hopes for the most fruitful outcome of the critical enterprise would be considerably deflated. Fortunately, it turns out that this is not so. When Kant is understood correctly, his claim that experience necessarily involves experience of objects that are independent of particular experiences of them is seen to have 'all the depth and interest which we were threatened with the loss of'.[35] The threat came from the now-rejected idea that what Kant establishes are at most 'analytic' or 'definitional' necessities. But for Strawson, Kant does not simply 'analyse' or seek a definition of the concept of a unity of experience; he asks what it would take, what must be so, in order for a set of experiences to be unified in the relevant way.

This leads to a series of necessity-claims which can be briefly summarized as follows. The set of experiences must satisfy the conditions of being united in a single consciousness. That requires that they satisfy the conditions which make possible the self-ascription of those experiences to the subject whose experiences they are. That in turn requires the possibility of consciousness on the part of the subject of the identity of that to which the different experiences belong and could be ascribed. And that requires further the possibility of some of those experiences' being experiences of objects which are distinct from and independent of experiences of them. Judgements about such objects are true or false no matter what the state of any experiencing subject might be. So, 'unity of diverse experiences in a single consciousness requires experience of objects'.[36]

This is a necessity-claim; one thing is said to be required for another. It is supported by all those intermediate claims leading up

---

[34] *The Bounds of Sense*, 72.   [35] Ibid. 73.   [36] Ibid. 98.

to it, and they in turn are to be further supported by looking for deeper or more general reasons why they must hold. Perhaps they can be derived, as Strawson tries to derive them, from something as basic to the possibility of thought and experience as the idea of particular items being thought of as falling under concepts. The strength of such claims can be tested, as Strawson tries to test them, only by seeing how they stand up to attack. There is no foolproof method here.

What is special about the project is not the method but the kind of necessites that are to be established. The question is what must be so in order for a person to be capable of certain thoughts or experiences. The possibility of having certain kinds of thoughts or experiences must be in a person's repertoire in order for experience to be possible at all. And further conditions must be fulfilled in order for those things to be in his repertoire. What other things must he be able to think or experience, what other distinctions must he be able to draw, or in what other ways must he be able to make sense of things? These are questions about what Strawson elsewhere has called 'conceptual capacities', and the necessary linkages between them.[37] They are not questions about the necessary connections between the concepts or meanings employed by a thinker. They do not seek simply to 'analyse' or lay bare the *contents* of a person's concepts or thoughts or experiences. They are concerned with the conditions of anyone's *having* thoughts or experiences with certain contents. Concept *possession*, or conceptual and experiential *capacity*, is what is in question, not just the concepts themselves. One concept's being known to be 'covertly contained' in another would contribute nothing to an understanding of how thought and experience are possible if possession and employment of those concepts were not required for thought and experience.

To establish such necessary connections between some of our conceptual and experiential capacities would reveal a certain distinctive character or status of some of the elements of our conception of the world. If a person had to be able to think in certain specific ways—e.g. to think of himself as a subject of experiences—in order to think or experience anything at all, and if thinking of the world as containing objective particulars that are independent

---

[37] See his *Skepticism and Naturalism: Some Varieties* (London, 1985), 21 ff.

of thought and experience was required in order to think of oneself as a subject of experiences, then those parts of our conception of how things are would have a special status.

They would not have been shown to hold necessarily, or even to be something we must think holds necessarily. It would mean only that thinking of the world as contingently containing subjects of experiences would require thinking of it as contingently containing objective particulars independent of experience as well. Nor would that imply that there *are* subjects of experiences or objective particulars. The truth of what we think does not follow from our thinking it, or even from our being required to think it.[38] Even the link between the contents of the things we think might not be necessary. If thinking that *p* requires thinking that *q*, it does not follow that it is necessarily true that if *p* then *q*. Of course, it is not ruled out either.

But if certain ways of thinking are required for the possibility of any thought and experience at all, then what we think in thinking in those ways has a special, and a specially invulnerable, standing. It must be accepted or acknowledged by anyone who thought or experienced anything. It could not consistently be exposed as a mere metaphysical illusion, as nothing more than a widely held belief which for all its familiarity fails to capture the way things really are. That there are independently existing objective particulars, for instance, would be a belief which must be held even by someone who claims to conceive of, or to believe in, a world in which that belief is held by many people but is not really true. No one could so detach himself from that indispensable belief as to find that the world is that way.

All indispensable beliefs are invulnerable to that kind of 'unmasking'. This is actually one of the sources of incoherence or inconsistency in transcendental idealism. That doctrine wants to say that objective particulars independent of experience are indispensable to any world we can find intelligible, and also that, transcendentally speaking, what we take to be independent objects are not really independent of experience after all; nothing is. That seems to take back with one hand what it offers with the other.

---

[38] This is the substance of my objection to what I have called 'ambitious transcendental arguments' which would draw conclusions about how things are from premisses about how we think. See, above, my 'Transcendental Arguments' (Ch. 2) and 'Kantian Argument, Conceptual Capacities, and Invulnerabilty' (Ch. 11).

Transcendental idealism tries to escape the charge by claiming that it is not the same thing in each of the hands.

Establishing that some elements of our conception of the world have the kind of standing that guarantees invulnerability to unmasking requires an 'absolute' or non-conditional understanding of the necessities discovered by metaphysical reflection. The indispensability of certain ways of thinking must be indispensability for any possible thought or experience at all, not merely for this or that conception of the world which we, or some other culture or epoch, happen to have. The 'historical' view challenges the assumption of this conception of the metaphysical task. So, in another way, does the Humean view. The questions they raise about the possibility of establishing such absolute necessities are perhaps as close as we can come to austere analogues of Kant's question of how synthetic a priori judgements are possible.

For any necessity-claim the Strawsonian Kantian project comes up with, the 'historical' view will find it true only 'for us', or true only 'for' those whose conception of the world is in question: for thought and experience with such-and-such particular form or structure, but not necessarily for all thought and experience. Even the apparently stronger Strawsonian claim to have identified elements that are necessary to any conception which we can make intelligible to ourselves is something the historical view might accept, by taking it strictly. It might see our inability to conceive of other possibilities as a result of our being so immersed in our period and culture that we cannot even make sense of things' being otherwise in certain ways. But still, it says, they could be. There could be forms of thought and experience of which we, for reasons having to do only with us, can form no coherent conception at all. But the fact that we can form no coherent thought of any such alternatives does not imply that there simply are no such possibilities.

The wisest response to this last point, it seems to me, is to grant it. From our failure to make sense of something we can recognize as a possibility, it does not follow that there is no such possibility. There is nothing in the austerely understood Strawsonian or Kantian project to guarantee without possibility of failure that the necessity-claims the philosopher comes up with must be true. Nor is there anything in our ways of trying to find out things in general that guarantees that we will succeed. That is a fact of life we just have to accept; and it applies as much to philosophy as to anything else.

This is something that I think Kant's own richly transcendental, non-austerely-understood project denies, at least with respect to philosophy. It was meant to give the philosopher such a guarantee. The knowledge sought by the project was to be a priori, therefore 'in us', even in some sense 'contributed by us' or by 'reason', and therefore directly available to us by the operation of 'pure reason' with complete certainty. Since the critique of pure reason 'has to deal . . . only with itself and the problems which arise entirely from within itself, and which are imposed by its own nature,' Kant writes, 'it should easily be able to determine [its limits] with completeness and certainty.'[39] 'Judgments [of reason] are never opinions' Kant says, '. . . it must affirm with apodeictic certainty.'[40] 'Otherwise we should have no guidance as to truth.'[41] This is how metaphysics can be put on the path of a science which we can know in advance is secure.

There is no reassuring epistemological theory of this or any other kind behind the austerely understood Strawsonian project. The metaphysical investigator can do no better than to reflect on whether or how it would be possible for one thing to be present without the other. He can try out necessity-claims, and try to defend them against potential attack. To understand more fully why something that looks like a possibility is not really possible after all would help explain the basis of the necessity-claim, and so would add further support to it. This is the most we can ever do in establishing necessities, when it is not a matter of explicit demonstrative proof.

To the 'historical' metaphysician's caution that there *could* be forms of thought and experience of which we so far have been unable to form any coherent conception, it is best to concede that, yes, perhaps there could be. But yet again, perhaps there could not be, either. What we have now found to be the limits of the possible could well be the limits of the possible. Anyway, that is what we now believe. To pursue the question further the only thing we can do is keep trying our best to find out what is necessary and what is not. To refuse to draw conclusions about the necessary features of

---

[39] Kant, *Critique of Pure Reason*, B23.   [40] Ibid. A775 = B803.
[41] Ibid. A823 = B851.

any possible experience simply because, after all, it is only *we* who
are drawing the conclusions, only we who live and think and experience in a particular culture at a particular time and place, would
simply be to give in to a different abstract and general theory of
thought and experience. And there is much in what we have discovered so far that does not support that subjectivist or relativist
theory.

One challenge represented by the 'historical' view was that it
would absorb all the necessities discoverable by metaphysical
reflection into merely conditional or 'analytic' necessities, and so
rob the project of its universality and absolute necessity. The interesting austere project was to avoid that deflation by concerning
itself with necessities among the conditions of the possession and
employment of certain concepts, not simply among the concepts
themselves. But it is just possible, I suppose, to see even that enterprise as yielding at best only 'analytic' or 'definitional' necessities.
They would express what is 'covertly contained', not in the concept
of, say, "experience", or the concept of "subject of experiences", but
in the concept "possesses the concept of experience", or the
concept "possesses the concept of a subject of experience". 'Analysis' might reveal that the quite different concept "thinks of the
world as containing objective particulars" is 'contained' in one or
both of those concepts.

As I say, it is perhaps just possible to think of an examination of
the necessary conditions of the possession of certain concepts in
this way. Devotion to the hopeless idea of analyticity apparently
dies hard. I think that is because analyticity is widely thought to be
the only possible explanation of necessity, and of our knowledge of
it. That double requirement on the idea of analyticity is what I think
is the source of its inveterate obscurity. It is expected to account
for too many different things all at once, and accounts for none of
them. So it adds nothing to a necessity-claim to the effect that
having one concept or capacity requires having certain others. The
'historical' view of metaphysics does not present a sharp, identifiable challenge when it makes essential use of the idea of analyticity in this way.

The Humean view is not 'historical' or social or potentially rel-
ativistic. It is universalistic, about all human beings. But it says that
any necessities discoverable by a priori reflection are merely 'analytic' connections, or 'relations of ideas' alone. Its differences from

the austere Strawsonian or Kantian project can therefore also be measured only in terms of the repudiated notions of analyticity and the a priori. Hume says that any non-analytic necessities we might discover about the ways we think and experience the world are merely 'natural' or causal necessities. If it is true that no one can avoid believing that there are objective particulars, or that every event has a cause, as he thinks it is, that is simply because of the way human beings are. Given the way the world is, and the way it affects them, they cannot avoid getting those beliefs. That is for Hume a causal fact of the world. But causal necessities are not absolute necessities. It is possible for things that are in fact causally related not to have been so causally related.

Does the idea that we are all caused to believe, and in that sense cannot help believing, in objective particulars and causal connections pose a threat to the idea that those beliefs have the distinctive character or status in our thought that I have identified? I don't think so. For one thing, if it is true that we must believe in such things, then we do believe in them. So we can see our being unavoidably caused to believe in them as an indication that the way we are unavoidably caused to believe things are is, in certain respects, just the way things are. Hume's more troubling view is not just the causal thesis that we inevitably get those beliefs, but that the beliefs in question are not true; we only think there are objective particulars and causal connections. But making that negative claim seems to overlook the positive part of the story that says that everyone has to believe such things. It appears to be claiming for the philosopher who discovers such bad news an exemption from the operation of laws that are said to apply to all human beings. But then the positive part of the story would not be universally true. So it is questionable whether Hume could consistently arrive at the negative part of his view, if the positive causal part about human beings and the world is also true. That again is the question of whether beliefs that really are indispensable can consistently be unmasked as illusions. It does not seem to matter whether the indispensability is only causal or something stronger, even absolute.

But the fact that causal or natural necessities are not absolute—that it is possible for two things that are causally related not to be so related—does not itself threaten the absolute necessity of the claims a defender of the austere Strawsonian or Kantian project would make. Suppose that Hume is right that we are all inevitably caused to believe in a world of objective particulars; that is a natural necessity. And suppose Strawson and Kant are right that believing in objective particulars is a necessary condition of the possibility of anyone's having any experience of a world at all. Then any world in which that natural necessity does not hold, and human beings in interaction with that world get no thoughts or beliefs about objective particulars, would be a world in which those human beings do not have experience of that world, or of anything else. They would not fulfil one of its necessary conditions.

Maybe the idea of possible human beings with no thoughts or experiences of anything at all is too much to accept. But, looking on the bright side, if Hume is right about the natural necessities, then human beings cannot fail to fulfil that necessary condition of the possibility of experience. It is inevitable, given the way human beings are and the way the world is.

So any conflict between the Humean view and the austere Strawsonian or Kantian conception turns again only on the negative part of the Humean view: the idea that no necessities are discoverable a priori except 'analytic' connections or 'relations of ideas'. I have admitted a way in which even that might be compatible with the search for conditions of the possession and employment of concepts. But the negative Humean view represents a challenge to the austere Strawsonian project only if some knowledge is possible 'absolutely independently of all experience', and if all necessities are knowable only in that a priori way. Even then the force of the challenge would be directly proportional to the degree to which some clear light can be thrown on the idea of purely 'analytic' connections, or 'relations of ideas' alone.

So the austere project appears to be left only with what looks like a standing challenge to all knowledge, or to all philosophical theory. Strawson takes up the question briefly at the end of *The Bounds of Sense*. 'How is it, after all, possible to establish that experience must exhibit such-and-such general features?' he asks.[42] He gives what seems like the only possible *general* answer to the question. We do our best to find out what must be so if something else is, and we test what we find against the best potential counterexamples we can muster. Of course, any particular necessity-claim can be challenged, and perhaps overthrown. But that will be done,

---

[42] *The Bounds of Sense*, 271.

as Strawson says, 'only by making us able to understand the possibility of an alternative'.[43]

But for many philosophers, and here I think we come to the crux of the matter, there is thought to be something special, and especially problematic, about necessity. It is thought to be in some way mysterious. That is why our knowledge of it is felt to need a special kind of explanation. The idea itself apparently cannot be explained or defined, except in terms like "possibility", "contradiction", and so on, which in turn can be explained only in terms of necessity. I think that is true, but if it creates a special problem about our knowledge of necessities, then there is a special problem about our knowledge of everything. What we know are truths, and the idea of truth cannot be defined in terms which can be understood independently of the notion of truth either. Reductionism is out of the question for truth, just as I believe it is for necessity.

But necessity has been thought to be especially problematic because, roughly speaking, it has been believed that there is and can be no such thing as necessity in the way things really are. It is said to be only something we impose on our thinking about the way things are. Necessary propositions have been said to be 'empty' or 'devoid of factual content'. That is harmless if it means only that necessary truths do not state contingent facts. If it means more than that, it expresses a conception of necessity in general that is analogous to Hume's deflating account of causal necessity: the idea that there is no such thing in the world as it really is, we only think there is because of the ways our minds work.

It is precisely this conception of necessity, and our knowledge of it, that I think the idea of analyticity has been brought in to explain. That is the real source of its continued appeal, despite the dismal record of attempts to explain what analyticity actually is. It is believed that some idea of analyticity must be accepted, however difficult it is to formulate it, because it is the only way we could explain how there can be necessary truths among the things we know, given that necessity is really only something we impose on the world by the ways we think about it. The source of whatever necessity we recognize is therefore thought to be ultimately only 'in us', in the meanings we build into the concepts we use to understand what exists independently of our thought. But if necessity has

---

[43] *The Bounds of Sense*, 271.

a merely human or conventional source, that source must somehow be found in what can only be contingent facts about human beings. That is why I think no such notion could do all the jobs demanded of it.

It is this broadly Humean picture of necessity as somehow coming 'from us' that I think generates the idea that there is a special difficulty about necessity and our knowledge of it. The picture is not far from the kind of 'transcendental subjectivism' that the austere Strawsonian conception repudiates in Kant. And to this version of the picture I think we should give the same response. We do think of some things as necessarily true; and perhaps we do so because of the ways our minds work. But if what we believe is that some things are necessarily true, and the idea of necessity is irreducible to any other notions which do not presuppose it, then no one could consistently reach the view that necessity is only something subjective and not part of the way things are. That some things hold necessarily would be invulnerable to philosophical unmasking.

Without the shrunken picture of an impoverished independent reality in which there are no necessities, and so without the special problem that picture gives rise to, perhaps we are left after all only with Strawson's very general question of how it is possible to establish that experience must exhibit such-and-such features. Nothing very interesting can be said with complete generality; we can only look at the details of particular proposals, and try them out. None of this suggests that it is easy. It is often very difficult to find out what is necessarily true. But then it is also often difficult to find out what is true.

INDEX